In Her Honor, For *His* Glory

In Her Honor, For *His* Glory

THREE LOVES MADE IN HEAVEN
"'TIL DEATH DO US PART" . . . AND BEYOND!

John O. Solano

FULL-SERVICE   BOOK-MAKERS
ESTD.   1999

*All Bible verses are from the New International
Version (NIV) except where noted otherwise.*

In loving memory of my beloved Dot who made the 64 years of our marriage the best ever. I am indebted to her for seeing a person in me that I could not see for myself. Till we meet again, my Beloved.

Acknowledgments

I want to thank Edwina D. Woodbury, publisher, and the Chapel Hill Press staff for their untiring, professional expertise in proofreading, editing, designing, and everything else they did to make sure this manuscript was given the best possible attention to get it to publication.

Contents

PART I

In the Beginning

PART II

Wandering in the Wilderness

PART III

And the Two Shall Become One

PART IV

Being Where God Wants You to Be

PART V

What Next?

PART VI

Your Ways Are Not My Ways

PART VII

Til Death Do Us Part

Introduction

We read in the Gospel of Matthew, chapter 22, verses 34–40, "But when the Pharisees heard that he [meaning Jesus] had silenced the Sadducees, they gathered together. And one of them, a lawyer, asked him a question to test him, 'Teacher, which is the great commandment in the law?' And he said to him, 'You shall love the Lord your God with all your heart and with all your soul and with all your mind. This is the great and first commandment. And the second is like it: You shall love your neighbor as yourself. On these two commandments depend all the Law and the Prophets.'"

The story you are about to read is the story of a troubled, confused, drinking young rabble-rouser whose life was completely transformed by the influence of a young woman who believed and lived the truth of these commandments. The following proverb that appeared on Facebook captures the heart of the love story that this manuscript is about: "God and a good wife are the two best things a man can have." The love story begins with a vow of promise repeated at most weddings, "'Til death do us part." That was the vow made in holy matrimony by 18-year-old John O. Solano and 19-year-old Dorothy Mariam Pratt on December 31, 1950. As with many young couples in later years, they were vows made in intended honesty and promise, but, as documented by huge statistics, many couples do not keep them. And the reason they are not kept is that "'til death do us part" is predicated on what precedes it: "honor and keep you ... forsaking all others ... in sickness and in health ... for richer or for poorer." They were vows that linked John and Dot on a journey of life where that link was tested, strained, weakened, and often stretched to the limit where it looked like the chain would end up broken.

It is their story, but in reality it is the story of a loving, caring, and forgiving God who can take the lives of two persons who were complete opposites—opposites in gender, self-esteem, family background, religious views, education, temperament, and cultural backgrounds—and form them into a unified team to fulfill the purpose for which God created them. As the old saying goes, "It was like mixing apples and oranges!" In actuality, their story is proof of the biblical claim, "With man this is impossible, but with God all things are possible" (Matthew 19:26), and "Everything is possible for him who believes" (Mark 9:23).

This story was initially written in third-person form because the author believed that too much personal reference would make the reader immediately think, *I hope he doesn't break his arm patting himself on the back.* But it was later rewritten in the first person because the story of how the Holy God has used His work of clay to glorify Himself cannot be told unless that risk is taken. It is within the confines of John's and Dot's flesh-and-blood personhood that God's marvelous work took place. Thus the reader is requested to withhold judgment until the story's conclusion.

This is a love story and a life of romance that many would say is fictitious and was made in Hollywood. Actually, it's real and was made in heaven. Some would say it's fictitious because it seems like the make-believes of the days of *Father Knows Best*, *The Adventures of Ozzie and Harriet*, and the days of "innocence" that some critics have labeled fairy tales. And those criticisms rightly come from those who have never experienced the true lasting love of each other and the unconditional love of God—a love that came *to* Dot and John *from* God when they found that love *in* God.

Without God's love as the foundation of this relationship, this story would not have been possible. Ephesians 2:8–10 reads, "For it is by grace you have been saved, through faith—and this is not of yourselves, it is the gift of God—not by works, so that no one can boast. For we are God's workmanship, created in Christ Jesus to do good works, which God prepared in advance for us to do."

The pages that follow tell the story of Dot and John. It is a story of hardship, uncertainty, traditional family values and typical family feuds, threats of divorce, patriotism, and faith in God. In other words, it's what current critics would call a fairy tale. It is not a fairy tale, but it is a rare tale indeed!

PART I

In the Beginning

I

The Birth of Two Opposites

Taylor Springs, New Mexico, and Warner Robins, Georgia, 1931–1932

The expression "Never the Twain Shall Meet" (meaning that two things, places, etc., are very different and can never be brought together or made similar) could easily have been applied to this unlikely love story. Dot was born in Macon, Georgia, on June 26, 1931. Although she was born in Macon, her parents, Mr. and Mrs. Royce Pratt, lived in a small community known as Wellston some 18 miles away. The town was later named Warner Robins for a general who had been the commander of the Air Force base across the railroad and main road from Wellston. At the time that we met, Mr. Pratt had a combination auto parts store and car repair garage, a trailer park, and some acreage, and was a well-respected business and civic leader. Dot's parents were members of

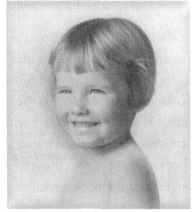

Dot at four years old. June 1935

the local Methodist church. Mr. Pratt had a fairly new Cadillac that played an important part in our initial relationship.

Dot was a high school graduate with high scholastic honors, and the recognition accorded her is highlighted next to her picture in the 1948 Warner Robins High School annual (the *Pioneer*) as follows:

President of 4-H Club 4; Advertising Manager of "Pioneer" 4; Sextet 4; Glee Club 3; Literary Guild 4; Commercial Club 3, 4; Science Club 4; Chemistry Club 4; Treasurer of Class 4; Christmas Pageant 4

Also printed next to her picture are the words "To Those Who Know Her All Words Are Faint." Obviously we have a future telescopic view of success for this person.

Much more could be said of my sweetheart, but she was under hospice care fighting for her life at the time of this writing. It was her intent to write this story, but because she was so busy during the prime of her life she didn't have the time to do so. When she finally did have the time, significantly bad health did not permit her to undertake the task. Knowing how important that dream was for her, I promised her that I would do so, praying that God's Holy Spirit would make up the difference in the necessary talent I lack to write it.

I was born in Taylor Springs, New Mexico, on March 31, 1932. I do not remember New Mexico at all. The first memory of my life was my dad as a farmhand for a Japanese American farmer next to the town of Fowler, Colorado. It had to be before World War II and the internment of the Japanese Americans in California, so maybe it was when I was around 5. I remember that we lived in a run-down shack that was covered inside with roof tarpaper to cover the cracks between the wooden boards to keep the cold out, and a woodstove for cooking and heating. There was no electricity, and we had to use kerosene lamps for light. I also remember that one day the Japanese farmer's son offered to trade me and my sister, Anita, his sandwich of white bread and bologna for a bowl of pinto beans. That was a real treat for us.

The unpaved road leading from the main highway to the farmhouse went along a water canal, and it was not uncommon for a car to get stuck on that road when it rained real hard. I remember once that when we went off somewhere, when we came back I was very depressed and wished that we didn't have to go to that horrible place we called home. One day when we had been away it had rained heavily, and my father had to walk to the barn through the mud and get a team of mules to pull the car back to the farmhouse. When he unhitched the mules, they spooked and ran away, dragging my dad, who was holding unto the reins. He was mad as a hornet—not because they had dragged him, but because he had lost his "chawing" tobacco! I recall fondly my father letting me sit on his lap and steer the car. Of course, Dad was holding on to the steering wheel all the time, but I thought I was doing something big and special.

From near Fowler we moved to Swink, Colorado, which had a sugar beet factory. My father worked in a plant nursery and was good at making things grow. I remember that one day a policeman came to our house looking for me and Anita because he had been told that we had been seen stealing peaches from an orchard. We were hiding under the bed. He told Mother that he was letting us off with a warning this time, but that it had better not happen again.

Next we moved to La Junta, Colorado. I was in first grade so I must have been 6. I remember hiding under a stairwell at noon in grade school because I was so ashamed that some of the other students might see me eating my lunch. My lunch consisted of tortillas with pickled sandwich spread between them that had unsightly soiled my lunch bag because we had nothing for wrapping them. It was pickled sandwich spread because we hardly ever had any kind of meat. Mexican food was standard in our home. In fact, when Mom would open a can of peaches, which was rare, I knew that my brother-in-law was coming to visit because those were his favorites. The bakery in La Junta would sell a large bag of what they called day-old bread for 50 cents that we bought occasionally. Boy, was that a treat! Among the stash we could always count on finding yummy, mouth-watering pastries with all manner of frosting, poppy seed, and other delicious goodies—all foreign to this poor family but scrumptious.

I was shy, fearful, and insecure in childhood. As they say, "I was afraid of my own shadow." The environment I lived in was pretty scary to me. I had recurring nightmares that my mother and father were going to die, and I wouldn't have anyone to take care of me. The neighborhood we lived in didn't have streetlights, and when I was out in the dark at night I always felt safe when I saw the light from the kerosene lamp calling through the window. However, I always felt like just about the time I walked through the door, the hand of a big monster was going to grab me by the collar and pull me back into the dark, which was terrifying.

As we all know, bullies have a way of sensing other children who are afraid of them, and one tormented me all the time in grade school. I was afraid of him, and he knew it. He would wait for me around the corner before and after school and chase me there and back. He made life a living hell for me. He had eyes that jutted out of his sockets and everyone called him "Egg Eyes." One day, I got tired of running and waited for ol' Egg Eyes to round the corner. When he did, in desperation I belted him with all my might and took off running with him flat on his back on the ground! That was the end of that scenario, and ol' Egg Eyes never bothered me again. Reminds me of an old saying I once heard: "We're like a used tea bag. We don't know our own strength until we get in hot water!"

One day when I was in the fifth grade, I started to walk across the street to the playground opposite the school. My teacher, Mrs. Brown-field, who had a rump as big as her chest, told me to walk across at the crosswalk. I mumbled something, and she asked me what I had said, and I replied that I had said nothing. Another boy who didn't like me told her that I had responded with some cuss words. She sent me to Mr. Crane, the principal, who used the rubber hose on me. Mr. Crane was a wonderful, caring person, so the whipping was more symbolic and instructive than hurtful—except to my pride.

My early upbringing can only be described as horrible—at least as I saw it through the eyes of a child subjected to extreme poverty and discrimination. The scenario of my upbringing was painted mainly in the city of La Junta, Colorado. As is clearly evident, discrimination and segregation have crippling effects on persons, especially innocent children. La Junta was located in the agricultural belt of eastern Colorado, where Mexican labor did the harvesting, much as blacks did in the South with cotton at the time.

As a result, whites stereotyped and profiled all brown-skinned people as below them, often referring to them as "dirty, stinking Mexicans" because of their smell from harvesting onions, sugar beets, watermelons, cantaloupes, and other varieties of produce. My family worked in these fields one summer before my father found regular work.

That kind of labor is a backbreaker. Take the harvesting of onions as an example. First we'd go down the row of onions pulling them out of the ground by hand and stacking them in piles in a bent position. Later we'd come along with a tool that had razor-sharp, knifelike blades that looked like the tips of swords. We'd use that tool to clip off the top of the onion. Then we'd place the onions in bushel baskets because the amount of bushel baskets we harvested in a day determined the amount of money we were paid. All of this took place in the blistering sun in a very dry climate. By day's end, all we wanted to do was crash and rest our weary bones.

Harvesting cucumbers from farms near La Junta was big business, so there was a pickle factory in town. The pickles were stored in a huge fenced yard in large wooden barrels before shipping. I would jump the fence at night, pop the plug on a barrel, and load up on pickles. My stupidity started early in life.

Our family was light-complexioned with hazel-colored eyes, unlike many of what we called "Mexicans," who seemed to be very dark-skinned by nature and made even darker by long days in the hot sun. Unlike those Mexicans, we came to Colorado from New Mexico—not from old Mexico. We called ourselves "Spanish," and in our minds that disassociated us from being Mexican. The name "Solano," according to Webster's Dictionary, is also of Spanish origin. Thus, in order to ward off the sting of discrimination, we mentally practiced another form of discrimination to fool ourselves into thinking we were different. "We're not Mexicans," we told ourselves, We're Spanish!"

Anglos (white people) didn't care what we foolishly thought. As far as they were concerned, we were Mexicans and treated as such. I saw signs in some restaurants in La Junta in the late 1940s that said, "No dogs or Mexicans allowed." Unless you've been a minority treated in this fashion, you have no idea what that does to a 9-year-old's self-image. You really don't.

That poor self-image was compounded by extreme poverty. My father was a common, unskilled laborer who lived from paycheck to paycheck. My parents were honest and upright citizens with limited education, my mother and father probably having reached third or fourth grade. Not until my mid-teens did our family have indoor conveniences in our home. I remember being on welfare for a number of months when my father was unable to find employment. We received food from the government as well as clothes in generous quantities. I was given a pair of long underwear with a flap that covered my rear end with two buttons to hold the flap in place and looked like the tailgate of a pickup. Instead of having to take off the entire underwear to do "number two," all I had to do was unbutton the flap and let 'er rip!

I remember my father being a very simple, but loving and caring man. I idolized him for that. He had a bad temper and could be severe when you got him riled up—but that was not often. I can't remember a time when he left the house without hugging every one of us children. He was a happy person, always humming a tune. As long as he was well fed, caring for his family, had a roof over his head, and paying his bills, he was happy as a lark.

He would take a lunch box to work and always brought back a little remnant of its contents for the three of us kids still at home to share. This was another of his ways to show us that he loved us and was thinking about us. He didn't have much, but he left us a whole lot to remember about him.

This description kind of reminds me of the 1950s movie *Cat on a Hot Tin Roof* with Burl Ives as the father, and Paul Newman and Jack Carson as the sons. The film is about a dysfunctional family at its worst. Ives is portrayed as a man who rose from being the son of a homeless bum who had nothing to the owner of a huge plantation. Carson is the oldest son and a greedy lawyer. Newman is the younger son, an alcoholic married to Elizabeth Taylor, and with whom he is always arguing. Ives is dying and in a quandary as to who will inherit his great fortune. Greedy Carson wants it and connives to try to get it, while Newman is quite happy with the comforts and securities of his bottle and could care less about the estate.

The point the movie attempts to convey comes at the last when Newman is bumping into everything in the basement drunk, and Ives comes down and they have a man-to-man talk for the first time in their lives. Ives is angry with Newman about his drinking and takes him to task, telling him what a disappointment it is that Newman doesn't want the plantation that Ives has worked so hard to amass.

Ives tells Newman about how he remembers his pitiful hobo father with only a suitcase to his name, and how his father dragged him from one place to another, ever at his side, but leaving him with nothing. Newman, hungry for that kind of close relationship with Ives, says to him, "It sounds to me that he left you a lot more than you think." My father was like Ives's hobo father—he had nothing of this world to leave me, but he left me a whole lot of who he was. If we humans could only realize that that close relationship is what our Heavenly Father wishes for all of us as well how much better would we be.

I have mixed memories of my mother. She didn't seem to be happy about anything, yet my father would make every effort on his part to make her so. I can still picture him always trying to hug her, kiss her, or make some kind of sexual advance and her always rejecting him. Maybe that's the reason he showered us kids with so much affection, because he didn't get any from her. This happens more than we think.

As I look back, I consider that, because I was the first and oldest boy, she spoiled me. When I was 16 and would go out partying at night she would secretly slip money into my hand as I left—money that, as I look back now, would better have been spent on necessities that the rest of the family needed more in the home. I was stationed abroad when my mother died, so I have no knowledge of her funeral service.

Both of my grandfathers had died before I was born, so I never knew them. I knew my grandmothers only slightly because one lived in another state and the other several hundred miles away. I vividly remember the death of my grandmother on my mother's side because the aftermath was a horrifying experience to see. I must have been around 9 or 10 at the time. She lived in Cimarron, New Mexico, so we went there for the funeral. They kept delaying the service, waiting for her son, Uncle Paul, to come from San Francisco. We waited and we waited, but no Uncle Paul. For whatever reason, he was delayed a long time.

Whether this was the custom in Cimarron in those times, I don't know, but her body had not been embalmed and so the body began to decompose in the wooden casket. Her body fluids began seeping through the casket, and as a result the Catholic priest would not let them have her funeral service inside the church. It was held outside on the steps leading into the church entrance. The fluids naturally attracted flies, which made the scene even worse.

Seeing this happening to my grandmother must have really hurt my mother badly because at the grave, when they lowered the casket, she went berserk and would have jumped into the grave with her mother had she not been forcefully held back.

I had numerous odd jobs when I was in my teens, none of which lasted long. In La Junta I worked at a potato chip factory, peeling potatoes in a peeler that looked like a cement mixer with a rough interior. I also had a paper route, but not for long. One day it snowed so much that I couldn't ride my bicycle with that big load of papers so I had to push it. I got tired of pushing it, so I dumped all of them down a drain in the street. Needless to say, the next day I was canned. I also worked at the Fred Harvey Train Station Restaurant, which lasted for one night. My job was scrubbing stinking pots and pans, and I wasn't about to do that. It didn't appear that stick-to-itiveness was one my fortes.

By the time I was 16 my father had bought a 40-acre farm outside of La Junta, so we were living out in the country. Some winters got so cold that we had to wrap old rags around a long stick, light it, and then place it under the transmission to warm the transmission fluid long enough for the car to start. Here at the farm I had my first introduction to smoking. I sat on the front seat of my dad's car when he was not there, facing out from the driver's seat. I lit up, took a big puff, inhaled deeply, got woozy, and fell backward, gasping horribly. I started smoking when I was 11 and quit when I was 28—one of the smartest things I ever did.

One day I was riding my bicycle to town from my dad's farm so that I could drink beer and shoot pool with my buddies (the wrong crowd). I was barely 16, but I looked older than I was and was never refused alcohol. Along the dark road I ran into a man alongside walking in the same direction and knocked him out cold. I didn't want to be responsible for the accident, but I didn't want to just leave the man there both moaning and dying. I knew who the man was, so I went to the man's family, told them where he was lying, and lied that I had just found him there. Needless to say, I was an accident waiting to happen.

At that same time I went to Pueblo, some 200 miles away from La Junta, to live with my father's brother, Ed, for a short time, and while there I worked in a broom manufacturing plant, a hide tanning shop, and did a short stint in the Pueblo Steel Mills. My job at the hide tanning shop was to turn hides that were stacked on top of each other with salt between them to keep them from rotting while they were being preserved. The smelly, wet substance that got on my clothes was pretty raunchy by the end of the day. On my way home on the bus, people would look at me with contempt and the unspoken assessment, "Dirty, stinking Mexican!" Shortly thereafter I joined the Air Force. The thing I liked best about La Junta was seeing it in the rearview mirror.

PART II

Wandering in the Wilderness

Interlude

When I was being inducted into the Air Force in Pueblo, the government paid for the inductee's meals in a restaurant nearby. I went with a group of other inductees, and I saw that the menu was written in a completely foreign language to me—I didn't see tortillas, frijoles, or tamales listed. I didn't know what any of the meals on the menu were. One of the others said to me, "Go ahead and order, John!" I hid my ignorance by saying, "You go ahead. I'm still looking!" That fellow ordered veal cutlets. I figured if veal cutlets were good enough for him, they would be good enough for me. I ordered the same thing, and the same thing every day after that, for a long time.

I had completed the ninth grade, dropped out of school, forged my baptismal certificate, lied about my age, and joined the Air Force for a period of six years as an airman. I think my father signed my enlistment papers because he thought that sooner or later I was going to be in big trouble. My father's parting words to me when I went into the Air Force were never forgotten—mentally that is, but not behaviorally. My father told me, "Son, I don't have much in this world, but I have a good name. Don't ever bring shame to that." It would take 10 years for me to seriously heed those words.

After my induction into the Air Force, I was sent to Sheppard Air Force Base in Wichita Falls, Texas, for basic training. How I was transported there I don't remember. I most likely was sent there by a commercial bus. Lackland Air Force Base in San Antonio, Texas, was normally the place where this training was conducted, and to this day it still is. But because of a potential Korean conflict on the horizon, the United States was building up its military forces. The number of volunteers had become so large that the Air Force had to open another basic training center elsewhere to accommodate the overflow, and Sheppard was selected.

The United States was not at war at this time, nor did it want one. But trouble was brewing in a far-off land called Korea, and we felt we might have to use our muscle to handle it. Being the mightiest force at the time, we were looked upon as the policeman of the world, an expectation that exists to this day. Korea was ruled by Japan from 1910 until the closing days of World War II. In August 1945 the Soviet Union declared war on Japan and, by agreement with the United States, occupied Korea north of the 38th parallel. United States forces subsequently occupied the south of the Korean peninsula.

By 1948, two separate governments had been set up. Both governments claimed to be the legitimate government of Korea, and neither side accepted the border as permanent. The conflict escalated, with open warfare starting when North Korean forces (supported by the Soviet Union and China) invaded South Korea on June 25, 1950. On that day, the United Nations Security Council recognized this North Korean act as an invasion and called for an immediate ceasefire.

On June 27, 1950, the Security Council adopted a resolution known as the "Complaint of Aggression upon the Republic of Korea," and decided upon the formation and dispatch of the UN's forces in Korea. Twenty-one countries of the United Nations eventually contributed to the defense of South Korea, with the United States (quite naturally, as always) providing 88 percent of the military personnel and other essential warfare resources.

I didn't join the Air Force out of patriotism but to get away from the depressing environment in La Junta that I hated. But wearing the uniform was always a love of mine. Even 27 years after my retirement in 1992 after over 32 years of active service, when I wear my uniform for special speaking engagements, being in that uniform is where I am at home—where I am truly myself. It probably brings me a sense of belonging and security, what I still desire after a childhood without it.

The style of the Air Force uniform has changed quite a bit since my retirement, and Dot was always after me to get one in keeping with the times, but my quick reply was always, "This is the one I wore when I was on active duty, and that's the one I'm going to wear 'til the day I die!"

Basic training was quite a new experience for me, but a happy one. I needed the strict, disciplined kind of regimentation it provided—and the security, of course. We had to learn how to wear the uniform, march in cadence with others, salute, and respect those of higher rank. In those days a corporal thought he was a god, but a staff sergeant really was. There was strenuous physical training to turn flabby flesh into ready-for-combat muscle if the time ever came.

Unlike the cozy single rooms of brick airmen's quarters today, we lived in wooden barracks with open bays and communal showers with no privacy. Neatly pressed uniforms were hung on simple wooden racks built on the wall, with our undergarments and toiletries stored in footlockers at the foot of our beds, which were double bunked. Air-conditioned? Not in 1949! We were taught how to make our beds so tight that when Corporal Kennderly or Sergeant Bramblett tossed a quarter on it during inspection, the coin had better bounce. Combat boots were tan colored on issue and in time had to be polished spit black.

There was a fellow in my flight whose laugh was so funny it also made you laugh. It was before the days of soundtrack. He had worked for a comedian who had hired him to laugh so that his laugh would also make the audience laugh at his jokes. It was interesting and a growing experience to mix with men from so many different backgrounds, parts of the country, and cultures. The big appeal for me was that I was looked upon as ordinary and equal to any of them, and not as a stinky, low-life Mexican. On the days that our flight was not out training we had to pull KP (kitchen patrol) duty or base detail, which consisted of painting fences or other menial jobs.

There was an airman in our barracks from Chicago whose last name was Smith. Doing some forms of menial work can leave fatigues (work uniforms), not to mention the people wearing them, dirty and smelly. Smith was pimply faced and nasty anyway. He would seldom shower. Well, I got tired of putting up with that and talked to two big guys who were also from Chicago: Morehead and Jones. Morehead was as big as a gorilla and Jones had broad shoulders that were probably 40 inches wide with a 28-inch waist. He was all muscle. (Names changed to conceal real identities.)

I told them, "If you'll hold Smith, I'll scrub him!" They did, and when I got through scrubbing ol' Smith, he was as red as a beet. The soap and brush I used were government issue, so you can imagine how rough that was. Any time after that, when I would say, "Smith, let's go shower," Smith was only too glad to get with the program. Sometimes you have to take the bull by the horns—or in this case, "The nasty by the rump!"

I'm a kidder like my father, and I was always kidding around, even then. If I found someone I thought I could outfight napping on a hot summer day, I would gently and carefully squirt shaving cream on the palm of his hand, careful not to wake him up. Then I would start tickling his nose with a feather or other similar object and run away and hide and watch from where I couldn't be seen. When the fellow would swat his nose thinking it was a fly he would get the cream all over his face. My middle initial is "O" for "Orlando," but many people thought the "O" was really for "ornery."

2

Three Sheets to the Wind

1949–1950

When I graduated from basic training I was sent to Scott Air Force Base in Illinois near St. Louis, Missouri, for training as a control tower operator. During time off we would take a bus to an amusement park in St. Louis where there were booze and women. There was a fellow in my squadron whom many of the other fellows didn't like. They didn't like him because he was a shyster. He would lend a $10 bill during the middle of the month when they didn't have any money, to be paid back with a $20 bill on payday. Guys didn't like it, but they borrowed from him anyway.

One day after we had arrived in St. Louis on pass, we soon saw him staggering down the street. We went to see if there was something wrong with him so that we could help. He told us, "Get away from me, I'm okay!" Before the class graduated, he was arrested by the federal authorities because what he was doing was pretending to be inebriated so that some homosexual would pick him up. Once in the room for hanky-panky, he would roll them (beat them up and take their money), and then run away. The arrest couldn't have happened to a better person.

I was unable to learn how to land airplanes due to hangovers from my partying in St. Louis and washed out (flunked), so they sent me to the 37th Communications Squadron in Orlando Air Force Base in Florida, which was also the headquarters for the 14th Air Force. My first time in the South with all that greenery as opposed to the flat, dusty, ugly landscape of eastern Colorado was stupendous. This was paradise—heaven on earth.

It was the first time I had to drive a jeep with four-wheel drive, common in automobiles today but rare then. My buddies and I would take it out in the swamps and get it stuck in wet sand to make it prove it could do what they said it could. There was a nice beach on the base to go and relax, and I spent a lot of off-time there sunbathing, swimming, and enjoying the good life.

I was doing on-the-job training to learn how to be a voice radio operator. It was in the same radio shack where they also had Morse-code operators: the "dit-dit-dit-dot" guys. Smart phones? You gotta be kidding! They didn't even have landlines. Smart phones were eons away. My job was to get the incoming call from some high official from my base who wanted to talk to another official at a distant base. When both officials were on the line, one would talk and when he got through with his end of the conversation, he would say, "Over." The operator on the other end and I would turn a switch, and that procedure was reversed back and forth until the conversation ended. Pretty up-to date stuff in 1949–1950.

Girls from Orlando and nearby towns would come to the Airmen's Club for dances. And that's where I met Sally Mae (not her real name). I was 17 and she was 22. Her father owned a lumber mill in a neighboring city near Orlando, and she owned a dress shop. *Pretty classy*, thought this snot-nosed Mexican kid from the barrios of La Junta. "I'd better make time with her." And latch on to her I did. I knew I couldn't tell her I was only 17, so I lied and told her I was 22. (I also lied to Dot about my age when we first dated, she being eight months older than I.)

I always looked older than I was, and that was why I was never questioned when I bought beer. I maintained a steady relationship with Sally Mae, who would come out and pick me up at the base and we would have party time together. She frequently picked up the tab, because how could a private making $75 a month match the income of a dress shop owner? That relationship ended when in June 1950 the Air Force moved the 14th Air Force Headquarters to Robins Air Force Base in Warner Robins, Georgia, and closed the base in Orlando.

I rode on one of the convoy trucks to Robins. I became good friends with Jack from Louisiana, who went on to become a millionaire civil lawyer, and a West Virginian by the name of Howard, who probably ended up behind bars or six feet under if he didn't change his ways. Jack, Howard, and I became drinking buddies from the start. Jack and Howard worked in the radio shack with me, both dit-dit-dit-dot operators. I liked Jack because he was a gentle, likeable guy who laughed at my silliness. I liked Howard, who was feisty and a scrapper like me, ready to fight at the drop of a hat. Back to back in a scrape, Howard and I were hard to handle. It was at Robins that I started my escalated wayward behavior, as well as becoming the 180-degree opposite of the one who personified the words of the Apostle Paul in 2 Corinthians 5:17: "Therefore, if anyone is in Christ, he is a new creation. The old has passed away; behold the new has come."

We'd buy beer cheap at the base and sneak it into a local club where we hid it under the table, and after ordering only one beer at the busy club's price we would tap the cheap stash that we had brought. Brawling and fighting in this club were not uncommon—nor Howard and I being in the middle of it. Instead of ID cards, airmen had passes to go off base. My misconduct got to the point that the squadron commander, Captain Adams, restricted me from access to my pass.

Didn't bother me—I'd borrow someone else's pass, flash it at the gate, and get off the base and back on without a problem. One night when we came on the base I must have been tipsy and weaving because I was pulled over. I got out of the car, and when the fellow approached me in civilian clothes he said to me, "I'm General So-and-So." I saluted and replied, "Glad to meet you, sir. I am Private First Class Solano!" He chewed me out and told me to get to my barracks and stay there.

In later years when I would visit my millionaire friend Jack, he would remember this incident and laugh. But he would embellish it by saying that when I had replied to the general I had said, "I'm Private First Class Solano, and I don't give a damn who you are!"

Captain Adams got wind of this and called me in and blessed me out. In exasperation he said, "Solano, what am I going to do with you?" I replied, "I don't know, sir." He ended up keeping me on base and my car off base for a certain period of time as punishment. For some reason, Captain Adams and the first sergeant liked me and let me get away with more than they should have. That would be called "enabling" in 2019.

If I had had the ability to look within myself in those days, I would have seen where and why and with whom I was behaving the way I was. I was furious with the society that had made me feel like I was nothing just because my nationality didn't fit in with theirs. I was furious with my parents who were responsible for bringing me into this world. I was even furious with God because He favored some with the good life, and punished others with a crummy life like mine for no apparent reason and through no fault of my own.

I had so much rage that one night in a drunken stupor I looked heavenward in a nightclub parking lot and cursed God. But, as you'll see in the later events of this story, God has big shoulders, can put up with any childish tantrum that I wanted to pitch, and always—always—has the last laugh and the last word.

Early in our days at Robins, my two buddies and I met two beautiful blondes who loved to party as much as we did, with all that goes along with it. One was from Warner Robins, and her cousin from Alabama would come and spend time in Warner Robins. We were three males and only two females, but that didn't bother us. Like the three musketeers, "All for one, and one for all!" We all had the time of our lives self-indulging in sinful pleasure—or so we thought.

Jack and I were like brothers and full of vim and vigor. Howard had been shipped out elsewhere. The Korean War had started, so we volunteered to go there so that we could get a piece of the action. They would take me, but not Jack because he had had a heart murmur when he was a child. If they wouldn't take us both, we wouldn't go. Ironically, the end of that story is that Jack ended up being sent to Korea, and I went to Japan.

Before Howard was shipped out, he, Jack, and I were asked to join the 37th Communications Squadron baseball team. Howard was an excellent pitcher. I was not much of an athlete but I filled the centerfield slot with the cap cocked behind my head so as to not mess up my curly hair. When it came time to play the championship tournament, we won. There was all manner of whooping and hollering by the 37th Comm team champs.

And that's how Dot Pratt comes into the picture. Her date was on the defeated team. Apparently Dot had had her eye on me throughout the game because at one point she said to me, "What are you whooping and hollering about? All you did was stand out in centerfield, looking pretty and showing off your pretty curls!" I was infuriated! I was a macho guy, and I wasn't going to let any woman talk to me that way. I told one of my buddies, "I'm going to get that woman in bed one of these days." After we married I told her what I had told him, and she said, "Yeah, you did. But you had to marry me to do it!" The rest is history, and the next chapter of this story begins to unfold.

God made us with a free will to choose what we want to do with our lives and how to do it. We are all given the choice to live life the right way or the wrong way. Finding the right way and doing it are two different matters—and both are matters of personal understanding and application. Bible-believing persons believe that the model and standards for the right way are found in Scriptures and thus translated into living a life under God's will. They believe that living life relying completely on what a person selfishly wants and does is the wrong way. We all struggle with trying to know what the will of God is.

Rabbi Rami Shapiro in his book *Recovery: The Art of Spiritual Living* has an interesting view of this concept that is food for thought. For Shapiro, God's will is Reality—everything that was, is, and ever would be. He believed that whatever was happening in the world at any moment was God's will, and that God's will for his life was different than God's will for yours and mine. We are meant to become as conscious as possible in the situation we find ourselves in, and our true desire is to navigate our reality in a way to maximize love. There is a right way to engage life, a foolish way, and a wise way. The wise way is an expansive one, enabling us to grow in compassion, courage, wisdom, truth, and trust. The foolish way is constricting, locking us up behind a wall of anger and fear, and robbing us of trust and trustworthiness. God's will is simply that we will respond in a wise way to whatever is happening in the moment. Finding that will means finding the current of godliness that enables us to live with love.

He explains that we all operate from a position of weakness by surrendering to God. Instead of an imposition of self, we tap into God's strength. Karma teaches us that we cannot change what is, but we can learn to work with what is in order to influence what will be. Everything is constantly changing; nothing is static. By focusing on the forces at play we can more mindfully engage in the reality unfolding around us and within us. Our objective is to live in harmony with God's will, always leading to actions that are loving and just.

The Christian practice of "kenosis," or self-emptying is referred to in Philippians 2:7, where we find the phrase "Jesus emptied himself." He did so in order to be filled with God. In this way we can put on the mind of Christ and see the divine in, with, and as all reality. Centering prayer is very helpful in self-emptying. Shapiro encourages us to practice constantly living out of the center of our being, living out of the fullness of who we are. He urges us to move from a conversation with Christ to communion with Him. To commune with Christ is to rest in His presence.

Not bad, coming from a Jewish brother!

In a more general sense, the pleasure principle explains that human behavior is motivated by what brings us pleasure and reward, and avoidance of what brings us pain and punishment. It's obvious that you can't give what you don't have, and up to this point I had very little to give to complete His story in my life. I was feisty, quick-tempered, and ready to fight at the drop of a hat. I was known to get drunk, walk up to the biggest fellow at a bar, and get in his face with the boast, "I don't like your looks and I'm fixing to change them."

It was all a stupid bluff, but the other fellow didn't know it. My bluff went unchallenged most of the time as my buddies calmed me down, but it was my way of gaining false respect and admiration from my drinking buddies. In retrospect, I see that if God and Dot hadn't come into my life, I would probably have ended up behind bars or six feet under. My I-don't-care attitude could only be described as bordering on antisocial behavior that would eventually destroy me if not corrected. I had come to the point where I didn't care about anything or anybody. As warped and false as it might seem, there was a sense of freedom being in a world of your own making where nobody tells you what to say or what to do, no matter the consequences.

I struggled my entire life balancing a trait that I inherited from my father, and that was either being too harsh or too tenderhearted. Living a life of right and wrong is a constant daily battle for all of us—even ministers. As you'll see later on in this story, even after surrendering my life to Christ I was sometimes too harsh. On the other hand I could see a heart-rending human-interest scene in real life or a movie and be driven to tears.

Another trait I inherited from my father was being a practical jokester. I learned to be witty, charming, and winsome and could be the life of the party. Sometimes Dot thought I bordered on simply being silly—which is probably true. Interestingly, the word "silly" is derived from the Old English word "seely," which means happy, blissful, lucky, or blessed. But I enjoyed making people laugh. To be honest, I think I sometimes I used this trait as a defense mechanism to control and steer the conversation away from more serious dialogue in which I felt ill equipped to engage. I also loved the attention.

In my early days I displayed an exterior superiority complex that covered an inner inferiority complex. Through 57-plus years of pastoral counseling, I came to realize that we all have imperfections. We're all screwed up. It's not a matter of kind, but degree. We can recognize these character flaws, take responsibility for them, and do something to correct them, or we can blame everyone and everything else for our predicament, as had become fashionable in the year 2019. The prime excuse was, "I'm in this bad state of affairs because of my race, my environment, my lack of education, because of this or that." Give me a break. Suck it up and move on!

There was little evidence of personal accountability, and finger-pointing was the norm in blaming anything and everything instead of taking charge for our own actions. I liked to tell a story that humorously hits the nail on the head about seeing imperfections in others. A minister was preaching about the perfection of Jesus. At one point he said, "I have never heard of anyone other than Jesus being perfect, have you?" A fellow in the congregation hollered out, "I have!" Shocked, the preacher asked, "And who might that have been?" The fellow responded, "My wife's first husband!"

When I was a child, the main developers of character in society were the family, the church, and the school. At the time of this writing, social media was the main influencer because the family, the church, and the school were in disarray.

And I have to be honest and admit that, in my early days of life, I also blamed everyone and everything for the story I inherited. I thank God that He gave me the opportunity, His power, and a wonderful woman to help me change my story. And that's where God's story in the lives of a man and a woman from two completely different earthly origins started in joint ministry. As you will see, it could only have been a union made in heaven because there was very little in common between these two to make it so.

PART III

And the Two Shall Become One

3

Garbage In, Garbage Out

Warner Robins / Columbus, Georgia, 1950–1959

"Dislike at First Sight Turns into Love at First Dance!" could easily be the title of the first chapter of our joint story. I had a car that I had conned my father out of. My father was working for the railroad and farming his 40 acres at the same time. He owned a pickup and a 1941 Plymouth sedan. I wrote my father a real sob story about how far my military base was from a sizeable town and how this poor boy was stranded out in the boonies and suffering so badly. I really laid it on heavy. My father had never deprived me of anything I wanted if he could manage it. I offered to buy his car now that I was making big money as a private ($75 a month). My father wrote back, "Son, if you want the car, come get it!" which I knew he would say, and I did—and shamefully never paid him a cent for it.

One of my big problems in my late teens was that I saw women as objects of amusement and pleasure to be used, and I didn't attach myself to one for long. Insight today leads me to believe that it was all about control and feeling important in the same way that many others use fortune and fame to control people and situations. Besides the casual baseball episode mentioned earlier, Dot and I actually met at the Warner Robins skating rink, which was a local hangout for teens and those in their early twenties. The rink was a large wooden building with a snack bar and a counter for renting skates. Nothing ornate. The skating area was surrounded by a waist-tall wooden railing for spectators to watch the skaters. A huge revolving ball made of chipped mirror pieces hung from the ceiling with a spotlight shining on it that would create spots of light all over the skating rink as the ball turned.

Dot says her second remembrance of me after that baseball incident was when I once passed by her with my tattooed right arm of a naked woman and my cigarette pack tucked under the sleeve of my T-shirt with an Elvis Presley hairstyle and strutting like John Wayne. One of the girls nearby sighed, "If only he would look at me." Dot responded, "You have a taste for horse manure."

In September 1950 my buddies had made plans to attend the Labor Day dance in Macon, Georgia. They had dates, but I didn't and at that late hour no list of prospects. One of my buddies suggested calling Dot Pratt. My immediate response was, "You have to be kidding! I don't even like her. Period. I wouldn't date her if she was the last person on earth." Little did I know that God would make me eat those words. After much pleading, and not wanting to let my buddies down, I consented and called her.

Her response was, "Call me back in 20 minutes." I was to find out later that I was her second choice. A boy Dot had been dating would either not show up or show up late. I called back in 20 minutes, and since the other fellow hadn't shown up or called, she consented to date me. The miracle of miracles happened. God's plan for these two opposites was starting to take shape for the long journey He had in mind.

The arrows that Cupid shot into our hearts on the dance floor created a love in both of us that was irresistible and would last for a lifetime. It was love at first dance, and the rest is history. Three months later, we exchanged wedding vows and rings, and through all the storms that came our way we lived up to those vows, especially the one claiming, "'Til death do us part."

Dot and I began our 64-year earthly journey together on December 31, 1950. It was a happy moment that soon turned into nine years of a stormy relationship with the strong possibility of ending in divorce. In fact, during our arguments, divorce was always discussed as the possible solution to our unhappiness. Dot would turn to the person who had earlier given her security, her father—I would turn to the bottle. In argu-

Our wedding day, December 31, 1950, First Baptist Church, Warner Robins, Georgia

ments during our early days, Dot would say, "I'm going back home!" I would respond with, "There's the door. But if you go, you're not coming back. The door's going to be locked."

Typical me. Bluff had worked before, and it was all bluff again. I would have taken her back in a heartbeat. But Dot didn't know that, and it worked. One day she called her father after an argument. He said, "Put Johnny on the phone." When she did, he asked me, "What's going on, Johnny?" I answered, "Why don't you come over and find out?" He knew from my tone of voice that he had better not. Her father never interfered in our affairs after that and let us battle it out for ourselves. More often than not I would storm out the door and use that as an excuse to go drinking.

The union was rocky from the start. We didn't really know each other, had very little in common, and courted but three months. And, in truth, we were a couple of mixed-up teenagers. Many who knew us predicted it would

Warner Robins, Georgia, 1952

not last. In later years, Dot would jokingly say, "The only reason we are staying together is to prove them wrong." She was something else, that girl!

As stated before, Dot and I came from totally different backgrounds and had absolutely nothing in common for building a relationship. We were opposites in every way, and most of our problems stemmed from that. As I look back, I have to admit that I was probably the main reason for our discontent because I carried a lot of negative baggage.

When I first had the opportunity to visit the southern part of our great nation, I was appalled at the way blacks were treated and shamefully referred to with the n-word. There were not many blacks in Colorado at this time, so the few who were there fit right in. Although I knew that was not the case in the South, I had had my fill of being put down, and as long as segregation didn't apply to me, I could live with it.

Dot's father was a staunch seg-
regationist at the time, and the
day after I came courting Dot,
her father said to her, "I'll bet
he has nigger blood in him." He
mellowed some as the years went
by as the national viewpoint on
segregation changed. Humorously, when I made full colonel in
the Air Force some 34 years later,
he would proudly introduce me
as "my son-in-law, the colonel!"
Slow learner, that guy!

Dot also was in for a huge
shocking surprise. On her first
visit to my parents in Colorado,
Dot heard some of my relatives

Warner Robins, Georgia, 1952

say, "Do you remember so-and-so? He married a white girl too." Dot's
reaction was, "What in the world are they talking about?" She probably
also wondered, "What in the world did I get myself into?" Had I married a Caucasian in Colorado at that time (which was rare, if at all), I
also would have felt that I had married a white girl because of the stares
and the glares. But I never felt that way with Dot in the South—maybe I
blended in well enough.

But I learned later that segregation and discrimination are part and
parcel of our sinful makeup as we try to make ourselves feel better by
thinking that others are beneath us. All minorities were referred to in
contempt in different parts of the country, with names such as "spics" for
the Mexicans, "micks" for the Irish, "chinks" for the Chinese, "wops" for
the Italians, "slant eyes" for the Japanese, and so on. Why do we do it?

Daniel Schachter has written, in *Searching for Memory*, that memory is a central part of the brain that attempts to make sense of experience, and to tell coherent stories about it. These stories are all we have of our pasts, and so they have a powerful impact on how we view ourselves and what we do. Yet our stories are built from different ingredients: snippets of what actually happened, and beliefs that guide us as we attempt to remember. Our memories are fragile but powerful products of what we recall from the past, believe about the present, and imagine about the future.

The Bible clearly says in 2 Corinthians 6:14, "Do not be yoked together with unbelievers. For what do righteousness and wickedness have in common? Or what fellowship can light have with darkness?" And Scripture says that for good reason. Dot was a professing Christian at the time, and I was not. She would talk to me about her faith in Christ,

Dot as a student at Anderson College, Anderson, South Carolina

and I would belittle her with such insults as, "I can have as much faith in this chair as you do in your Jesus with the same results!" Not only did I abuse her verbally, but I even slapped her around a couple of times—until—until—one day she picked up the frying pan and gave me that Dot Solano you-know-where-you-can-go-to look—and that was the end of that. They say that "opposites attract." But opposites also cause each other a lot of grief.

This was true of us. We were not evenly yoked in many ways, including education. As I indicated earlier, Dot was very smart and had completed several semesters at Anderson College in South Carolina. I was as dumb as a mule, going nowhere fast. Dot didn't like me because of my cocky, (false) self-assurance, and I didn't like her because I thought she was "Miss-It-on-the-Stick," strutting around town in her father's Cadillac.

One may find it strange that two people with such differences with and dislikes for each other would end up writing a romantic saga of a 64-year blessed marriage. Quite frankly, some would say, "It was a twist of fate." In actuality, "It was a fate designed by the good Lord above."

In February 1953 our first son, Keith, was born at Robins Air Force Base in Warner Robins, Georgia. I remember the cost of his birth as being around $5.35—quite different from what it would have been in a civilian hospital. Keith went on to become a physician with two specialties, internal medicine and nuclear medicine, and served in the Army in that capacity for a period of over 28 years, retiring in the rank of full colonel. Upon military retirement he joined the largest group of physicians in the civilian sector in Colorado Springs, Colorado. In 2019, after 39 years of seeing patients, he tapered his patient load so that he could teach younger doctors about nuclear medicine.

Oftentimes when children argued and misbehaved, the parents said to them, "Time out," and sent them to their room to cool off and regain proper self-control. Our heavenly father did that to us. He gave Dot and me a lengthy time out. He kept Dot in Warner Robins and sent me to another part of the world, giving us sixteen months to cool off and show us about proper relational composure.

In May of our second year of marriage, we got a break from a fractured relationship when I was sent to Misawa Air Base in northern Japan. Japan at that time was still recovering from all the devastation caused when we bombed the daylights out of them for a war they dastardly caused with their sneak attack on Pearl Harbor, known as "the day of infamy." Japanese women still dressed in kimonos, wore wooden clogs for shoes, rode bicycles, and got rid of human waste by channeling it down in drains (known as "benjo ditches"). They used this human waste for fertilizer and grew the biggest produce I had ever seen. The smell floated horribly all over the area, but the Japanese were very gracious people.

I was assigned to a squadron out in the boonies whose mission was to intercept and interpret conversations of other nearby foreign countries, and crypto was the vocabulary used. All of this was secret stuff behind a barbed-wire fence that I knew nothing about. I was a staff sergeant in the field of journalism at the time.

My job was to report news, and there was no news to report, so in essence I didn't have a job. I spent most of my time catching a bus to the main part of the base, drinking and shooting pool at the Non-Commissioned Officers' Club. One night I had called a cab to take me back to my barracks. When the cab arrived, another drunk sergeant got into the cab by mistake. I wasn't about to let this guy take my cab, so I grabbed him and pitched him out and took the cab for myself. Not one of my finer moments.

Typical of other mean things that I was capable of doing is the following story: My roommate was a technical sergeant from North Carolina with poor eyesight who wore thick glasses. It was the practice of the Non-Commissioned Officers' Club to award a bottle of champagne to sergeants during their birthday month. When I was given mine, my roommate and I drank it with the understanding that we would drink his when he got it the following month. In the interim, my roommate and his brother, who was stationed in Korea, made plans to meet in Tokyo for what is called R&R (rest and recuperation). My roommate decided he would take the bottle of champagne to Tokyo so that he and his brother could celebrate. In the meantime he kept the bottle in his closet.

One day my buddies and I went out partying in the local village. When we got back to the barracks pretty well tanked, we wanted more booze. But everything was closed by that time. I remembered my roommate's bottle of champagne stashed in his closet. My roommate was at work, so we drank it. To make matters worse, I filled it back up with water and placed the cork back on as neatly as I could. My roommate, having poor eyesight, didn't discover what I had done until he and his brother went to drink it in Tokyo and discovered it was water and not champagne. He was mad as a hornet. But knowing my reputation for being a scrapper, he didn't press the issue. It's obvious that with that kind of behavior, I did indeed need salvation of some sort. And that did miraculously happen.

It was at Misawa Air Base in a makeshift chapel that I came to know Jesus Christ as my personal Lord and Savior under the ministry of an American Baptist chaplain. That happened in a strange way—what many of us consider to be a "God thing." The squadron had devoted a section of a warehouse into a makeshift theater, and also decided to use it as a chapel. The Protestants arranged for the Army chaplain at the main part of the base to conduct services in that makeshift chapel on Sunday instead of having to transport the personnel to the main part of the base for worship over a bumpy, unpaved road.

The squadron commander thought this was a novel undertaking and he asked me to attend and do an article about the proceedings. I attended on official duty but kept coming back on following Sundays because I found the good news of salvation in Jesus Christ very interesting, and actually irresistible. With every Sunday that I came back, I found that message to be overwhelming and overpowering.

One Sunday at the end of the service, this tough, macho phony was so moved by the Christian gospel that I started shaking like a leaf and then broke into uncontrollable sobbing. As is typical among Baptists, the American Baptist chaplain extended an invitation to come forward to accept Jesus Christ as Lord and Savior, and the Lord used me to lead a group of eight others by going forward and committing my life to Christ. To this day, I am convinced that the hand of God reached down from heaven and carried me forward because I would never have made such a spectacle of myself of my own volition.

To me, my Christian conversion experience was as dramatic as that of the Apostle Paul's on the road to Damascus (Acts 9:1–9). I had been raised in the Catholic Church and baptized, but my family was not much of a churchgoing family. Sunday mornings I would leave the house to attend church, but would stop under a bridge to smoke where I had my cigarettes hidden instead. If my parents suspected, they never said anything. Why go to church only to be reminded of the only God I knew? My picture of God was the same as many people's— God is an unforgiving, severe Creator up yonder who is taking note of your every action, recording it, and one day will punish you for all your bad behavior. *Zap*— and it's all over!

That was not the God I met that morning in that makeshift chapel. This was a personal, loving, caring, and forgiving God who loved humanity so much that He would come in human form and take the penalty for our bad behavior upon himself so that we wouldn't have to.

"For God so loved the world, that He gave his one and only Son, that whosoever believes in him, shall not perish, but have eternal life. For God did not send his Son into the world to condemn the world, but to save the world through him" (John 3:16–17). "There is none righteous, no not one. For all have sinned, and come short of the glory of God!" (Romans 3:23). "For the wages of sin is death, but the gift of God is eternal life in Christ Jesus our Lord" (Romans 6:23). After my personal experience with the Living Christ, I would lie in bed in my barracks at night wishing that I would die. Not because I was suicidal or had a death wish, but because that first taste of God's wonderful, merciful, forgiving love was like water to a thirsty man in the Sahara Desert.

No longer did I feel like I was that dirty little Mexican kid from La Junta. I had had a spiritual transfusion—I now had royal blood—I was a child of a king—the King of kings, in fact. I became a prince! I came to realize for the first time in my life that "God was not mad *at* me," but that "God was mad *about* me!" I was taken under the wing of a Christian technical sergeant in the orderly room and a corporal in the supply room, and they helped keep me straight until my return and discharge in September 1954.

As I was writing this manuscript, I started reading Laura Hillenbrand's book *Unbroken: A World War II Story of Survival, Resilience, and Redemption*, which was later made into the well-received movie *Unbroken*.

Unbroken is the story of the famous Olympic champion runner named Louie Zamperini, who later was captured by the Japanese, subjected to terrible torture, and survived. He credited his ability to endure their torment to his untiring, never-give-up tenacity on the track. An example of that tenacity is related in Hillenbrand's book. On the night before the race, a Notre Dame coach told Louie that rival coaches were ordering their runners to sharpen their spikes and lash him. Halfway through the race, just as Louie was about to make a move for the lead, several runners surrounded him, boxing him in. He couldn't break loose, and he couldn't get around the other men. Suddenly the man beside him swerved in and stomped on his foot, impaling Louie's toe with his spike. Seonds later, the other man ahead began kicking backward, cutting both of Louie's shins. A third man elbowed Louie's chest so hard that he cracked Louie's rib. The crowd gasped. But even with all that pain Louie stayed in the race. Nearing the final turn, he saw a tiny gap open in front of him, and he burst through with his shoe torn open, shins streaming blood, and chest aching, and won the race easily.

Because of his ordeal as a POW, and later going back to Japan to find his tormentors to forgive them after he became a Christian, he was hailed as a hero. I saw the movie based on Louie's life while reading the book and was disappointed that the movie didn't credit his conversion under Billy Graham as Louie's main reason for going back to Japan in later years to locate his tormentors in order to forgive them in person.

In reading about Louie's early life of drinking, stealing, womanizing, and all the rest that came to an end when he accepted Christ as Lord and Savior at one of Billy Graham's early tent revivals, I was surprised how our early wayward lives paralleled. In my 32-plus years of military service, I never saw action in a war zone like Louie Zamperini, but the enemy I was battling within myself was just as real to me and could have destroyed me had I not found God as my liberator to help me win my inner struggle. Of course, it goes without saying that He used my wife as His powerful instrument to do that. And I was not unique in my struggles. We all have demons to conquer. In fact, truth be known, even you who are reading these words have demons you're battling right now.

Neither Louie's transformation nor mine was self-generated, but came by the will and doing of the Almighty God to accomplish His purpose. Such transformation of a tarnished object of God's creation is described allegorically in Jeremiah 18:3–4, where the prophet writes, "So I went to the Potter's house, and I saw him working at the wheel. But the pot he was shaping from the clay was marred in his hands; so the potter formed it into another pot, shaping it as seemed best to him"—the Potter, of course, being God, and the marred pot being none other than God's creatures disfiguring his precious creation with their sinful ways.

As I said earlier, I was befriended by two fine Christians, a technical sergeant and a corporal who helped me in my beginning baby steps as a new believer. The technical sergeant was a Master Mason in the Masonic lodge and petitioned me to become a 3rd degree Master Mason as well. And that I did. In attending Masonic meetings I found a brotherly love that I had never experienced, and the importance of good character and wholesome living.

You would think that after having such a dramatic personal conversion, my life from this point on up the spiritual ladder would be smooth and easy. Such was not the case. As many other Christians have found out, we are still free-willed to pick and choose where and how that journey will take us. That unforeseen road has many twists, turns, and temptations luring us toward the high road or the low road. Things don't always work the way we plan, nor might God's plans align with our own, for that matter—and the reason is that we have the personal choice to do our will or His.

I had somewhat of a problem integrating back into family life when I returned from Japan. Things are not the same way you left them after being gone for 16 months, so you can't expect to pick up where you left off. I didn't have sense enough to know that. When Dot, Keith, and I would be in the living room, Dot would say to my son, "Keith, go and give Daddy a kiss," Keith would go past me to kiss my picture, which was

With Dot's relatives, 1956
1st row: James M.H. Pratt, our son Keith Solano, Dot Pratt Solano, John O. Solano
2nd row: Revere Pratt, Meredith Pratt, Doyle Pratt, Peggy Pratt
3rd row: Royce and Naomi Pratt, Dot's parents

the only daddy he knew. The problem in the adjustment period was not Dot's but mine. Like too many of us, I have always been very controlling: it's my way or the highway.

As many military personnel in the Middle East war discovered after long deployments, you can't come back and immediately take control of a situation that another has handled very well in your absence. Unless the shift of power is done gradually and cooperatively, you can expect the fur to fly.

We had some friction at the beginning but weathered it well, mostly because Dot was able to put up with a lot of my stupid ways. For nine years she said she was sorry after an argument when I wasn't man enough to do it when I was at fault. We were both professing Christians, but I was still in spiritual diapers.

I had acquired my GED and entered Mercer University, in Macon, Georgia, as a predental student under probation with financial assistance from the government GI Bill. At the time, Dot's brother, Doyle, was in dental school at Emory University in Atlanta, and I, in my naiveté, thought *I'll pursue the same course and when I finish, Doyle will have been in practice and we'll go in together.* There really was no basis for entertaining that thought because at the time we married, Doyle didn't like me and I knew it.

In time I reverted back to some of my cocky ways, and it didn't take long for Dean Burt at Mercer to size up ol' John. In essence, in one of our counseling sessions, he told me, "I've seen your kind come through here before, and it doesn't take long for us to weed them out." Looking back, Dean Burt was giving me a challenge in reverse psychology, and I would eventually decide to prove the dean wrong. After struggling with chemistry for several semesters and the sum of my knowledge of chemistry only being that H_2O = water—and believing that if you couldn't actually see molecules they didn't exist—I decided I needed to pursue another course of study.

I met up with two fellows—Don, who later became a school superintendent, and Wayne, who God only knows what happened to him—and we became drinking buddies. For about a year I, the professing Christian, made Dot's life a living hell. There were times when Dot would come home and find me either passed out on the couch or out partying with the boys. I could write a book about my foolish behavior.

I was like the town drunk in a small town in Alabama. The only time he came to church was during revival meetings. He would get religion that would last for about a week, and then he'd go back to his old drinking ways. One year when he went through the same phony routine, he was heard to pray, "Oh Lord, fill me with your Spirit. Oh Lord, fill me with you Spirit!" The third time he said that, this little old lady who was behind him and had heard this chatter time and time again, looked heavenward and said, "Don't you do it, Lord. He leaks." That was my problem: "I had leaked," and the wonderful relationship with God that I had experienced in Japan was no longer there.

By this time, I had become a 32nd degree Mason and a Shriner. One day, a fellow student by the name of Harold, also a Shriner, and I went to a Shriners convention in Atlanta. While there, we tied one on, as some Shriners are known to do. As we started our way back to Macon, I suggested to Harold that he jump in the backseat and sleep, and I would drive the first part of the leg back, which Harold did.

Roads were only two lanes in those days. Halfway home I noticed that we needed some gas, so I pulled into a gas station and filled up. I woke Harold up, and I jumped in the backseat to sleep. However, I failed to tell Harold that when I pulled into the station the car was facing back in the direction from whence we had come. About an hour and a half later, Harold woke me up saying, "John, I think we're back in Atlanta!" With all of my shenanigans, a lesser woman than Dot would have pitched me out on my ear with full justification.

But she saw a person in me that I didn't see in myself and stuck with me. My grades were atrocious that first year. Then I got my act together, beginning a job at nearby Robins Air Force Base at night and attending school during the day. Dot and I could have been the model for the song "Strangers in the Night." We saw each other in passing, but life still took on a semblance of normality.

While working at Robins, I was befriended by a female in her 60s who almost caused us to divorce. She had recently been widowed and had received a sizeable amount of money from her husband's insurance policy. Our friendship blossomed and she became like one of the family—too much so. She showered me with all manner of gifts, even to the point of buying me an expensive diamond lapel Shrine pin. And she always had liquor available for me in her house trailer, which I happily consumed. I felt obligated to include her in all of our social life, and Dot rightly resented this deeply. This widow even offered the use of her brand-new car and joined us on a trip to Colorado to visit my relatives. In retrospect, I believe she felt that I would care for her, when I became a thriving dentist, as she was caring for me. In time I realized what was happening and saved our marriage by severing the relationship.

My grades improved to the point that I made the dean's list and remained there until my graduation in June 1958 with a major in psychology and a double minor in speech and Spanish. I also became involved in theatre and appeared in numerous plays.

Our second son, Don, was born in June 1955 in Macon, Georgia. Don went on to earn several college degrees and served as a computer specialist, retiring as an Air Force lieutenant colonel, and doing the same job he was doing at the time of his retirement as a civil servant government employee in the grade of GS-13 in Oviedo, Florida, until his second retirement in June 2018. Of all our children, I remember Don as being on his knees praying first thing out of bed in the morning and the last thing before going to bed since the earliest days of his life. One of my early part-time jobs for a short period of time while a student at Mercer was as a dance instructor for Arthur Murray Dance Studios. I mention this to make a point later on in the story.

4

Prodigal Son Comes Home

Columbus, Georgia–Wake Forest, North Carolina, 1959–1964

I had planned on seeking a master's degree in speech therapy, but mounting bills made it necessary for me to go to work, and Dot was pregnant with our third child, Mike, at this time. So upon college graduation in June 1958, I took a job as a retail store management trainee with Montgomery Ward in Columbus, Georgia. From my boss, the store manager, C. E. McAlister, I had my first lesson in looking at things optimistically instead of negatively. When I encountered a problem I would come to him and say, "Mac" (as he was fondly called), "we have a problem." "No, John," Mac would say to me, "we have an opportunity!" I always wondered if Mac purposely created these problems to see how I would handle them.

We joined the First Baptist Church in Columbus because we were told it was good for business. We had been only occasional church attenders in Warner Robins and didn't do much better in Columbus. I was told that I showed great promise, and that I would likely be a store manager within a five-year period. But God had other plans for me. For some strange reason, I decided to attend a worship service at First Baptist on the night of February 19, 1959. That seemed rather odd to Dot since I didn't even attend morning services that often.

At the conclusion of the worship service, an invitation was offered to come forward to accept Jesus as Lord and Savior, for rededication of life or to full-time Christian service, as is customary in Baptist Churches. I had accepted Jesus as my Savior in 1953 in Misawa, Japan, but it was at this moment, like a bolt of lightning out of the blue, that I came to know Christ as my Lord.

I honestly surrendered my life to Him as fully as I knew how—for God to do with me as He wished. And I discovered that there is a world of difference between knowing Jesus as Savior and knowing Him as Lord. As Savior, it's all about what He did and can do for me. As Lord, it's about what I can and must do for Him. I went forth and gave my life to full-time Christian ministry. Like my going forward in Japan six years before, I truly believe it was God's doing—with me willing, of course! I knew nothing about what church work involved, and absolutely nothing about what the ministry required of a minister.

Furthermore, just two months earlier at a Montgomery Ward Christmas party, the assistant store manager and I were so drunk that we were out on the dance floor dancing together like a couple of fools. I was the least likely candidate to be a minister. But that's where it all began. Everybody thought I was crazy, including my wife and myself. But I was undaunted. Nothing felt so right. I felt like the square peg in the square hole. There was no doubt in my mind, as ridiculous as it all seemed at the time, that I had been created for this purpose. As with Esther in the book of Esther in the Old Testament, God had brought me to this point in my life "for such a time as this" (4:14)

With all the bills facing us from years past due to college expenses, and with Mike about to be born, Dot refused to go back to work to support my decision to go to seminary to prepare for the ministry. But I, in my usual take-charge manner, gave her three ultimatums: (1) "You can go and we can live off of what I make part time," (2) "You can go back to work to help me secure my education," or (3) "You can stay, but I am going!" Dot gave in, which was the beginning of a wonderful team effort where God used us both in a multitude of settings to minister to thousands of His people for the next 54 years in America and across two continents.

In later years Dot would often say, "I used to pray for God to save John when he wasn't a Christian. But when God called him to the ministry, I said, 'Lord, I didn't mean for you to go that far!'" She would add, "People talk about miracles. I'm married to one!" Mike was born in Columbus, Georgia, in March 1959. He went on to secure his undergraduate degree from Auburn University and his master of divinity degree from Duke University. He then served churches in North Carolina, eight years as an Air Force chaplain, and ended up as chaplain for the Texas Air National Guard in San Antonio, retiring in 2016 in the rank of lieutenant colonel after 30 years' service.

I was often asked, "How did you know this was God's will for your life? Did you hear an audible voice tell you?" How do you give a satisfying tangible answer to something that is so intangible? You just know! What proof is there that there is love in my heart? My heart tells me, even though I can't see it, smell it, or feel it with my fingers. How do I know there's air? I know because my lungs tell me so, and when I need it and breathe it I experience it to my satisfaction.

My call to the ministry is but one of thousands of questions that remain unanswered, but that we accept on faith. Such decisions have significant implications for how we live. As ingenious as man has been in his knowledge of the nature of life, he still has human limitations and multitudes of questions that will always remain unanswered. The true vastness of the earth and human life is still mind boggling to human understanding, even with all of our technical advances in so many fields.

Our earth is just a dot in the Milky Way system, with its millions of heavenly bodies, and the Milky Way system is only a small cluster of

heavenly bodies in the limitless expanse of the universe. In the midst of
that, we are but a grain of sand in the gigantic ocean beach. The whole
human race, all seven billion of us, is but a tiny speck on the earth.

Being that small in comparison, it's only natural to feel alone in all
that vast space. Our finite minds can't comprehend the mind of the all-
knowing, invisible Almighty God. God knew that, so He came in human
form in the person of Jesus so that we would know that God is at least
like Jesus—and even more, to let us know that He loves us more than we
could ever imagine, even in our sinful nature. The Psalmist in Psalm 8:1,
3, 5, and 9, struggled thousands of years ago with the same unanswerable
question for understanding.

He wrote, "O LORD, our Lord, how majestic is your name in all the
earth. When I consider your heavens, the work of your fingers, the moon
and the stars, which you have set in place, what is man that you are mind-
ful of him, the son of man that you care for him? You have made him a
little lower than the heavenly beings, and crowned him with glory and
honor." The Psalmist's conclusion is the only one we can come to and leave
it at that. "O LORD, our Lord, how majestic is your name in all the earth."

I sold our car, bought a used pickup, rented a U-Haul trailer, and
packed all of our belongings, and all five of us crammed into the small cab
of that pickup and idiotically headed for Southeastern Baptist Theological Seminary in Wake Forest, North Carolina. We looked like the Beverly
Hillbillies come to town. We had no job and no place to live. All we had
was the name of an unknown Methodist minister by the name of Wesley
Jones and a trust in God that was unwavering. Within a week we found
a two-bedroom house in the low-income section of Raleigh, and settled
down to see what the Lord would do next and where He would lead.

A few weeks later, Keith, 6, Don, 4, and I headed to Wake Forest to
scout out the seminary. On the way there, we passed Gresham's Lake,
where we saw people waterskiing. The boys asked if they might stop and
view the skiing on the way back, and I consented. After spending time

watching all the people skiing, we journeyed back to the main road on the bumpy, washboard-like, unpaved road. I decided to drive along the shoulder of the road on the right to keep the pickup from bouncing so much.

At one point the front tire dropped into a rain washout and the pickup tumbled down a 40-foot embankment into the lake. Luckily we were not hurt, and a man in a linen supply truck came to our rescue as the pickup was slowly ebbing partly into the lake. Little Don was screaming up a storm, and I kept asking if he was hurt. He replied that he wasn't. He was crying because he had lost his candy corn.

Later the pickup was pulled out of the lake, all the water emptied from the engine, and new oil replaced. There, embedded between the cracks of the cardboard interior of the pickup were little pieces of Don's candy corn. The total cost for that service was $24.21, and I still have the faded receipt. We needed a sedan more than a pickup, so I traded it to a mechanic for an old Chrysler clunker with a Dynaflow transmission that burned oil as quickly as you filled it up. Smoke billowed out of the exhaust so badly that on our way to visit in Georgia, no one would pass us because they couldn't see around us to see if another car was approaching. I kept that oil guzzler filled with reprocessed oil.

Those early seminary days were difficult for us financially. Money for a loaf of bread was hard to come by, and Dot was wearing two-for-$5 dresses. But Dot and I could give testimony after testimony of how the Lord took care of us. It was not uncommon for us to be at church, and for someone who knew our trying circumstances to come up and offer us money in an envelope, or for some monetary gift to come from our former church in Columbus that would always—always—be the exact amount needed to meet our particular immediate needs.

We are convinced that was God's way of assuring us one step at a time that we were precisely in His will, and that He would care for us as promised, no matter what. We were terribly poor in material and monetary possessions, but we were very rich in so many other, more important ways.

That first Christmas was skimpy in gifts exchanged and received, but one of the most memorable because we were totally dependent on God's provisions on faith. Wesley Jones gave me two of his girls' old used bicycles, which I repainted for our two older boys. Ralph Byrd, a commercial painter in the church we belonged to in Raleigh, had befriended us, and he said he would take care of Christmas for the children, which he did most generously.

Dot, in her creative genius, made a Nativity set out of cardboard, construction paper, small balls, pipe cleaners, and bits of cloth that endured 60 years, 13 different moves around the world, and is still our most treasured of heirlooms. It has now passed on to Mark, who displayed it on his fireplace mantle in his home for the first time on Christmas of 2014.

While in seminary, I learned some very important lessons that greatly influenced my future role as a minister. One of the first lessons was when I went to ask Mr. Brown, the personnel officer for Wachovia Bank and Trust in Raleigh, if it looked like I might be hired for a part-time job about a week after I had applied. Mr. Brown's answer was as follows: "Yes, John. We've checked all your references, and they all look good. We haven't checked with your minister, and we probably won't. Ministers have a way of saying something good about everybody." That was not a compliment, and I determined that that would never be said of me. My word would have credibility. If you had the makeup of a snake, that's exactly the way I was going to describe you.

A lot later in my career, in Okinawa, Japan, a fellow colonel called me asking me to provide a letter for his son who was working on his Eagle Scout award. I told him that I couldn't do that. When the perturbed colonel said, "Why not? You're the senior chaplain!" I told him, "I've never seen you or your son in church, and I'd have to fabricate something. And I won't do that." The colonel was angry with me, but I could sleep at night with a clear conscience.

Another thing that influenced me was a casual remark that a seminary professor made that became the guideline of my ministry. He said,

"Eloquent preachers will soon be forgotten, but loving, caring pastors will long be remembered. They may not remember what you said from the pulpit, but they will remember if you were there with them during a time of need." And that turned out to be true. Every place that I left, people remembered that I was always there for them when they needed me.

Another lesson I learned was that you have to walk the talk if people are going to believe who you say you are. That first semester, I was working part time and taking a full load of courses, including Greek. I was straining under the load, so it made sense for me to drop Greek, which required daily study, and pick it up at a later time. I decided to go talk to my Greek professor, who was also my counselor.

I was bleeding all over the place, and the professor, instead of being caring and compassionate, proceeded to lecture me. He said, "Sir, when we accept people in this institution, we expect them to be mature and govern themselves accordingly." I didn't say it, but I thought, *If this is Christianity, you can take it and shove it!* Needless to say, I graduated without the study of Greek or Hebrew, which didn't seem to have hurt my career one bit.

Soon after moving from Columbus, Dot secured a job as an administrative clerk with the U.S. Attorney's Office in Raleigh. Although Dot did not complete her college education, she displayed exceptional intelligence and common sense, and within a few years was promoted to administrative supervisor of the entire administrative staff and the chief liaison between them and the attorneys. One of the attorneys once told her she had a "college education on her shoulders."

One day a clerk who worked for Dot told her she was going to Houston, Texas. Dot remembered that one of my old drinking buddies, Jack, the one who became a millionaire civil lawyer, lived there, and would she call him and tell him about my call to be a minister? When she got back she said that Jack kept saying, "Well, I'll be damned. Are you sure we're talking about the same person? John ought to be a good one, because if anyone knows about sin, it's John!"

In addition to my part-time job with Wachovia, during those first few years I also worked as a night clerk at a Holiday Inn, delivered mail during the Christmas holidays, and in the summer measured tobacco allotment for Wake County. Interfacing with some of those jagged-toothed tobacco growers was an education in itself. When some of them opened their mouths, the wisdom of Solomon came out. I remember one of them saying to me once, "Reverend, there are two things in this world that I am going to buy the best that money can buy. You know what they are? One is a good pair of shoes, and the other is a good bed because when I'm not in one, I'm in the other." Made sense to me!

Academic teaching is absolutely important in its own right, but you really don't get the true value of learning until that knowledge is applied in real life. That's where we learned what ministry is all about. At that time, North Carolina had the most rural churches per capita of any other state in the union. As a result, most seminarians would end up pastoring a rural church at one time or another. What a seminary professor once told the class, I found to be true. He said, "Rural folk won't know much about theology, but they'll sure teach you about the love of God." My understanding of that truth came from being part-time pastor of two small rural churches, Rock Springs Baptist Church in Bynum, North Carolina, and Pleasant Hill Baptist Church in Pittsboro, North Carolina. That's where my real pastoral education really started. I treasure wonderful memories from both experiences.

At these churches we were first introduced to what is called "dinner on the grounds," tables loaded with succulent southern cooking that could never be duplicated in restaurants. Here we also experienced a love from God's down-to earth farming people, who showered their pastors with a caring, genuine love like no other.

One of the deacons at Pleasant Hill was almost totally deaf and lived with three old-maid sisters. His name was Paul. It was told that after the service when I had preached my trial sermon, the head deacon asked

Paul, "How did you like the preaching?" Paul responded, "I didn't catch but three catfish, and the maskitoos liked to have ate me up!" The first Sunday after I assumed my position as pastor, I told that story from the pulpit. The congregation, fully aware of Paul's past mistaken responses, exploded in laughter.

These were simple, down-to-earth rural people who gave my family a Christian love that helped form our loving and caring ministry, and which we never forgot. Of interest at Pleasant Hill was the fact that not one of the members of the Deacon Board would consent to pray in public. It was all up to the pastor. Behind the pulpit at Pleasant Hill sat two leathered chairs and a settee near windows that had no curtains. As a result, the leather was sun beaten and terribly cracked.

There were cotton mills in the area with fabric outlets where cloth was fairly reasonable. Without the congregation's knowledge or consent, I took it upon myself to purchase from my own funds some red velvet material and reupholstered the chairs and settee. Seeing this, the congregation felt that if I thought that much about the church, they ought to do something as well, so they had red carpet to match installed down the middle aisle and on the floor in front of the stage. You never know how a little gesture in Christ-like spirit will influence others to do another good deed.

One day I was visiting the son of one of the members at the Rock Springs church who owned a nearby barbeque place but was not a church attender. He asked me if I had ever eaten any "turnings." I told him I didn't even know what they were, much less having eaten any. He replied, "Preacher, you're in for a treat!" And what a treat it was! "Turnings" turned out to be that portion of meat that sticks to the hot irons when the meat is turned over to cook on both sides. We learn something new every day.

Education is not limited to the classroom. The barbeque fellow never did come to church while I was there, but that didn't stop me from visiting him often (no ulterior motive, of course). I graduated with a master of divinity degree from Southeastern Seminary in June 1963 and moved on to writing the next chapter of this story.

A very popular program offered in those years was what is called a Clinical Pastoral Education (CPE) internship offered at the Baptist Hospital in Winston-Salem, North Carolina. It was a course of academic study as well as on-the-job training to learn proper hospital visitation techniques as well as basic counseling skills. It went a step further in including personal counseling time for the interns with staff counselors for personal growth. The personal counseling required a lot of introspection. The training was offered as a short one-quarter course, one-year duration, or a two-year segment that carried with it supervisory certification. I elected to take the one-year program.

I consider my seminary education extremely valuable training for later ministerial positions, and my CPE as a rare treasure in learning how to better my relationships with other people, especially in my 57-plus years of counseling with congregants. I considered my personal counseling so valuable that I arranged for Dot to drive all the way from Wake Forest to Winston-Salem every Saturday so that she could receive counseling from a staff chaplain to better know herself as well.

There was a home for alcoholic women near the hospital. Part of the requirements for admission was for them to come to the chaplain interns for counseling. We chaplain interns needed the training and the alcoholics needed the counseling, so it worked out well for both of us. One of the first things taught in our training was, "Always clarify what the other person is saying for proper meaning and understanding—don't just assume." Making assumptions can lead to misunderstanding and hamper hospital visitation and the counseling process. The standard illustration the counselors provided went like this: "When a certain chaplain walked into this patient's room one morning, the patient gleefully said, 'Chaplain, I've been saved!' The chaplain responded, 'Isn't Jesus wonderful?' The patient said, 'I don't know about that. But I found out that the insurance policy I thought had elapsed, had not, and it's going to pay for my entire hospitalization!'"

Seeing so many patients suffering and dying that year was heartrending, but extremely valuable later during my 57 years of active ministry. Ministering to different needs in the hospital can affect your emotions in roller-coaster fashion, and by the end of the day you're thoroughly exhausted. You go from the maternity ward where there is such joy over new births, to a room where the patient is nervous and scared awaiting test results, to another room where the patient is terminal, and then to the Intensive Care Unit where a hallucinating patient is tied up to all manner of wires and tubes. No one size fits all, and each requires a different kind of emotion for proper ministry.

I had been baptized in the Roman Catholic Church as an infant and had joined the Baptist Church simply because Dot had been a member of that church. Like many nominal Christians, I knew very little about either one of them. During my year of CPE, I learned to forget about labels and extend my parameters for a better, more inclusive ministry to all in need.

One night when I was the chaplain intern on call, I was summoned to the hospital at 2 in the morning because a 3-month-old baby had died. Upon arrival I discovered a terribly heartbroken, grief-stricken couple who professed to be Methodist. In their guilt-ridden conversation, they said to me, "We didn't know she was that sick. We had planned to have her baptized. Would you do that?" I had never baptized a baby, much less a dead one. A typical Baptist response might have been. "I would like to. But we Baptists believe in believer's baptism by immersion. We don't baptize babies. I'm terribly sorry!" Instead, seeing this heartbreaking scenario, I wondered, *What would Jesus do?* Without hesitation, I said I would. I got a pan of water, read Scripture, concocted some form of ritual, and prayed with them.

The couple went away satisfied that they had been ministered to by a representative of God, instead of hurt, disappointed, and maybe even turned off by religion. The next day, I called their minister in a distant city and told him what I had done; why I had done it; and that if I had erred, God forgive me; and that if I had done something wrong, it would be up to that minister to correct it. The fellow minister responded that under the same circumstances he would have done the same thing.

I had befriended the editor of the newspaper in Waynesville, North Carolina, who had been one the patients I visited. One day after he had gone home, he called and told me, "John, we have one of our city fathers who has just been diagnosed with terminal pancreatic cancer in your hospital. He's a good man, but he's not a Christian. With your personality I think you can sneak up his blind side and lead him to the Lord. Would you visit him?" I did both! Claude, knowing he was dying, asked me if I'd come to his hometown of Hazelwood in the North Carolina mountains and do his service.

I had the oddest experience at Hazelwood. Ordinarily it takes a while for mountainfolk to extend their welcome to strangers. Of course, Claude was known by all, and because I had been the chaplain who had led Claude to the Lord, the town was mine for the asking. While I was there, the First Baptist Church of Hazelwood was looking for a new pastor, so they asked me if I would preach a trial sermon as a possible candidate. I did, and Dot and I left knowing for certain that this was where the Lord wanted us to do ministry. Words fail me to describe the setting. Hazelwood is nestled in the valley surrounded by the most gorgeous mountains—the only way to picture it is heaven on earth. So we anxiously waited for the Lord to do His work. We were so sure we almost started packing, but decided it might be wise to wait—until He actually signed on the dotted line.

I called the chairman of the search committee the next week and asked him how it looked. He said, "I'm pretty sure we're going to issue you a call to be our pastor, John. But we have promised this other fellow in High Point that we would listen to him before we make our decision and we have to keep that promise." I told him, "Take my name off the list of possible candidates. I'm not in competition with anybody else. It should be pretty clear to you that this is where God wants me to be or not!" I called Dot and informed her of what I had done, and she was completely devastated. We thought that the Lord just wasn't listening. Ever had that feeling?

But leave it up to God! As always, He knows exactly what He has in mind, even if we think He doesn't. This was one of the first of a number of times when what we thought was a mistake turned out to be a blessing in disguise. If we had gone to Hazelwood, we might not have gone into the Air Force to minister to God's people in uniform. We realized in retrospect that the Air Force was exactly where He really wanted us to serve Him. I was called to a church in Raleigh instead of Hazelwood.

A few months later I had occasion to pass through Hazelwood and stopped by to visit Claude's widow, Sarah. She said to me, "John, if you don't mind wearing a dead man's suits, I think Claude would have wanted you to have his." As poor a preacher as I was at the time, I took them gladly. I told her, "My name is Jimmy. I'll take whatever you gimme!" I had them altered, and I was the poorest, best-dressed preacher in Raleigh. As time went on I passed them on to my dad, who eventually gave them to my sister who used the material to make a quilt. She later gave that quilt to my son Mark, and we named the quilt "John B" after my dad. At times when it was cold we'd ask Mark, "Were you cold last night?" He would respond, "No, I had John B to keep me warm!"

Through personal introspective sessions with my counselor, I learned many things about myself—some things that were deeply buried in my subconscious that were painful to resurrect. One example was my college graduation six years prior. As stated earlier, my relatives were relatively poor and uneducated people. Even though I never finished high school, I am the only member of my family who ever finished college. My relatives would have hocked everything they had and traveled through hell to attend this very special graduation.

As I was digging deeper into my subconscious for self-actualization in counseling, I painfully discovered that I had been ashamed of them being there for my graduation. I was "Mr. Big" who felt better than they. I broke down and cried uncontrollably, facing that I could have entertained such terrible thoughts and feelings. But as painful as it was, it turned out to be one of many other painful admissions that proved therapeutic and invaluable in my later years of counseling others.

The name "Solano" was not a familiar one to southerners, and numerous times was not grasped on first hearing. One family that I was ministering to at the hospital had that problem. I told them one way to remember my name was to think of it in syllables like the musical scale: "so-la-no." They said that would be easy to remember. After visiting other patients, I saw them in the lobby and one of them called me over. She asked, "What did you say your name was?" I replied, "I told you to remember it by thinking of the musical scale." She said, "I did. But all I could think of was 'Chaplain Do-re-mi!'"

As I advanced in my CPE training I was recruited by the department to travel to churches in the area to promote the CPE program to fellow pastors. One of my travels took me through the city of Leaksville, North Carolina. Since the Reverend Harry D. Wood, pastor of First Baptist Church there, had been instrumental in my completion of my seminary education, I made it a point to visit Reverend Wood. I related this story to Harry.

Midterm at seminary, the devil dug his claws deep into my heart and mind. I started enviously hearing about some of my fellow college graduates buying fancy cars and houses and living the good life. And here my family and I were, poor as dirt. So I decided that we would quit seminary and go back to my old job with Montgomery Ward and get on the bandwagon with the rest. I was going to tell Dot that evening when she got home from work. That never happened because of a letter Harry had sent me.

When I went to the mailbox, I found a letter from Harry, a total stranger. I didn't know Harry from Adam's housecat. The note said, "Dear

John. I recently was on a cross-country flight seated next to a Montgomery Ward District Superintendent by the name of C. E. McAlister, your former employer. He told me about all the wonderful things that you are trying to do for the Lord. I know that things can be tough sometimes because I have been there. I come to Southeastern [Seminary] on occasion. Maybe we'll meet. If you *ever need anything*, please don't hesitate to call on me." It was signed, "Harry D. Wood, pastor, First Baptist Church, Leaksville, NC."

I took that message to be from God telling me to hang on, that His will was for me to stay put. I told Harry how God had used his note to tell me to stay where I was, and that He would take care of everything just as He always had. The irony of that story is that Harry didn't even remember having written it. Harry and I embraced, gave glory and praise to God, and wept like babies. We never know how God is going to use us to influence others for His good, even with a simple note like Harry's. As Dr. Seuss said, "To the world you may be one person; but to one person you may be the world."

5

Learning to Walk

Creedmoor Road Baptist Church, 1964–1966

Upon completion of my Clinical Pastoral Education program, I was called as pastor of Mount Zion Baptist Church, located on Creedmoor Road on the outskirts of Raleigh, North Carolina. It was a small congregation with just over 200 people, but with a full church program. Mount Zion was located very near to Jefferies Grove Elementary School for African American children, so people thought that with a name like Mount Zion it was a black congregation. In time I recommended to the members that we change the name to the Creedmoor Road Baptist Church, which would not only eliminate that mistake but also identify the church's location.

The church was located in a semirural area. Galatians 5:22–23 points out that "the fruit of the spirit is love, joy, peace, patience, kindness, goodness, faithfulness, gentleness, and self-control." I never quite mastered patience and self-control. One night after the evening service, I caught Mike, who was then 6, and another boy of the same age running around in the church. I called Mike over and told him not to be running around in the church.

The little boy looked up at me and said, "Why don't you shut up and leave him alone?" I grabbed him by the collar and told him, "I don't know who taught you to talk to grownups that way. But if you ever talk to me that way again, I'll whip your tail until you can't sit down. Do you understand me?" When I later told Dot about it she asked me, "What if he tells his father and he comes after you?" I said, "I'll whip him too." Both Mike and the other boy went on to become ministers as well. Tough love sometimes pays off.

This was my first full-time pastorate, so I received a wealth of education and experience from these good people. One of the biggest influences was a petite lady in her late fifties who was a ball of fire. Her name was Mildred McCall, affectionately called "Chick"—probably because of her untiring energy in getting things done in quick fashion. She was fired up for the Lord, and she taught me the absolute crucial ingredient of the pastoral heart—loving, caring, and visiting the congregation. In visiting church members, Chick was either in front of me or right behind. It was primarily by Chick's example that I became a loving, caring pastor. We had many rewarding conversations over a slice of pound cake and a glass of milk that she always managed to have available for me.

Chick's example of a loving, caring, compassionate heart—an essential quality for a successful pastor—was coupled by one that I had seen and admired in a former pastor in Warner Robins, Georgia, by the name of Jim Dorriety, who also became a dear lifetime friend. Jim was an outstanding preacher, but even more a caring pastor who loved everyone and had no favorites. He was an excellent example for me to emulate and influenced my ministry greatly.

Another mentor was Dr. Broadus Jones, Pastor Emeritus of First Baptist Church in Raleigh, where he had pastored for many years. He and Dot were the best of friends but agreeably at odds because he was a progressive Democrat and she a staunch conservative Replication. He taught me several valuable lessons. For one, he said that rather than lock horns with the Deacon Board on issues where they might differ, he would befriend the most influential deacon on the board, and since this deacon had the confidence of the others, he would convince that deacon the importance of what Broadus wanted passed and let that deacon be the person to spearhead it. Broadus said it worked every time.

One day he asked me what kind of literature I was reading. Since I was conservative I mentioned the name of the magazine I was reading. He mentioned the name of a certain magazine that was liberal with completely opposite views, and asked me if I was reading it. When I answered that I wasn't because I disagreed with their opinions, he said to me, "John, if you're going to reach both sides you need to know their differing opinions. You don't have to agree with them, but you do need to know what they are thinking. Be sure you know what you're talking about." Broadus sparked my interest in trying to be well read and well rounded.

I and another young fellow pastor by the name of Allen, played golf with Broadus on occasion. One day I was late, and Broadus asked me why. I told him I was counseling a lady. Broadus replied, "I don't know, John. Women will get you in trouble. I normally just pat them on the back and send them on their way." I, ever the jokester, winked at Allen and told Broadus, "That's fine with you, Dr. Jones, but Allen and I still have a shine for the ladies." Broadus smirked and said, "Guess you're right, John. At my age, I'd just as soon have a good BM." In our declining years when sex was less of importance and constipation more of an issue, Dot and I would grin and say to each other, "Ol' Broadus knew what he was talking about!"

It's amazing how God uses the littlest of things and situations to teach us lessons. And the journey of life is full of these teachings if we just keep our eyes, ears, and hearts open to those possibilities. This happened to me one night when I was studying in seminary. The apartment we lived in was old, and I was studying in the kitchen where the faucet over the sink had a small drip. The constant drip on the aluminum sink made a small noise that bothered me and interfered with my studying.

Finally I got up and placed a rather large plastic pan under it to cushion the sound. The next morning when I got up I saw that the large pan was full and overflowing. Lesson learned? "Inch by inch, everything's a cinch!" "The journey of a thousand miles begins with one step!" "Don't look at the top of the mountain, which looks insurmountable, but concentrate on each and every small step that will finally get you there!"

Every minister has stories about embarrassing moments in the pulpit. Mine came early when I first began preaching. I was preaching my first sermon on the celebration of Palm Sunday. I very carefully painted the historical setting of that time, pointing out the Jews being under Roman oppression, and the Old Testament prophecy of a coming messiah to set God's people free. Under those conditions they fully expected a warrior in the likeness of David riding on a white steed with sword in hand fully prepared for war. Having that as a backdrop, I said, "Can you imagine how disappointed the people must have been to see Jesus enter Jerusalem, being hailed as the coming messiah, on a simple donkey with his feet dangling from his ass?" Realizing how that might be taken, I quickly did my best to recover and move on.

In the fall of 1965 the Creedmoor church sent me as part of a group of 17 North Carolinian Baptist pastors on a six-week preaching mission to Brazil. On the way there, we visited Lima, Peru; and in Brazil, Rio de Janeiro—where we saw the famous Corcovado (the huge statue of Christ overlooking the city)—Brasília, the new capital; Belo Horizonte; and finally landed in Belem. In Belem I was housed with a missionary couple whose home was near a coffee bean roasting factory. The tantalizing aroma that wafted to my nostrils from the roasting coffee beans was one I had never smelled before or since. Belo Horizonte is known for its precious gems, and I had several rings made for Dot while there.

From Belem we were farmed out to numerous remote locations. I ended up at Braganza, a small, very primitive village at the end of the Amazon River. In Braganza, I was able to see that the poverty I was raised in was a paradise in comparison. The poor conditions here were awful.

The church was adjacent to a small shack where the pastor and his family lived under very meager conditions. There were all kinds of small animals walking in and out of the house and church as if they were part of the family. I even saw tarantulas crawling around. It gave me the willies, but it didn't bother these poor people. I wrote Dot about how poorly I was eating and the harsh conditions I was experiencing. She had that story told in church, and a couple of widowed sisters with means gave her money with the instructions, "When you meet John in Miami Beach, y'all go to the best restaurant and get yourselves a big steak dinner."

In the meantime, when all of us who were on the mission trip got back to Belem, we were wined and dined royally. They even had us on television. I didn't have time to write Dot about this new treatment. Dot in the meantime ate cautiously in preparation for that steak dinner she was going to devour. When I got off the plane with my belly full from all that good hospitality and she told me about the offer, I told her about our dilemma. I should have known to keep my mouth shut. This is exactly what she said: "If I starved myself in order to have that steak dinner, you are going to have a steak dinner if I have to shove it down your throat!" I didn't want to have it shoved down my throat, so I forced myself to eat a steak dinner.

During my stay at Creedmoor Road, I led the church to add an education building to provide for possible potential church growth since the city of Raleigh appeared to be moving in that direction. In January 1966 I resigned as pastor of Creedmoor Road when I was commissioned as a first lieutenant to serve on active duty as an Air Force chaplain. I went on to serve as a chaplain for 32 years, five months, and two days, which included my six years of enlisted time.

Thinking about my chaplaincy career reminds me of my blessed mother. Even with all of my behavioral mishaps, I had attained the rank of staff sergeant during those six years in the enlisted ranks. My parents, in their limited understanding, were ever so proud. In the commissioned ranks, I advanced to the rank of full colonel, of which there were only 86 in that rank among the 869 chaplains on active duty at that time. During that entire time, when my mother was asked what my rank was, she would proudly answer, "He's a sergeant!" She didn't know what else was important to the military, but she knew that sergeants were, and by gosh her son was one of them.

This act of commissioning chaplains is interesting and one that few people know about. First of all, we had to have four years of college, four years from an accredited seminary, and at least two years of pastoral experience in a church setting for commissioning as a first lieutenant—four years to be commissioned in the rank of captain. Clergy just couldn't go to a recruiter and say they wanted to join the military. They had to have an ecclesiastical endorsement from their denomination, which amounted to a letter of approval and certification. These endorsements came about only when there was a vacancy created by retirement, commission resignation, or death of a person belonging to that specific denomination. The quotas for the various religious denominations were controlled by law.

These denominational endorsements carried dual chaplain ownership—by the military, but also by the denomination, whose authority could supersede the military's. For example, if a priest was on active duty by approval of his bishop, at any time that bishop felt he needed that priest more in a local parish than the military, he could instruct that priest to leave the military and come home. If the priest refused, all the bishop had to do was pull the priest's letter of endorsement and the priest would have no basis for staying on active duty. The chaplain's commission was contingent on the endorsement.

In 2007, after my retirement, I was invited to be the principal speaker for the 200th anniversary celebration at Creedmoor Road Baptist, with all of the other six pastors who had succeeded me in attendance. During the years since my resignation, the area surrounding the church had exploded in growth, with the building of housing subdivisions and commercial businesses. Sadly, the Creedmoor Road church, instead of growing with the times, had actually declined in membership.

PART IV

Being Where God Wants You to Be

1966–1992

6

Stepping into Uncharted Waters

Keesler Air Force Base, Biloxi, Mississippi, 1966–1968

I attended the basic eight-week Chaplain Orientation School at Lackland Air Force Base, San Antonio, Texas. During one of my sober moments in 1949, I had had a tattoo of a naked woman placed on my right forearm in St. Louis. I later had panties and a bra tattooed to cover her private parts. Unlike 2019 when a huge segment of the population seemed to think tattoos were a sign of acceptance, in 1966 a tattoo was not a good image, especially for a chaplain. Tattoos were associated with drunken sailors.

One of the chaplain instructors at the school arranged for me to have it removed. At that time they didn't have the sophisticated means to remove tattoos that they have today (but seeing so many people tattooed today, I doubt that tattoo removal is much in demand), so they used what is known as the "abrasive method." They took a tool similar to what dentists use for drilling, and scraped the top layer of skin down to the epidermis, allowing the wound to scab. After scabbing, the skin with the tattoo was simply peeled off.

Blacks and other dark-complexioned people have a tendency to form what is known as keloids where the skin buckles up, making the area look like it was burned badly. I developed bad looking keloids, and my forearm looked like I had been badly burned in a fire. One good thing that came from that tattoo removal was, because of my surgery, I didn't have to participate in a rigorous training session at Lackland where the other chaplains had to crawl under barbed wire under simulated enemy fire.

The chaplain instructor who arranged for that tattoo removal, who was also good at handball, taught me a valuable lesson. He said in one of his presentations, "Some people have the mistaken notion about it being okay for chaplains to be fat and sloppy because they have their head up in the clouds. I don't agree with that. I'm going to be well groomed with a good haircut, shined shoes, and pressed uniform, and psychically fit. I'm going to be as good as any line officer because it might be a way of possibly having a religious influence on them because we have that in common." Having spent six years enlisted, that made sense to me, and I embraced that philosophy and did my best to do the same during my entire career.

One day I received notice to report to the firing range at such-and-such a date to qualify shooting with a weapon. Having done the same thing in airman basic training in 1949 I willingly obeyed. When I got back, the sergeant took me to task, saying, "Chaplains are noncombatants. You weren't supposed to do that!" I replied, "I was only obeying orders like a good soldier." I knew it all the time, but I thought it was a good opportunity to have some fun.

My first permanent assignment was at Keesler Air Force Base, Biloxi, Mississippi. It was a large academic setting for every manner of electronics. God could not have picked a better place for me to get indoctrinated. The senior chaplain, a full colonel by the name of Grover, proved to be a good role model for me. Even though he held that coveted rank, Grover was admired and respected because he was unmistakably a man of character and integrity, fully committed to the Lord's work, and he didn't let his rank go to his head. He preached, sang in the choir along with his wife, Ethel, and taught a Sunday school class for the choir members between services, even though supervising 22 chaplains along with at least that many enlisted personnel and other demanding duties was no small task.

Grover and I hit it off immediately because we both were witty and liked to kid around. His wife was just as witty and a match for both of us. Shortly after we arrived at Keesler they had a buffet in the main chapel annex to greet the new personnel, and we wore stick-on name tags. After eating, Grover took off his name tag and left it on his paper plate while he wandered around talking to other people. I went over and picked up his name tag and placed it over my left breast in place of mine and sat down next to Ethel. She looked me straight in the eye, smiled, and said, "Are you interested in the responsibilities or privileges that go with that name?" Since Dot sang in the choir with Ethel, she became a good friend and role model of a chaplain's wife for her as well.

It was at Keesler while serving as the hospital chaplain that I had the keloid from the previous removal of my tattoo repaired. The dermatologist, who was Jewish, took skin from my right hip and

"Brand new captain," Keesler Air Force Base, 1967

grafted it over the keloid. It remained lightly scarred, but the appearance was so much better. God again provided me with another Jew to get rid of my sinful ways!

Because of the huge number of personnel assigned there, and with numerous chapels located throughout the base, it required the large number of chaplains mentioned to adequately provide for the spiritual needs of that large population. Having that many clergy to run an operation is unheard of in civilian life, and that's not counting the equivalent number of airmen and secretaries we had to complement the same number of chaplains to assist them. No other base in the entire Air Force compared with this operation in size.

Those chaplains represented religious persuasions and denominations of every description. With my hunger for expanding my horizons, this was the perfect place for me to start. I borrowed a little from here and a little from there, and became a well-broadened chaplain, a quality that would serve me well as I progressed up the ladder of leadership. The first two things I learned were the importance of being a team player and the need to set labels aside and focus on providing for the needs of everyone, regardless of religious persuasion or lack of it.

Since I had become a Christian under the leadership of an Army chaplain, I had some idea of what chaplains did. But being one was a whole new ball of wax! Quite different from the civilian ministry, and I give thanks to God for that. Civilian congregations at the time had some unrealistic expectations of their pastors and their families. They expected for the pastor and his family to be perfect because they believed that Christian perfection was what preachers preached, and they should themselves be the perfect role models.

This was especially difficult for the children who were expected to walk on eggshells and not be like other ordinary children. Preachers' kids had it tough for another reason. Congregations see their ministers at their very best in the pulpit only on Sundays, but their children see them on a day-to-day basis in their humanity with their flaws, weaknesses, and clay feet.

Some churches also expected to get two for the price of one, meaning that they felt that the pastor's wife should be as involved as the pastor in the operation of the church and not be employed elsewhere. Some churches wouldn't even call a minister to be their pastor if the wife worked elsewhere, or if they did they resented it. I guess they thought that the poorer they kept the preacher, the better he would preach.

That never worked for me. The quality of my sermons was determined by the amount of time I spent with the Lord and His good book, and not from the amount of hunger pains I experienced. Some members even took issue with the way the pastor wore his clothes, combed his hair, and so many ridiculous things that caused some pastors health issues, and some to even leave the ministry.

We didn't have any of that in the military chaplaincy. My wife and children could be themselves without absurd expectations. We didn't have church roles because we didn't have membership like they do in civilian churches. Personnel attended chapels wherever they were assigned base after base, and some still kept attending chapel services at nearby bases after retirement, or became affiliated with a local church.

We didn't have to worry about funding. Our salaries were supplied by the government according to our rank, and we competed for rank among other chaplains just like any other line officer. Because we wore the same uniform, our role as chaplains was seen completely different from that of our civilian counterparts. We were their "padres." We budgeted for government money for maintenance of our facilities, supplies, and other needs just like everybody else, and our standards of behavior were no different from any other military member—above reproach!

Because of my previous Clinical Pastoral Education training, I was assigned as the Protestant hospital chaplain for Keesler's large hospital. My office was in the basement along with that of the nutritionist, a Jewish major with the last name of Frielander, and the Red Cross representative. Because of the name Solano, people were always mistaking me for being a Catholic priest. It cropped up so often that I developed the habit of dismissing the subject as quickly as possible without long explanations to the contrary.

One day I met Colonel Henry, the hospital commander, walking alongside a little old lady. On behalf of the lady who apparently was Catholic, he asked me the time of Catholic mass. When I informed Colonel Henry, the little old lady chimed in, "Oh, Father Solano. I am so looking forward to hearing you say mass. I hear you say mass through the

Mobile TV station all the time." I had never said mass, much less through the TV station she mentioned. I politely bowed, dismissed myself, and went about making hospital visits to patients. When I finished I took the elevator all the way down to the basement floor.

As I was exiting the elevator, this little old lady was getting on, having just finished lunch in the cafeteria. As I was backing out of the elevator, the last words from her were, "Oh, Father Solano. I am so looking forward to hearing you say mass." As the elevator doors closed, I turned around and almost kissed Major Frielander, who was standing in my path. She said, "Oh, Father Solano, I, too, am looking forward to hearing you say mass!"

I guess word had gotten around that "Father Solano" was not a Catholic priest because one day I was riding the elevator when a lieutenant colonel nurse said to me, "I understand you aren't Catholic." I told her that I used to be, but now was a Baptist. That set her off! She got red in the face and said, "Well, I think it's such a shame that you would leave the one true faith," and proceeded to dress me down as if she were a nun and I an altar boy beneath her. I simply said, "I'm sorry that you feel that way" and left it at that. I have to be honest and confess that I really wanted to tell her where to go. People like that usually speak with such superiority because in fact they really feel inferior and threatened for one reason or another.

We became good friends with the family of Dr. Currie, head of the ob-gyn clinic at the hospital. Like Grover, he was also a full colonel. One Saturday, Dr. Currie invited me, Keith, and Don to join him and his teenage son on a boat ride on the Gulf Coast waters. The boat was very fancy, with sleeping and cooking accommodations. Keesler was bordered by water on one side so the boat was housed at the Keesler dock. This was a wonderful experience for us since we had never been on a boat like this.

At one point during the trip, Dr. Currie allowed his teenage son to take the steering wheel. Typical teenager, the son pushed the throttle full force in the takeoff and sheared the propeller pin. Dr. Currie tried to replace it by leaning over the back of the boat backward with me holding his legs so he wouldn't fall in. It didn't work, so we were stranded a long way from the Keesler dock. Dr. Currie said not to worry, that his wife, Eleanor, would call the Coast Guard if we were not back by a certain time.

Nightfall came and no rescue. We were in total darkness with only a hint of moonlight aglow. Currie shot off a couple of flares, but no rescue in sight. Eleanor had called the Coast Guard, but not knowing the exact location of the boat, it was like looking for a needle in a haystack. Currie had some cans of soup left over from previous trips, so he prepared that for the group. Unfortunately, the son had brought along his dog, and while we were eating the dog knocked over the pan of the leftover soup. The smell was horrible, and dealing with it throughout the night in those close quarters was sickening. Even worse, the soup had wet all the matches, so there was no way to set off another flare. Midnight came and still no Coast Guard rescue.

Finally at 2 in the morning a barge came by and pulled us back to shore and safety. We were fortunate that there had not been a storm, as was quite common in that area, as Hurricane Camille later proved in 1968 with its destructive results just after we left for our next assignment. Dr. Currie had been raised in China while his parents were missionaries there and was scheduled to speak that morning in chapel. Needless to say, he was so tired that much of what he had to say was rather disoriented.

I was made the custodian of the Protestant Chaplain Fund, which came from Sunday morning collections for expenses that had not been budgeted and covered by the government. It was policy that in order to make purchases over a certain amount, one had to have my prior approval as the custodian. The education director was a retired full colonel and was accustomed to making purchases without that approval, and then coming to me with the claim, "John, I bought such and such an item for Sunday school," and wanting reimbursement. I would remind him of the policy and gave him fair warning. One day he came with the same explanation, "John, I bought so-and-so," to which I responded, "That's right, Sid. That's exactly what you did. You bought it!" I didn't reimburse him one penny, and that took care of that.

Chaplains were initially commissioned as reservists and after two years were considered for regular augmentation. Another physical examination was required. I saw several doctors for the examination, and ended up seeing the last doctor who would do the evaluation. He looked at my fingers and said, "Look at those clubbing fingers!" and let it go at that. Then he took my blood pressure and said, "Boy, your blood pressure is sure high. Have you had trouble with high blood pressure?" I replied that I hadn't and asked, "What would cause it to be high?" The doc replied, "Oh, it could be a number of things—coming in here for the first time for example." I asked, "How about hostility?" And the doc said, "That could do it. Are you hostile?" I said, "Yes!" "At who?" asked the doc. I replied, "At you. You talk about my clubbing fingers and then don't tell me what that means." The doc said, "Oh, don't worry about it."

But I did worry about it, and told Grover. I explained to Grover that while doing my CPE, I had had a bout with ulcerative proctitis, which is an ulceration of the upper rectum wall. I wondered if there was a connection, and worried that it might affect my regular commissioning. Grover took me to see his good friend Colonel Henry, the hospital commander. Colonel Henry explained that there was nothing to worry about, that all it meant was that persons who had what they call clubbing fingers could be susceptible to respiratory problems in later life. In his usual way, Grover said, "What's that got to do with his rear end? That's where his problem is!"

At a hospital party one time, a doctor came up to me and jokingly said, "Chaplain, you chaplains are indebted to us." "Why is that?" I asked. "Because we patch them up so you can take another crack at them," he said, laughing. Not to be outdone, I told him, "Actually, you doctors are indebted to us." The doctor raised an eyebrow and asked, "What do you mean?" I smiled even more than he had and replied, "Because we bury your mistakes!"

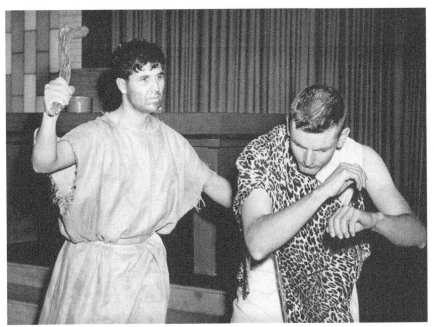

Performance of "Cain and Abel," February 1967, Keesler Air Force Base, Biloxi, Mississippi

I applied my theatrical training from college in several plays at Keesler. In one, I played the part of the biblical character Cain who slew his brother Abel. Dot used to tell me that I had been typecast. I later performed soliloquies of different biblical figures in the Air Force as well as in later civilian parishes.

This assignment was also a training ground for Dot, who learned a lot about the chaplaincy and the Air Force from the wives of other senior chaplains and officers as she started her work with both the Protestant Women of the Chapel (PWOC) and the Officers' Wives' Club (OWC). It was valuable training and experience that in our next assignment would put her in the limelight in many places in Europe.

Dot could be a kidder herself. At one of their Hospital Wives' meetings when I was the hospital chaplain, their assignment was to compose a humorous parody. She wrote the following:

On Monday evening, June 3, 1968, Dr. and Mrs. Edward H. Currie entertained at an abominable dinner party in their dirty quarters honoring Chaplain and Mrs. John Solano. The hostess greeted the guests in a cruddy way. Dot Solano wore a poontangish dress and John's shirt was stinky. Fred Stowe was his usual turdy self. Marge Smith had a crummy hairdo and John Alexander was smoking his revolting pipe. The host told some of his nasty jokes and Barb Stowe laughed in a bitchy way. The food was crappy, the drinks were slimy, and a sweaty time was had by all.

I had been told that my second assignment would probably be Vietnam, so I prepared myself and my family for my going there. Much to my surprise, when my assignment did come down, it was to Aviano Air Base in northern Italy. That news turned out to be even more of a joy when it was further revealed that because the government was trying to save money, all overseas assignments would be extended to a period of four years instead of the previously normal three years.

Dot put to good use her poetic gift and came up with the following poem to present to the OWC members at their monthly "Hail and Farewell" meeting where they greeted new arrivals and said good-bye to those leaving for another assignment.

GOODBYE TO KEESLER

Hi-Bye Coffee, May 1968
'Twas at a coffee like this 'bout two years ago
I stood up here and said, "Hello."

A new Air Force wife I was then
With nary an idea of where to begin.

But with the help of new friends—or were they foes?
I soon had more interests than fingers and toes—

Coffees and luncheons, meetings and teas
And everywhere, everyone busy as bees—

It's been hectic and frantic and sometimes a chore
For this old gal to do just one thing more.

But looking back now and about to say "Bye,"
I look back with joy, and I'll probably cry.

'Cause it's been a good tour and I've gained a lot of
know-how
So to Italy I go and to Keesler—Goodbye now!
                                    —Dot Solano

I bought a used Volkswagen camper from the dental hospital commander that was mechanically in good shape, but had some rusty places that I proceeded to repair in preparation to ship to Italy. It was the best we could afford on a first lieutenant's salary, and would serve us well. By some quirk we were given first-class accommodations on the commercial airlines that booked us, and all five of us flew from New York to Milan like big shots.

7

Evenly Yoked

Aviano AB, Italy, 1968–1972

Of all our thirteen different assignments during a 26½-year span in the chaplaincy, Aviano turned out to be our best and most enjoyable. Aviano is nestled at the beginning of the pre-Alps about 80 miles south of the Austrian border and about 60 miles north of Venice in a very picturesque mountainous setting. I think the Lord gave us this gorgeous garden spot as a substitute when we wanted to go to Hazelwood, North Carolina back in 1964 when we thought He wasn't listening.

We were picked up in Milan by the chapel senior sergeant in his late-model Volkswagen camper. On the way to Aviano, the sergeant got lost and we arrived too late for our accommodations at the *pensione* (hotel), so the sergeant said we could stay at his house, even though space would be rather tight. I was helping unload the luggage from the top rack of the camper when I had an accident.

I was experiencing jetlag, and as I stepped down my college class ring got caught on the side of the luggage rack atop the camper and embedded itself through the flesh down to the bone on my right ring finger. I immediately was taken to the base clinic where the wound was cleaned, medicated and stitched. When we got back to the house, Dot was told that they had to cut it off. She gasped and started crying. They were referring to the ring having to be cut off, and she thought they had meant the finger. Interestingly enough, on the underside of the finger where the ring was embedded, I have carried a blue spot for the rest of my life where apparently some of the slivers of ring metal had remained when the ring was cut off. Although I had the ring repaired, I never wore it again.

I discovered that the Major, Chaplain Harold Henderson, a classmate from the basic chaplains' orientation class, had also been assigned to Aviano the month before. But since Harold had missed the beginning of the new four-year overseas tour policy beginning on July 1, the Hendersons only got to stay for three years. But during those three years, we traveled together as families to nearby countries and became the best of friends. Our two older sons were the same age as theirs and they became like brothers and remained so for the rest of their lives.

I also soon discovered that the previous group of Protestant chaplains had been fighting among themselves and left a very discontented congregation and a disheveled Protestant chapel program. For me and Harold, there was only one way our efforts could go—and that was up. Or so we thought—until Rufous appeared upon the scene. More about him later. Harold and I made an outstanding team. I was feisty and a charger, and Harold was more pastoral and laid back. I would stir the waters with my bubbling energy to get things moving, and Harold in his quiet manner would smooth them over. I was promoted to the rank of captain shortly after arriving at Aviano.

We had an outstanding base chaplain by the name of John who was a priest and a full colonel. He was fun, humorous, always brimming with enthusiasm, and very pleasant to work with and for. An example of his humor was when I went with him to the personnel office for him to fill out his "dream sheet" (desired future assignments).

"Regular commissioning," Aviano Air Base, March 1969

Father John put down "angel." The female airman said, "Father, you can't put that down!" He said, "Why not? That's what I want to be." We had two chaplains of general rank: the chief, who was a major general (two star), and the deputy, who was a brigadier (one star). Their offices were in Washington. She said, "You need to put something down that's realistic, like chief of Air Force chaplains!" In his usual way, He said to her, "Sweetheart, my chances of making angel are a whole lot more realistic than making chief of Air Force chaplains!" He loved the Protestant hymn "How Great Thou Art" and had the Catholics sing it at every mass until they were sick of it. At mixed gatherings, he would have us sing it to his heart's content, lovingly saying, "All right, you Catholics. Let's show these Protestants how to sing it."

Ben, the senior chaplain in the rank of major, was in charge of the Protestant program. But Ben was running scared and was somewhat ineffective in that position because he had been accused of heresy by the base commander, who was a very conservative Southern Baptist. As a result, Ben dreaded getting into the pulpit.

At that time there were military communication sites along the Italian and Austrian border, and chaplains had the responsibility of regularly visiting the personnel at those sites for morale purposes. Because Ben was afraid of the base commander, he wanted Harold and me to run the Protestant program so that he could be the sole person to visit the sites and be out of the commander's wrath. Because he was the ranking Protestant, that arrangement was not possible. Ben sort of worked in the shadows, and Harold and I built up the chapel attendance to the point that folding chairs had to be placed in the center aisles to accommodate overflow attendance.

But Ben was soon transferred back to the States, and in comes another chaplain, a major by the name of Jerald who was very negative. Spiritual halitosis, you might say. (We called him "Rufous" to his back because like a Rufous, the aggressive, troublemaking hummingbird, that description fit Jerald to a *t*.) If Rufous had ever taken the course "How to Win Friends and Influence People," he would have flunked the course with an F minus—nothing could please this man. After a few weeks, his assessment of the outstanding program Harold and I had built up was, "Worst program I've ever seen. We're gonna have to do something about that." The relationship with me and Harold with Rufous started bad and grew worse. It became so bad that it started to show and affect the congregation, who could sense it.

In time, the bickering and morale got so bad, Father John got wind of it and decided to get us together for a pow-wow. In Ephesians 4:3–6, the Apostle Paul says, "Make every effort to keep the unity of the Spirit through the bond of peace. There is one body and one Spirit—just as you were called to one hope when you were called—one Lord, one faith, one baptism; one God and Father of all, who is over all and through all and in all." The Holy Spirit just cannot operate where there is division. Knowing this to be true, I went to Rufous to make peace, eating whatever crow was necessary to make amends. When I left Rufous, I felt that reconciliation had been achieved and I thought the issue was settled.

A few days later, when Father John had us all together, he began by asking, "What seems to be the problem?" Rufous quickly blurted, "Oh, nothing, Father. A couple of little boys got caught with their hands in the cookie jar. But I've taken care of it!" I guess if I had to compare my temperament to one of Jesus's apostles, it would have to be Peter—impulsive, quick tempered, and ready to whack off the enemy's ear. (In reality, I guess at that time I was a Rufous myself!)

I won't make excuses for my method of dealing with righteous indignation, but it's who I was at the time. Sometimes the end justifies the means, and I believe that's just the way it is. I asked Rufous, "What did you say?" Rufous made the bad mistake of repeating what he had said. I came unglued, got in his face, and said, "Jerry, you're very lucky that I am a Christian. If you had said that 15 years ago, I would have dragged you outside this chapel and stomped the daylights out of you. And if you provoke me any further, that's exactly what I'm going to do."

Unfortunately, it would take me many more years to finally understand what the well-known Christian author, Max Lucado, is fond of saying: "God loves you the way you are, but He loves you too much to let you stay that way!" Father got us settled down, but there never was any love lost between me and Rufous. I've matured some in my relationship with Christ, and now at age 87 I know that the right thing for me to have done was to keep my mouth shut ("Vengeance is mine, I will repay saith the LORD" [Deuteronomy 32:35]). Or at least I should have gone to Rufous later on and asked for his forgiveness.

Harold and I remained the best of friends throughout our lifetime, and every time we got together, Harold would laugh and say, "You were so mad, I thought you were going to yank him by the collar and do it anyway." I could have been court-martialed for insubordination to a superior officer, but Father John, who had a special fondness for me, never let the matter go beyond the confines of that meeting.

Since we lived in the economy (off base) we didn't have telephones nor radio pagers to carry to be reached like the commanders. So when we were assigned on-call duty, the military security police had to come get us at our homes whenever we were needed for an emergency. One night at 2 in the morning I was called to the dispensary to talk with a couple who had had a domestic dispute. When I got there, the master sergeant, whom I knew and who worked in the dispensary, said to me, "Counsel her, Chaplain, I'll be back to get her in about an hour."

It was obvious that he had been drinking. I said to him, "Sit down!" The third time I had to tell him to sit down I said to him, "I've told you to sit down twice. You get me out of bed at 2 in the morning, and now you're telling me she's the one who needs counseling. If I have to tell you again, I'm gonna sit you down. Do you understand?" He knew he had better sit down, and he did, as quiet as a mouse. She said to him, "You've needed for someone to talk to you like that for a long time!" This was one of many situations where tough love came in handy. (As is obvious, I still had a lot of growing up to do myself.)

The chapel secretary, a native Italian by the name of Rita Urbani, had been there for years and had seen chaplains come and go. She didn't like Rufous either because of his divisive nature, which had disrupted the previous harmonious program that we other three chaplains had built up. Rita was invaluable to us because she could translate for us and knew the ins and outs of the base and where and how to get things done. She liked me, and the Solanos and Urbanis would socialize quite often—with us at the Urbanis for excellent Italian meals, and us taking them to local restaurants and an occasional gourmet dinner at our home. Rita had a rosemary bush in her yard and kept Dot supplied with rosemary for Dot's wonderful recipes. Dot was a gourmet cook and had the gift of adding or subtracting from existing recipes to make them even better.

Dot had a maid for a few hours three days a week by the name of Giovanna, who was a devout Catholic and initially apprehensive about working in the home of a Protestant chaplain. But Dot won her over, and they became the best of friends, even to the point of us occasionally being invited to her house to have dinner with her and her husband. One day when Giovanna had not been with us long, I came home and Dot told me about all the things she and Giovanna had talked about. I said to her, "I didn't know you knew any Italian!" Dot responded, "Oh, gossip is a universal language!"

One day there was an exercise on the base where everyone was to practice doing what they would do if there were an actual enemy attack. It was early in the morning, and we chaplains decided we'd go to the dining hall and have breakfast. Soon the deputy base commander walked through and saw us eating breakfast. He was known to be pretty strict, and asked us what we were doing there. We should have been at the chapel in case we were called to a simulated casualty scene. We told him the obvious, that we were having breakfast. What else would we be doing in the dining hall? He said, "I'm going to the kitchen, and when I get back you'd better not be here!" We got the message loud and clear, and we chaplains boogied out of there pronto.

Aviano was a small base, and I, with my gregarious personality, was soon known as the friendliest chaplain there. I would stop and talk to people and wave to them as I went about the base. One day I was walking from the chapel to the Post Exchange (PX; the convenience store), preoccupied and waving at everybody and not paying close attention. In front of the library I stepped out into the street, and a big Chevrolet came to a screeching halt in front of me, almost hitting me.

Realizing that I had nearly caused an accident, I went to the window of the driver's side and embarrassingly apologized to the lady. She felt no harm had been done and said, "It's okay!" About that time she looked at the backseat where this humungous dog the size of a Shetland pony had been lying, and hollered out, "Oh, Koko!" When she slammed her brakes to keep from hitting me, the dog had messed up all over the backseat.

One time Dot accompanied Father John and me on our visitation to the communications sites. In order to get to the location of the sites atop the mountains, we had to travel by chairlift, and at some sites by enclosed lifts called gondolas. Climbing up the mountains, the view of the beautiful valleys below was breathtaking. Simultaneously, all three of us started singing,

> Oh Lord, my God, when I in awesome wonder,
> Consider all the worlds thy hands have made.
> I see the stars, I hear the rolling thunder,
> Thy power throughout the universe displayed.
>
> Then sings my soul, my Savior God to thee,
> How great thou art, how great thou art!
> Then sings my soul my Savior God to thee,
> How great thou art, how great thou art!

While stationed at Aviano I was sent on six weeks' temporary duty to Thessalonica, Greece, where an exercise was being held in what is called "a bare base operation." Civil engineers go into a completely remote area and build a tent city of all the essential facilities required to establish a base of operation to fight a war. Everything is flown in by military aircraft that is required to get military operations fully operative, including building a chapel for worship services. I represented the Protestant side and the priest, Father Tom, came with the civil engineers squadron from Ramstein Air Base, Germany, where they were permanently based.

We got so well acquainted with the initial civil engineering personnel that they lovingly decided to pay tribute to us by placing the following inscriptions on two commode lids: one said, "Father Tom," and the other said, "Chaplain Solano." The story is told that two airmen were straddling the commodes side by side doing their business when one of them noticed the writing. He said to the other, "These belong to the chaplains. Do you think we ought to be using them?"

At Aviano we had a very conservative older lady who was a participant in a Bible study group we called "The Quest," a study that helped all of us to grow a lot spiritually. Our endeavor was to use Scripture selections as a springboard to probe our inner spiritual beings to see how each of us thought the teaching of that Scripture applied to our individual lives. We were pretty forceful and straightforward with each other to try to be as honest and as transparent as we possibly could to get beyond much of the surface façade that many of us Christians hide behind. We became very close to each other and grew by leaps and bounds.

There was a first sergeant (the sergeant in charge in a squadron) who would bring his wife, then sit outside in the hall and read while he waited for her. His name was Don, and one day after the class, Dot asked him, "Don, why don't you join us?" He answered, "Because no one has asked me!" Dot said, "Well, I'm asking you!" He came regularly after that invitation. Studies have shown that a large majority of attending church members became that way because someone personally invited them.

Don was very smart and immersed himself in the study of the Scriptures and became one of our best workers in the chapel program. Eventually God used this Bible study as a way of reaching out to Don to lead him to accept Jesus Christ as Lord and Savior. In later years Don had stomach cancer and had to have a colostomy created to replace his bowels. Typical Don, he served the Lord gloriously by learning all he could about the effects of this kind of condition and would minister to others in support groups who were unfortunate enough to undergo the same procedure.

As indicated earlier in the chapter about my call to the ministry at the church in Columbus, Georgia, invitations by Baptists after a sermon is very traditional. I normally didn't extend invitations because our congregations were made up of persons from all denominations, but felt led to do so one year after my Easter Sunrise service. The service was held outside of a Catholic church atop a mountain slope overlooking the village of Aviano. It was fondly called the Silver Dome. What a wonderful experience that was as the sun showed its face over the horizon just as we started our sunrise service on that chilly early morning. Most who were there huddled together with teeth chattering to keep warm.

Attending that service was a young couple by the name of Dee and Herb. She was in the choir and he in the congregation. They had both been professing Christians but apparently had never had a personal experience with the living Christ through God's Holy Spirit. They did that morning! During the invitation Dee and Herb came forward to accept Jesus Christ as their personal Lord and Savior. Dee describes how it happened in her own words for an addition in this narrative: "We thank you for the inclusion of our conversion which happened at your Easter Sunrise service up on the mountain. Herb came forward on one side and I left the choir and came forward on the other side—we met at the top where you were waiting. We were both Catholic at that time but I was baptized as a baby in the Lutheran Church and again at age 5 into Catholicism. Love to all, Dee and Herb."

As they greeted me after the Easter service, they said, "We would like for you to baptize us." I said, "I would be honored. Let's meet in my office sometime this week and we'll schedule it for a time when it's convenient to both of us!" They shocked me when they said, "You don't understand, we want to be baptized today—this afternoon!" They wanted to be immersed in the manner that Jesus was baptized by John the Baptist, so we went to a nearby lake called Barches where I had done baptisms before. We found the lake to be short of water and very muddy. So I went to the base lifeguard, Walt, and secured the keys to the lock at the swimming pool and baptized them there. That night Walt and his wife were in line at the base theater waiting to secure tickets. They knew each other, and Walt said to them, "Guess what that nutty Chaplain Solano did today? He borrowed my keys to baptize a couple of other nuts in the swimming pool." Dee and Herb smiled from ear to ear, and responded, "Guess who those two nuts were?" and they pointed to themselves.

As nutty as this seemed to the keeper of the swimming pool keys, the Keeper of the key of heaven used Dee and Herb to bring Walt and his wife to the Lord themselves. All four of them became great supporters of the chapel program. Dot and I were privileged to stay in touch with these two couples and visited each other after our retirements from the Air Force.

After writing the first draft of this story, I sent copies out to various persons whose opinions I highly valued to read and give me some candid feedback to help me in rewriting it. Among those were Dee and Herb. Following is part of their testimony to that experience:

One more thought I've had all day and that is that you, my "father" in faith, were quite the tough guy—a hardened piece of steel. God took that steel and honed it over a long period of time and circumstances until it was shiny and sharp—like a surgeon's instrument. Then He sent sinful, spiritually ill folks from all walks of life. The instrument was now a tool He could use to address these needs. And the one who has been sin sick himself knows just how the unsaved sinner feels and where he's coming from. Your early rebellious years, no doubt, enabled you to bring Christ to places others might never have felt they could go.

And one more personal note—there was a young couple who responded to your altar call and came to Christ one Easter sunrise. Months later, they would learn that they would never have natural children. God's perfect timing—through your sharing scripture and personal knowledge of God's love, we were able to weather the storm, holding on to our faith and believing He had a plan to supply our need of having children. You know the rest of the story. PTL. Love, Dee

The rest of the story is that Dee and Herb were later able to adopt a boy and a girl. The adopted girl followed a straight and narrow path in her journey of life and blessed them by having a successful career of her own and presenting them with grandchildren. The son, as I had heartbreakingly seen in a number of adopted children before, became resentful and rebellious and followed a path much like mine in my early days of life. His, however, actually involved the law, while mine did not. But through Dee and Herb's prayers and continued love throughout those years, the prodigal son finally came home and the entire family is now enjoying a relationship that they should have had all the time. Better late than never!

One of the best examples of how God will use every occasion at His disposal to accomplish His will is the story of Master Sergeant Dave Gwaltney. Dave was a faithful member of our choir on Sunday mornings. But Saturday nights he was also a faithful guzzler for his alcoholic addiction at the Non-Commissioned Officers' (NCO) Club. What is interesting about this story is that the chapel and the NCO Club were separated simply by the same parking lot between them. Dave came to me for counseling as he battled between these two masters—the Lord symbolized on one side at the chapel and the liquor demon on the other side at the NCO Club.

I saw a perfect analogy of Dave's problem with this constant tug-of-war, and asked Dave if I might use his situation as an illustration for a sermon without revealing his identity to show how we all battle between doing what is good and doing what is evil. I titled the message "On This Side of the Parking Lot," making the center of my message that victory over our battle with the evil that the NCO Club represented with its lure of alcohol could come only from remaining on the side of the parking lot that symbolized God.

Dave left Aviano for another assignment without any indication that he had whipped his problem. However, several years later he wrote me that he had retired from the service, was no longer drinking, and had enrolled in a seminary to prepare for Christian ministry. He said he credited the turning point of his life with Christ to that sermon he gave me permission to preach. In later years I had the privilege while I was in one of my travels to visit Dave and his wife (he was single at Aviano) in California where he was a pastor. In the year 2012 I received notice from his wife that Dave had died in a Methodist nursing home after a very successful ministry.

It was at Aviano that Dot's ability as an excellent organizer, eloquent speaker, and people person began to be noticed. She got involved in the Officers' Wives' Club (OWC) and the Protestant Women of the Chapel (PWOC). She attended the PWOC retreats in Berchtesgaden, Germany, one of the most beautiful mountainous areas of that country. It's at the base of Eagle's Nest, which was one of Hitler's hideaways. While on one of those retreats, the president of the PWOC for all of Europe saw Dot's potential and asked her if she would serve as president of the PWOC for all of Italy the following year. Dot consented and did such an outstanding job that the next year she was asked to serve as the president of the PWOC for all of Europe. Again she consented and proved herself to be worthy of the trust.

As president for the European PWOC, it was Dot's responsibility to coordinate PWOC matters at military installations throughout the European region. These tasks sometimes included personally speaking at some of these military installations, presiding at all PWOC retreats at Berchtesgaden, and traveling with invited high-powered speakers from the United States at military installations at various countries in Europe. On one occasion, the speaker was Dale Evans of Hollywood fame, primarily in Westerns. Dot and her speakers traveled on military aircraft under GS-16 invitational orders, the equivalent of a two-star general. Needless to say, they were hosted with all the courtesies accorded that high rank. In those days, Dot was in the limelight, and I was in the shadows. Proof of that was a coffee cup presented to me at a gathering that read, "Dot's Husband," that I fondly still have.

One time, Dot and I were asked to be resource leaders at a Baptist retreat at Berchtesgaden to teach a class on marriage enrichment. At one of the presentations I had told Dot she would have 20 minutes to speak. I was long-winded, and when I was through I told her she would have to cut her presentation short. Typical Dot, she got up and told the class what I had said. Then she turned to me and with every bit of authority said, "You promised me 20 minutes. And by gosh, I'm going to take 20 minutes!" Since it was so fitting for a class on marriage enrichment, she was given thunderous applause.

Don and Mike, both teenagers at the time, were with us at the Baptist retreat. They had the adjoining room to us at the hotel. One night they were raising such a fuss that Dot told me to go check on them. When I entered the room, I found Don leaning up against the wall and Mike under the sheets of his bed angry as a hornet. When I asked what the trouble was, Don said, "Tell him to put the knife away!" Apparently they had had an argument. Mike was saying, "I'm gonna kill him! I'm gonna kill him!" I told them to settle down and asked Mike to give me the knife, which was a small one with a one-inch blade.

I scolded them and told them to go to bed—and that I'd better not hear another peep out of either one of them. When I got back to our room Dot asked me what it was all about. I told her not to worry, that she'd read about it in the papers the next morning. The headlines would read, "Chaplain's son stabs brother at Baptist retreat at Berchtesgaden." She didn't think it was funny.

One of the ladies attending the class who had on a beautiful outfit is an example of the negative baggage that all of us carry. When I complimented her on the suit, her blush was as red a beet. When I asked her if I had said something wrong, she replied, "I'm so ashamed. It's something I made myself. When I was growing up we were so poor we had to make our own clothes, and that always made me feel inferior. I'm so mortified that I take Sears labels and sew them inside the collar so no one will know." And she showed me the label as proof.

I told her, "It looks better than those professionally made, and you have nothing to be ashamed of. It's a gift God gave you. You should be proud of it. I have a sister who makes her own clothes, and she sews labels on them that say, 'Handmade by Rae.' You should do the same." The embarrassment she carried was too deeply rooted and she said, "Oh, I could never do that!" I took her hands in mine and said, "Let's put it in the Lord's hands, let's pray about it." About six months later I got a note from her saying, "I took the first step. I've ordered the labels."

I just can't say enough about Dot's abilities. She was gifted in so many ways. She took classes in flower arranging, interior design, and also painting. She even wrote some poetry. Following is a poem she wrote about Christmas.

At Christmas
Look all around you, my friend,
At the now most popular trend
Of buy and sell and advertise
Things which people idolize
At Christmas.

What is Christmas, anyway?
Why is it a special day?
Have we forgotten the tale so dear
Of when the angels did appear
At Christmas?

They came to tell of a little Child born
On that long ago Christmas morn.
He was God's own Son come down
From heaven to little Bethlehem town
At Christmas.

Have we forgotten why He came?
The truths of God to proclaim,
To live and love and die for men
Why can't we love as He did then
At Christmas?

Let us resolve this Christmas day
To turn our hearts to God and pray
That He might truly this day bless
And help us restore the sacredness
Of Christmas.

—*Dot Solano*

During the time when Dot was president for the PWOC for all of Europe, we were invited to Torrejon Air Base in Madrid, Spain, to be resource leaders for a retreat. The base chaplain was a full colonel, and I was simply a captain. During the week, Dot and the colonel's wife, Eileen, became good friends and took daily walks together. Their intimacy got to the point that they shared some very private things with each other. At one point, Dot confessed to Eileen that she initially felt uncomfortable with Eileen because she was a colonel's wife. Conversely, Eileen also confessed to Dot that she initially felt uncomfortable with Dot because Dot was so well known as an effective leader in PWOC.

I discovered in my 57 years of counseling that their problem was not a matter of kind but of degree. We all have poor self-esteem to one degree or another, some to the point of destructive behavior. A case in point was my last assignment in Albuquerque, New Mexico, in 1992. I had a young black chaplain who was outwardly very effective and confident. That proved to be a façade. For some reason he fabricated lies about himself to pretend he was someone he was not.

He had a football on his desk that had been made to look like a watermelon. He said he had played for the Cleveland Browns and had fumbled the ball in one of their important games, causing them to lose. The other players gave him the football resembling a watermelon in jest because he was black. No one had cause to suspect he was lying because people believe that chaplains are men of God who don't lie, but that's not true in all cases. He also wore ribbons indicating he had been a paratrooper and a veteran of the Vietnam War.

The senior Protestant chaplain smelled a polecat because he didn't think that the chaplain was old enough to have been in Vietnam nor that he might have been a paratrooper, so he started checking. None of this turned out to be true. Among other infractions, this resulted in his being discharged. From all outward appearances this young chaplain had it together, but that was not the case.

Most commanders tried to be lenient with personnel who landed in trouble the first time. But they were never lenient with chaplains, their mind-set being, "If I can't depend on my chaplains to set the spiritual example, then on whom can I?" And they had a right to think that way! You have to walk the talk for credibility.

An even more extreme example of the destructiveness of fabrication was the case of a chief of naval operations a few years earlier. He had risen all the way from private to a four-star admiral. It was discovered that he was sporting a ribbon on his uniform that indicated he had earned a medal that turned out to be false. It received widespread publicity. He felt such shame that he committed suicide.

Back to life in Aviano. There is a performance on the life of Christ called *The Passion Play* performed in the village of Oberammergau, Bavaria, Germany, every 10 years as a tradition by the village inhabitants. It was first performed in 1634 as a promise to God that if he would spare them from the bubonic plague that ravaged that area in 1632, they would do the play to glorify Him. At first the *Passion Play* was performed with some regularity, but then it was decided that it would be done only every 10 years in the year ending in zero.

The production is five hours long, with a meal break, and is repeated over a course of five months of that specified year. It consists of 16 acts and is attended by around half a million people per year. Dot and I were privileged to see this spectacular performance by the locals in an open amphitheater in 1970 in Oberammergau while stationed at Aviano.

Aviano proved to be a maturing experience for our oldest son, Keith, and the Henderson's oldest son, Royce, as well as for our second, Don, and the Henderson boy, Marty. Don and Marty were both very smart and took numerous scholastic honors all the years they were in junior high school in Aviano.

Since there was no high school at Aviano, those of high school age had to be bused about 100 miles away to the high school at the Army post at Vicenza, Italy, where they were also housed in dormitories. They were bused back to Aviano for the weekends, and they spent weekends with their parents when they were not involved in games away from Vicenza. Keith and Royce both played football and basketball. Their coach was a no-nonsense Army master sergeant. This demanding military leadership served to instill commitment and discipline in all of his players.

On those weekends when Keith was unable to come home, Dot would send him some "homemade goodies." He was always grateful for what he called "the bennies!" By the time he attended college he had already experienced his independence from his parents, which most new college students don't, and they sometimes become unruly.

Keith knew at this age he wanted to be a doctor, and was influenced by a doctor at the Aviano Medical Clinic by the name of Robert Cockcroft from Memphis, Tennessee. He talked Keith into going to Mississippi College in Clinton, his alma mater, where the ratio of premed students accepted into medical school was quite high.

Aviano gave my entire family much opportunity to travel in parts of Europe, including Germany, France, Spain, and other parts of Italy, in the old Volkswagen camper. Needless to say, living in Italy was a broadening education for our boys. The embassy in Belgrade, Yugoslavia, had a status of forces agreement with the military to have a chaplain from Aviano provide worship services for them in Belgrade on Sundays once a quarter.

Services were attended by people from all nations represented at the embassy complex. We chaplains would hop the sleeper in Trieste, Italy, on Friday evenings, sleep all night, and wake up in Belgrade Saturday morning. Sunday night we would reverse the order and wake up in Trieste Monday morning. Yugoslavia was under communist rule, and we were told that we should be careful about what we said and did there because there were cameras in the rooms watching our every move. Dot was able to accompany me on one of my trips to Belgrade. The embassy people were grateful for our service and treated us chaplains with royalty.

I had never been much of a jock, but it was at Aviano that I first took up racquetball. I played it every day for 17½ years and later became "tournament material" in my league. One day when I had gone to Belgrade by myself, I called Harold and told him to reserve a court at the gym to play racquetball shortly after my return. This would be prior to going to see Dot after being gone all weekend. I told Harold to go by the house and get my gym stuff and I would meet him at the gym. Dot was furious and told Harold she was going to strangle me with my jockstrap.

Another exciting and memorable event while at Aviano was our visit to Berlin with the Hendersons while the city was still separated by the Berlin Wall. We drove to Ramstein, Germany, where we caught a military troop train that took us to Berlin for four days. Dot knew a friend from Warner Robins, Georgia, who was assigned to the U.S. Embassy there, and he arranged for Harold and me to have a helicopter ride over the city. We felt pretty special because we were told that not many Americans who visited Berlin had had that kind of experience.

Master Sergeant Jim was the chapel manager in charge of the enlisted troops at the Aviano chapel, and he taught me a valuable lesson. Jim and I became the best of friends and socialized off duty. One Sunday when communion was served, the chapel managers mixed Kool-Aid and served it as a substitute for grape juice that they had failed to buy. You can imagine the congregation's reaction. The next day I found the sergeant talking to some of his chapel managers and proceeded to chew him out royally. That caused a rift between us, and when I confronted him to make amends, Jim said to me, "Chaplain, you had every right to dress me down. But not in front of my troops." That was a lesson in forgiveness and humility that I would remember, but failed to apply in later years when the same thing happened to me in Madrid, Spain. Toward the end of our four-year tour, I received orders to go to Richards Gebaur Air Force Base in Belleville, Illinois.

8

Surprise! Surprise!

Richards Gebaur Air Force Base, Bellville, Illinois, 1972–1974

Richards Gebaur was known as "Dickey Goober" by those stationed there. The two years here proved to be a maturation process for me and a shocking experience for Dot. It was here that Don graduated from high school and went on to receive an undergraduate degree and several master's degrees from several universities. He later joined the Air Force as a communications officer and retired in the rank of lieutenant colonel after over 22 years of active duty in Orlando, Florida, and transferred into that same position as a civil service employee. He did that for 16 years attaining the rating of a GS-13 and retiring in June 2018.

My boss was a lieutenant colonel by the name of Harry, who, like Grover previously, proved to be a man of God with many talents. Harry played the ukulele along with several of our church members and provided music for worship on occasion. Harry must have thought I was the dumbest chaplain he'd ever had because every time an opportunity for a school would come up, he would recommend that I go. (In actuality, he saw my potential and knew what these schools would do for my career advancement.) Dickey Goober was the headquarters for the Air Force Communications Command, and enlisted personnel came there for all types of advanced courses. I was the chaplain for the Non-Commissioned Officers Academy. Still ever cocky, at the beginning of each class, I would introduce myself, speak to them, and offer this challenge. "I play racquetball and I offer you this challenge—if anyone beats me, I'll buy you a steak dinner. If I beat you, you come to church." I never did have to buy a steak, and our church attendance did increase slightly in attendance.

By this time I had advanced to the rank of major. Dot was in the choir with another chaplain's wife of the same rank as mine, and they would ride together to choir rehearsal. On rehearsal night the other wife would often tell Dot that she had to get home early because the night of the rehearsal was also the night her husband liked to make love. One night when that wife didn't seem to be in a hurry to get home, Dot asked her, "I thought you had to get home early so you and Dale could make love?" Joyce replied, "Oh, I told him if I wasn't home in time, to start without me!" and laughed hysterically.

In 1973, Dot asked me what I wanted to do for my birthday party. I told her I would like to have a kiddie party since when I was a child we were too poor to have a party. So she invited about 20 guests and they all came dressed as kids and we played kid games, including pin the tail on the donkey blindfolded, and had the best time of our lives. Those attending brought a toy for me, which we donated to a locate orphanage.

Midway through my tour, the senior chaplain received notice that a new chaplain by the name of Bill was coming to replace one who was departing. Over time, the 869 chaplains on active duty would each create a reputation that would precede them, good or bad. (That reminds me of a story I once heard. There was a little old lady who rode a bus daily in inner-city Los Angeles. She made it a habit to study people to determine what they might be like. One day this big young man boarded the bus and rudely shoved people aside as he looked for a seat. She sized him up immediately as a bully. Just about the time he was to disembark, she hollered out, "Hey, fellow! You left something behind!" He roared back, "What did I leave behind?" She smiled smugly and replied, "A bad impression!"

At a staff meeting, the Dickey Goober chaplains asked each other if anyone knew Bill, the new incoming chaplain. The priest said he did. He was asked the typical questions: "Is he a team player, lazy or committed, what are his gifts," etc.? The priest said, "Well, it's like this. At a certain base when the chaplain leaves, everyone is sad because they really liked him. At another base, when the chaplain leaves, they're glad he's gone because nobody liked him. When Bill leaves, nobody knows he's gone!" How is that for a legacy?

There are three service schools that officers, including chaplains, had to complete to advance in rank. They were Squadron Officers' School (SOS) for lieutenants and captains; Air Command and Staff College (ACSC) for senior captains, majors, and lieutenant colonels; and the Air War College (AWC) for senior lieutenant colonels and full colonels. These could be accomplished through correspondence or in residence at Maxwell Air Force Base, Montgomery, Alabama. I was selected to attend the four-month SOS course in residence while at Dickey Goober. Mixing with representatives of all professions as well as different military services turned out to be quite a broadening experience.

Dr. Robert Cockroft, Keith's mentor, had called recommending that I go to Marks, Mississippi, where his father-in-law was a lawyer, to do all that was necessary to become a resident of Mississippi so that Keith could go to the Ole Miss medical school as an in-state student, which would make his tuition much less. So on the way to Montgomery to attend SOS I went to Marks, the only time I ever went there. Then after graduation from college, Keith went to the Medical College of Wisconsin in Milwaukee, and I, who never went back to Marks, paid state taxes in Mississippi for the next sixteen years as a resident.

Halfway through the SOS class, I was allowed to come home for Don's graduation from high school. While at home, Dot became pregnant at age 42, and Mark was born nine months later in February 1974. Dot was furious when she found out about her pregnancy, but I strutted around with my chest out like a bantam rooster. Dot's ob-gyn physician gave her a warning in the following words: "Since I am Catholic, I cannot advise you on an abortion. But you need to know that at your age, reproductive cells began to break down significantly and the chances of this child being born with Down syndrome are rather high." To Dot and me, abortion was never a consideration, believing that this child was God's will and gift for us and we would accept that child in whatever condition he was born. This is the letter that Dot wrote to Mark, who was yet to be born:

February 1974
Dear "Baby" Solano:

You don't know me yet and I don't know you except to know that you are a very active part of me. You see, you have not been born yet.

But your Daddy suggested to me one day that some of these long nights when I cannot sleep, I should write you a letter to be given to you years from now after you've grown up as our little girl or boy.

When I found out some seven months ago that I was pregnant with you, I have to admit I was not too happy about it. You see, I had just turned 42 years old, your dad was 41, your brothers were 20, 18, and 14—we thought our family was complete. I had been "footloose and fancy-free" for some years doing some things I enjoyed outside the home while the boys were at school—women's club work, church work, shopping, even golfing, learning a little painting, and going and coming as I pleased so long as Daddy didn't mind—now this—a baby at my age! I'd be all tied down again—formulas, dirty diapers, night feeding, worrying over little childhood illnesses. UGH! I was even angry with your Dad because I thought it was all his fault for impregnating me (which of course it wasn't—I enjoyed our very active, loving sex life as much as he did). Then I even blamed it on your brother, Don—Why? Because your Dad had been in Alabama in a four month school, April–August 1973, and came home to Kansas City one day in May (22nd to be exact) to attend your brother Don's graduation from high school. Dad had flown back to Alabama on May 23rd—some 24 hours at home and I got pregnant!

Then I even blamed it on a doctor I had seen in Italy in June of 1972 for my annual check-up. I had had an IUD contraceptive device for five years that had worked perfectly. This young doctor had a "fit" when he found out from my records that it had not been changed—said it should have been after two years at least (I found out later this was not necessarily true—just his "medical opinion"). So I followed his instructions and had a new device inserted. I had some problems from the start with the new IUD, but they finally went away, and I didn't worry about it anymore. I was due another check-up in June 73 and thought I'd just wait and have it at Maxwell AFB in Alabama at a larger hospital when I went down to be with your Dad after school was out. Well, I went to the hospital there all right, but to have the pregnancy test not just a check-up! I'll have to tell you, your Dad was elated about you from the beginning. But he understood my feelings and helped me to work through them.

When we returned to Kansas City and I contacted an Obstetrician, one of the first things he suggested was that I might be worried as to you being abnormal because percentages are high for abnormal babies after a mother passes 40. He suggested an "amniotic fluid" test with which results we could determine health (also sex) and if something were wrong, I could abort. ABORTION! It was very prevalent in our country at the time as laws had been changed legalizing it and it was a very controversial subject. I sort of knew how I felt about it generally, but now I had to be personal. You were by then a 3 month old "fetus" growing inside of me— "fetus"? No, you were a baby—a human being—a miracle of life— which only God could give. Could I decide on my own to "do away" with you? NO! I did not have that right! God was giving you to me and Daddy for a purpose—whether normal or abnormal. You were our baby, conceived in love, and meant to be. So you see, I'd worked through my disappointment to being resigned to the fact "I am pregnant."

Now came the part of getting excited about it all. God was giving us a new life to love, to mold, to see grow up, and be a part of our happy family. You see, with your brothers, Daddy was in college and seminary and I had had to work all the time they were little. Now with you, I was going to have the opportunity to cuddle, to rock you, to enjoy you—and probably spoil you—to be a real mother. And how I began to hope and pray for a little girl—your Dad and your brothers did too. And I admit even now so close to your birth I'm "thinking pink," and praying God will grant this request.

But I know even if in His wisdom He gives us another boy, you'll still be loved, cherished, and spoiled—and grow up to be a fine young man like your brothers are. One thing I do know, you are the most active baby I've carried and we've dubbed you our little "Mexican jumping bean." If you are as active after you're born, your old mother will have a time keeping up with you. We're so anxious for your birth now—besides my being so uncomfortable with carrying you. We're just anxious to hold you and love you. Your room is all ready. Dad and I have so enjoyed fixing it up. It's the first time we've had the extra room or the money to fix up a really pretty nursery. And, oh how excited our friends are also. I've been given two showers for you and nearly 100 people have given you gifts. Mike says you'll be the best dressed baby in town with all that "loot." Think he may even be a bit jealous after nearly 15 years of being "the baby"—especially now with his brothers gone to college. He thought he'd be an "only child" and "chief honcho" for about four years—and now you come along as an "intruder" on his time. But knowing old Mike as we do, once you are here he'll be right in there loving and spoiling you, too—especially if you're a little sister. If you're a little brother, he'll probably be teaching you football and basketball before you are a year old.

You are going to be born into a chaotic, confusing world—at a time when we are experiencing one crisis after another in our country. What will the future hold for you? We're very uncertain. But this we do know—your Dad and I have a very deep abiding faith in our God and in His son, Jesus Christ. We know God has been guiding our lives for some years now and as long as we stay in the center of His will and serve Him first in our lives, all other things will fall into place. So we also have a responsibility with you, to dedicate you to God and dedicate ourselves anew to being the kind of parents God would have us be. We will love you and discipline you in love and guide you in the ways of God. Then when you are old enough, you will accept or reject these principles as an individual in your own right. We feel very keenly God is giving you to us at this time in our lives as a very special gift, and that He has a purpose for your life, as He has had for ours.

So someday in the distant future, when you read this—your Mother's "ramblings" in the middle of the night while awaiting your birth—maybe God will speak to you in a special way. I can only say you are very special and wanted very much by me and your Daddy and *right soon*! Our love for each other has grown so over

these past 23 years that you are indeed our "love child"—more so than your brothers—for we were so immature then and not dedicated to God as we are now. You will assuredly be a very "blessed event" in our lives. So now we anxiously await your birth—and you.
Your loving Mother-to-be

Little did Dot know how much worse things would get by 2019 when Mark would be 45 years old.

America in 2019 was divided almost as much as it was during the Civil War. No longer was it looked up to as the world leader nation. Women and children were using profanity without restraint, and a selfish "me and mine" mind-set plagued society. A new clause was invented that gripped the nation and had everybody fearfully walking on eggshells. The term was "politically correct," and it meant that you had to watch every little word you said for fear that you might offend someone of opposite thinking or makeup, and exercise tolerance to the extreme because you might be labeled "racist," "bigot," or "out of touch with the times" at best. It got so bad that someone who saw a program that children watched on television with the main character being a white choo-choo train puffing black smoke said this was racist.

The socialistic trend was fast on the move. The Robin Hood mentality of taking from the rich and giving to the poor had swept the country, and redistribution and entitlement replaced the previous mind-sets of being rewarded for hard, honest labor and learning to be independent. The government became a "big daddy" that would provide for your every need, without regard that the money had to come from somewhere besides the government, which had no money of its own to give.

The church, the family, and the educational system, which had been the main sources of character building, were in disarray. Typical of the times was a lawsuit brought by a young girl who sued her parents for not consenting to pay her full tuition to send her to Harvard. How different the world had become since the days of Dot's and my childhoods, which came at the heels of the Great Depression. Someone rightly said, borrowing from Oscar Wilde in the 1890s, "This generation knows the price of everything, but the value of nothing."

The women's movement (also known as women's liberation or feminism) refers to a series of campaigns for reforms on issues such as reproduction, domestic violence, maternity leave, equal pay, women's suffrage, sexual harassment, and sexual violence, all of which fall under the label of feminism, that began in the Western world in the late 19th century and has gone through three waves.

It was much needed and had moved slowly, until around the late 1960s when it spread like wildfire and has been taken to extreme. In so doing, we threw the baby out with the bathwater. In the early days of my life, women were treated with a higher regard than they are today. In one good sense, society didn't regard women as equal with men, but of a higher stature because of their tender makeup and mothering capability.

We treated women as being special in a very unique way. It was a time of chivalry. Men opened car doors for them, tipped their hats when women walked by, and things of that respectful nature. Dot captured this feeling of being special in a statement she made to me when the current women's liberation movement began its rapid spread. She said to me, "I don't want to be your equal. Why should I lower myself and come down from this pedestal, I like it up here!" That special, tender quality of a woman cannot be provided by a man. You can't give what you don't have. It has rightly been said, "A man can build a house, but it takes a woman to build a home." Another saying goes, "The husband may be the head of the home, but the wife is the heart of the home." Dot had a large wooden plaque on the wall over the stove with a fairly big rooster carved into the wood. The lettering said, "He rules the roost, but I rule the rooster!"

I loved Dot for her physical beauty, but even more so for her inner beauty. Physical beauty can only last for a limited time—age takes care of that. But that inner beauty can only come from the source of it all, God, and increases and lasts forever. The godly example by which men should view women should start in the marital relationship and be good examples for the children. The biblical standard for that treatment is found in Ephesians 5:25, 27, and 28, where it says, "Husbands, love your wives just as Christ loved the church and gave himself up for her . . . to present her to himself as a radiant church—in this same way, husbands ought to love their wives as their own bodies. He who loves his wife loves himself." If that teaching had been ingrained in each previous generation, we might not have the unintended negative results brought about by the women's liberation movement. The saying "If Mama ain't happy, ain't nobody happy!" is more truth than humor.

Another problem plaguing humanity in 2019 was the insatiable hunger for the acquisition of things to satisfy a hunger for meaning and purpose. And two of the worst culprits were the news media and television, with their tempting advertisements of all descriptions that fed the appetite and mind-set that the more you had the more you needed and the more important you were. We didn't buy because we needed, we bought because we wanted—and it never seemed to be enough.

A story told about the late Dr. Albert Schweitzer puts this dilemma in proper perspective. Schweitzer was a theologian, accomplished organist, philosopher, physician, and noted medical missionary who was awarded the Nobel Peace Prize in 1952. But he never let that go to his head. He was content with the simple things of life, glorifying God and making a difference in this world with his godly gifts. In making plans to attend the funeral of a friend of his who had died, Schweitzer went to his locker and pulled out an old, wrinkled tie.

His nurse said to him, "Dr. Schweitzer, you can't wear that tie!" "Why not?" he replied. "It's the only one I have!" She said, "You, a man as famous as you are has only one tie? Why there are men in the United States who have as many as 30 ties!" He was heard to mumble as he walked away,

"My, my, 30 ties and only one neck!" Unfortunately all of us get sucked in by the myth that we are identified by what we have or what we do instead of who we are.

That elusive quest for happiness and meaning that we seek in things and fame can only be found in a personal relationship with our Heavenly Father, Creator of us all, through Jesus Christ. St. Francis of Assisi said it best: "Thou has made us with a restlessness that will not rest until we find our rest in Thee."

Violence was aflame all over the world, and the United States was so preoccupied trying to bring peace out there that it failed to see the unrest and moral degradation taking place right under its nose. While its leaders rhetorically mouthed the existence of a false peace, the godly Judeo-Christian underpinnings of America were dangerously being strained and eroding. Even one of its presidents publicly proclaimed that America was not a Christian nation. Too many Americans were like the ostrich with its head stuck in the sand, in denial that many of their precious constitutional rights were slowly but intentionally being taken away by socialistic-minded politicians.

Studies have pointed out that the lifespan of nations that ruled the world like Rome typically lasted around 200 years, and some predicted that the United States, soon to reach that mark, would go the way of Rome—defeated from within instead of from without.

George Santayana, a noted philosopher, poet, and literary and cultural critic of the past, has insightfully written, "Those who do not learn from history are doomed to repeat it." The Great Depression of the late 1920s and early 1930s was a great tragedy for this wonderful country, and I hope Santayana's prediction never comes true for us. And yet Professor Alfred McCoy, who has taught history at such places as University of Wales and written 11 books of history, says that there is solid evidence to indicate that this downfall is inevitable. He states this in his book *How America Will Collapse by 2025*, which he published in 2003. He says, "In spite of the aura of omnipotence most empires project, a look at their history should remind us that they are fragile organisms. So delicate is their hold of power that, when things start to go truly bad, empires regularly unravel with unholy speed; just a year ago Portugal; 2 years for the Soviet Union; 8 years for France; 11 years for the Ottomans; 17 years for Great Britain; and in all likelihood, 22 years for the United States from the crucial year 2003." The three main reasons for this demise, he says, "are (1) loss of economic clout, (2) the decline of American technological innovation, and (3) the end of the dollar's privileged status as the global reserve currency, and the fact that we are so indebted financially to other countries." During the dark hours of late summer 1940, Winston Churchill said to his people, "Let us embrace ourselves to our duty and so bear ourselves that if the British Commonwealth and Empire lasts for a thousand years, people will say, 'This was their finest hour!'" Oh, how America badly needs a rallying cry from such a trusted leader today!

Mark turned out to be completely normal and went on to live a very productive and successful life. He married and had three wonderful children of his own. In 2018 he was hired as a vice president for a company at a six-figure salary. Two months after Mark was born, I received orders to go to Kwang-Ju, Korea, an isolated assignment that did not allow for my family to go with me. My boss, Harry, called the office of the Chief of Air Force Chaplains to see if he could have my assignment cancelled because of Mark's recent birth, and he wanted to spare Dot the task of having to raise him that first year by herself.

Harry had underestimated Dot's capacity to rise to the task. This woman was made of granite. True to form, Dot would have none of it, believing that they might think she was some dingbat weakling who wasn't able to handle the year separation. "No way, Jose!" She had managed quite well with Keith when I was away for 16 months in 1953–1954, and by gosh she would handle this with Mark in the same way. "No, Sir, not Dot Solano!" So she had Harry call back and tell them to disregard his request.

She called her closest friend, Helen Gurganus, who was more like a sister, in Raleigh, North Carolina, telling her about my impending assignment. Typical of Helen, she told Dot, "You come and live nearby and we'll look after you while John is gone!" Within a few days, Helen had an apartment close by for Dot, Mike, and Mark, and look after them they did—and many times with her famous, delicious pound cake, which was always at hand.

Dot also had a witty streak that could put you in your place. One day while I was in Korea, Mark was sick, and Dot took him to see a pediatrician. When he asked Dot what seemed to be wrong with him, she told him she thought he had the colic. Obviously opinionated, he said to her, "Oh, colic is a lot of hullabaloo!" When Mark didn't get well after some time she brought him back to see him. When he asked again what was wrong this time she said, "He still has the hullabaloo!"

9

Sodom and Gomorrah

Kwang-Ju Air Base, Korea, 1974–1975

Kwang-Ju turned out to be a very interesting and profitable one-year assignment for me in terms of career progression. It was my first opportunity to serve as the senior chaplain. The military created Kwang-Ju AB as a result of the capture of the *Pueblo* by North Koreans years before. Kwang-Ju's main mission was to store munitions and have them easily accessible in the event such an attempt on one of the U.S. ships was ever tried again. Working under me were a staff sergeant (four-striper) and an airman second class (two-striper), a priest of the Passionate Order (reserve Air Force chaplain in the rank of captain), and a Presbyterian missionary who was my auxiliary and served as needed. The interesting thing about me and the priest was that I had converted from Roman Catholic to Baptist, and the priest had converted from Baptist to Catholic.

Sex was the rule of the day at Kwang-Ju. Almost every male had a live-in Korean female in the village they called their "Yobo." The term "Yobo" means "my wife" in Korean and in its original meaning was a good term. In this cheapened context it meant "the woman I am shacking up with."

Sex was cheap, and it was available. For the men, it satisfied their sexual appetites, and for the Korean women it was a lot better than working out in the rice paddies in the blistering hot sun for low wages.

Sexual promiscuity was so common and accepted that as soon as you got off the plane from the States, the mind-set one encountered immediately was, "It's there for the taking and everybody's doing it." I found out that even a former chaplain and base commander had had Yobos. It was the Old Testament story of Sodom and Gomorrah playing out in real life.

The only men who remained faithful to their wives and sweethearts were those who stayed closely associated with the chapel program and supported each other. Since we didn't have the typical programs normally provided in the chapel—choir, youth, and so on—one of my main ministries was night visitation of the bars in the local village of Kwang-Ju so that I could be friendly and visible to the airmen to establish a relationship in the event any ever needed counseling, as well as briefing the commander on morale from time to time. Since I owned a motorcycle, I had a jacket made with Snoopy atop a motorcycle embroidered on the back of my jacket with a cross over the left breast of Snoopy's chest.

One day I was at a bar when a barmaid came up and said in broken English, "You buy me drink?" The men around me, knowing who I was, and she not, eyed me closely to see what I would do. I said, "I don't think so!" She said, "I go home with you!" I again said, "I don't think so!" She said, "I think I have what you need!" I, in my usual quick-witted way, replied, "No. I think I have what you need!" The fellows broke out laughing, knowing that she and I were talking about two totally different things.

I established a good relationship with the personnel at the Presbyterian Missionary Compound and spent a lot of time there eating some good meals and sharing in good Bible study and Christian fellowship. The base commander was a Southern Baptist from Raleigh, North Carolina, and the two of us struck up a fellowship from the start.

I had become a hot-shot racquetball player by this time and had that kind of reputation. There came a time when a team of chaplains from Pacific Air Force Command Headquarters in Hawaii came to review the chapel program at Kwang-Ju. The team was comprised of Chaplain Colonel Ransom Wood, and the Catholic priest, Chaplain William F. Mattimore, also a colonel. Chaplain Wood thought of himself as a hot-shot racquetball player, so he challenged me to a match. Mattimore whispered to me, "Beat hell out of him!" I, much younger, did, and badly. Not to be outdone, Ransom asked me if I could get the keys to the gym. When I said I could, he challenged me to a repeat match—at 5 the next morning—before their plane returned to Hawaii. I whipped him again.

I used to run daily with two black airmen who were very much involved in the chapel program. One day they were running with me in the middle. One jokingly said to the other, "Do you realize that we three look like an Oreo cookie?" One of those airmen eventually left the Air force and went into full-time Christian ministry.

In those days, international phone service was limited, and Dot and I would talk occasionally by voice radio made available to us from the communications station at Kwang-Ju that tapped into the phone in my trailer and some ham voice radio operator in the States who would patch into Dot's phone in Raleigh. One of us would talk on one end while the other listened and then would say, "Over." Then we would reverse the order. The only cost to Dot was the telephone service from wherever she was being patched in to her phone from the States to Raleigh, which could be anywhere. There was no cost to me, of course. Very primitive, even in 1974, by today's standards.

Midway in my tour, I was able to come to Raleigh for a few weeks to visit Dot, Mike, and Mark. (No, she didn't get pregnant this time!) She confessed to me that periodically she would smell my uniform in the closet and imagine she felt my presence. The only uniforms I had in Korea were my work clothes called fatigues because there was no need for my blue uniform. As she had done with Keith previously during my 16-month absence, Dot did an outstanding job being Mom and Dad to our boys during my Korean tour, no easy task when one of the children is fifteen years old. While at Kwang-Ju I was invited to be the speaker by the commander of the flying squadron in Osan, Korea, the commander being Colonel Grover Pratt, Dot's cousin who later retired as a three-star general.

The only thing I learned in Korean was, "Hananim sarong kamnida!" In English it means, "God loves you!"—and if all I know is that "God loves me," that's good enough for me. Near the end of my one-year tour I was notified that I had been selected to attend the one-year course, Air Command and Staff College (ACSC) in residence. So I picked up my family in Raleigh, and off to Montgomery, Alabama, we went to write another adventurous chapter in our life story. Mike, 15 years old, hated leaving his sweetheart in Raleigh and cried for several miles to Montgomery—he was that saddened. He wrote her a letter that I happened to glance at as I passed by. I said to Mike, "You might want to rewrite that heading." He had started the letter, "Dear Sweaty," instead of "Dear Sweetie."

10

Sowing Seed for the Harvest

Maxwell Air Force Base, Montgomery, Alabama, 1974–1975

Air Command and Staff College (ACSC) proved to be an enriching, career-enhancing opportunity for me. There were two other chaplains attending as well. The huge class was broken into sections and was made up of military and civilian government personnel and officers representing many different branches, as well as countries from the Far East, Europe, the Middle East, and other parts of the world. In later years when I looked through my ACSC pictorial directory of the students, I often wondered what might have happened to those foreign students, especially those from Iraq, Iran, Afghanistan, and other countries in that part of the world where so much warfare has taken place.

Among the American students were nurses and line officers representing many different careers. This interface with such a mixture of professions helped me to move out of my comfort zone into many areas of life with more understanding. Being selected to attend in residence was considered a high honor, quite a feather in one's cap. With an estimated total annual cost to the government of $52,000 per student in 1974–1975,

Student at Air Command and Staff College in the rank of major, Maxwell Air Force Base, 1975

it was almost a given that one would get a good follow-up assignment after completing the school.

Much of what went on in the classroom, stage lectures, and exercises was beyond the natural part of a chaplain's thinking and normal ministerial life. During one of the exercises, I said to a classmate who had a cigar in his mouth all the time and who later went on to become a general, "I sure am glad we have people like you to understand and figure these things out." He repaid the compliment by saying, "Well, I sure am glad that we have people like you to keep us straight." He and his wife came to the section Halloween party dressed in costumes that were rather suggestive, she as a brick and he as a brick layer.

When it came time for graduation, the other two chaplains received assignments to what were considered bases of good visibility and good for promotion opportunity. When I got mine, it was to Vance Air Force Base, Enid, Oklahoma (Podunkville), a very small base out in the boonies north of Oklahoma City. I called Dot and told her we were going to Vance AFB. Dot asked, "Where is Vance AFB?" I said, "In Enid, Oklahoma!" In a more forceful voice she asked, "Where is Enid, Oklahoma?" I told her Enid was the wheat capital of the world. She said, "I don't care if it's Fort Knox. I thought you were supposed to get a good assignment from here!" Dot and I were naturally disappointed, but as always, the Lord knew what He was doing. He answers prayer with, "Not what I have in mind," "Not time," or "I have something better in mind for you!"

What appeared to be a minus turned out to be a real plus—a blessing in disguise! Vance gave me an opportunity to show what I could do in running the base as the senior guy again after Kwang-Ju. Military personnel received ratings of performance every year and those ratings were crucial to promotion in order to select the best. Prior to this time, all officers' efficiency reports (OERs) were inflated, and it was hard for promotion boards to distinguish between the true ratings and the inflated ones. To correct the problem, the Air Force marked the ratings as 1, 2, and 3, the 1 being the top rating. They also limited the number of 1s and 2s the com-

Air Command and Staff College, Maxwell Air Force Base, Montgomery, Alabama, in the rank of major, 1975

manders could issue. I was a major at this time with only one other chaplain, a priest in the rank of captain serving under me. However, since I was the head chaplain, if I did a good job, I was in a better position to receive the top rating of 1, which I did, as opposed to the other two chaplain ACSC graduates who were serving in lesser positions. One of those chaplains did go on to become a full colonel, the other didn't.

11

Disappointment Becomes a Blessing

Vance Air Force Base, Enid, Oklahoma, 1976–1979

Although Vance was a small base out in the boonies, it was an important one: an undergraduate flight training base. They started the students out in the T-37 fighter jet and later in the T-38—the T-38 being a pretty sophisticated aircraft in those days. In fact it was the T-38 that the famed Air Force Thunderbirds used for their awesome acrobatic demonstrations all over the world. The classes were made up of highly intelligent personnel, coming from graduates of the Air Force Academy, the Reserves, and other important groups—those considered to be the cream of the crop. Vance was known as a "contract base," meaning that the essential support comfort needs of the base, such as dining and security, were supplied by civilians, so there were few low-ranking airmen to go into Enid to get drunk, misbehave, and chase the women, as some were known to do. Thus, there was a great relationship between Vance and the town of Enid.

Sadly, there was not that good a relationship between me and the priest (Pat). The priest resented me as his boss, and was distant most of the time. Remembering what happened with Rufous at Aviano and sensing the need for a brotherly spirit, I talked to Pat about it. Pat's answer was always, "It's not you, John. It's your style of leadership. I had a superior in civilian life who led the same way, and that causes a division between you and me." Pat knew the problem, but apparently he didn't know the solution or didn't want to do anything about it.

Since it was Pat's problem, I realized it was Pat's to resolve so I learned to live with it. As the Polish are fond of saying, "Not my circus, not my monkey!" I was who I was and I wasn't going to change simply to appease Pat. We never did come to terms, and Pat went on to another assignment with that division unresolved. This fractured relationship ate at me, and after about a year I wrote to Pat and told him how it was bothering me and wished to make amends. Pat wrote back and told me that he had experienced the same thing, and wished he had had the courage to reach out and was glad that I had done it. I saw Pat in later years when I retired in Colorado Springs. Pat had left the Air Force and the priesthood and had married a divorcee with two children and was very happy.

Pat was replaced by Father Sam, who turned out to be a real plus for me and the Catholic parish. Sam was a good cook, a team player, and with Dot being a gourmet cook, they hit it off immediately. The Catholic and Protestant congregations had numerous functions together during the remainder of my tour at Vance. One of the most memorable times was at Christmas when members from both congregations went wassailing (a celebration with joyful drinking) from the chapel annex all around the housing area on base. We started out with two buckets of liquid refreshments, one with booze and the other a mixture of soft drinks.

As we approached each home, we sang to the occupants, asked them to take a swig from whichever bucket they preferred, replace some in the bucket from their own home, bring an egg, and join the group singing as we worked our way back to the chapel annex. There we would have a group of men from the chapel cooking a breakfast-type meal, to which all the eggs would be added and scrambled to complete the meal. Almost the entire neighborhood joined in by the time we completed our night's wassailing. What a joyous, festive time we all had, and I don't know of another base that ever did this.

Another fond memory was going on a training flight aboard a T-38. One of my congregants, who was a flight instructor, got permission from the flying wing commander for me to have this rare opportunity. I went through the flight chamber, donned the flight suit, and up into the wild blue yonder we went. I was having the time of my life in the backseat chasing those clouds at such top speed. What an exhilarating, unique experience!

At one point, the pilot asked me if I would like to take the stick, and I did. The pilot warned me that when we would exit the clouds the plane would be upside down. Either I did it inadvertently or the pilot purposely, but that's exactly what happened. When we came out of the clouds, I looked up expecting to see the sky and saw the ground instead. I had done fine up to this point, but when this happened I got the dry heaves badly and had to reach for the plastic barf bag.

Receiving a certificate after completing my first flight in the T-38, Vance Air Force Base, Enid, Oklahoma

Pilot training is very demanding and requires the utmost discipline and commitment. Furthermore, it's very expensive to the government because of the expense of training a pilot as well as the cost of possible airplane crashes that might take place. And many of those disastrous mishaps did happen in flight training throughout the Air Force due to student pilot error. After realizing how much graduation demanded, some of the students came to the conclusion that this was their father's dream for them, or their childhood dream now passed, and weren't willing to put the effort into it and would self-eliminate.

Those who did eliminate were required to see one of us chaplains for our assessment, which we provided the commander. Since this was an official assessment, it did not fall within the understood policy of privileged communication between clergy and counselee.

Among those I counseled was this tall, handsome, seemingly very intelligent captain who self-eliminated. During the counseling, I explored all possible reasons for his decision to leave, including depression and possible suicidal thoughts. The officer passed the test with flying colors. However, the next day while working in the orderly room waiting for orders to assign him to a future assignment, he told them he had forgotten something at home and was going there to get it and come back. Once home, he took a shotgun and placed it under his chin and pulled the trigger. Unfortunately, he only succeeded in blowing off a part of his jaw and survived the blast. Even worse, the first person to see him in the emergency room was the nurse, who also turned out to be his wife.

With myself being the only Protestant chaplain assigned to Vance, there were multitudes of opportunities for ministry. The wife of the hospital commander was a Christian and one of our choir members, but he was not a church attender. In time, through personal interaction with the family he accepted Christ, and I was privileged to baptize him by the means of immersion in the base swimming pool. There were only two base chapels in the entire Air Force that had baptismal tanks, and Vance was not one of them.

It was at Vance that I took the singles racquetball championship at a tournament at age 43. A write-up in the base newspaper showed me in a killer's stance, and the headline read, "Chaplain Shows No Mercy!" I loved the game so much that I even played it in my dreams. In those days Dot would sleep at my side with her head in the crook of my arm. Apparently I would get so involved in the game while I was dreaming that my arm would be shaking and it would wake her up. It happened often, and she would wake me up and say, "You've been playing racquetball again, haven't you?"

I know I'm getting ahead of myself, but because we're talking about dreams I want to fast-forward 37 years to 2013 when we lived in Colorado Springs. I was dreaming that I had been a witness to a homicide and was being questioned about what I had seen. I felt very uncomfortable being questioned and didn't want to get involved. I felt at ease in the next frame of my dream when I found myself riding in the engine compartment of a train—for a while, that is. I soon heard this hideous laughter that seemed to be coming from a jackal that really terrified me. I saw him to be some form of evil person who definitely didn't have my best interest in mind. I thought that if I didn't kill him, he was going to kill me—so I lunged for his neck. Dot woke me up screaming, "What are you doing? What are you doing?" Finding myself with my two hands around her neck, I broke into a sweat thinking of what terrible thing might have happened. Talk about being scared!

While writing this story I was finishing reading the book *Unbroken*. I found it interesting that Louie Zamperini had done the same thing with his wife that I had done with Dot. Before he came to know Christ he had turned into an alcoholic and was obsessed with going back to Japan, finding the guard who had tortured him so badly, and killing him. One night he was dreaming that he was strangling the guard when his wife woke him up and he found himself sitting on her chest with his hands around her neck the same way I had done with Dot. Talk about coincidence.

At Vance, the base commander, Colonel Wall, also taught me a valuable lesson on thinking before you speak—in other words, learning when to keep your mouth shut. At one of his staff meetings, Colonel Wall stated that they were planning to do some renovations to the chapel annex. I opened my big mouth and told Colonel Wall that the Air Force regulation stated that chapel facilities at the bases belonged to the chief of chaplains, and that they would have to get his permission. Actually, the regulation simply inferred that a courtesy notification was recommended, but I was wanting to show my stuff.

Colonel Wall was very gracious, and said, "Thank you, John," and let it go at that. However, no sooner had I returned to my office when Colonel Wall's secretary called and said Colonel Wall would like to speak to me. I reported to Colonel Wall as ordered. He said, "John, I don't know what the hell they taught you at Air Command and Staff, but I am the mayor of this base and I can do whatever I dang well please. Do you understand that?" I replied, "Yes, sir, I do. I was out of line."

Colonel Wall and I became good friends. One day he and his wife came to our home for dinner. Dot put on the dog, as she was known to do—a splendid gourmet meal with her finest European china, crystal, silverware, and all the rest. Sitting next to the plates was a small crystal triangular fancy object about three inches in width she had purchased in Germany. Very impressive, but unfamiliar to most. Colonel Wall asked me, "John, what in the heck is this for?" I replied, "I don't know. Ask Dot." He did, and Dot replied, "It's to place your knife on. You are so uncouth!"

One of the ladies who worked with Dot in the Officers' Wives' Club once told her a humorous true story. Her name was Cindy. She said, "Last Halloween I took off all of my clothes, put on a housecoat, slipped out the back door of the house, and went to the front and rang the doorbell. When my husband came to the door, I pulled open the housecoat with nothing but my birthday suit and said, 'Trick or treat!'"

Apparently this couple had been having a lot of marital problems because they went to another base where she received counseling from a chaplain, and she ended up divorcing her husband and marrying the chaplain, who had also been divorced. They ended up being assigned to a base in Maine, where in 1991 I was working for a priest named Chaplain Bill Mattimore, who was the head chaplain of Strategic Air Command that that base came under. In that capacity, Bill had occasion to visit that base, and Dot, knowing this couple's full story, told Bill, "When you see Cindy, tell her, 'Trick or treat!'" Bill did, and Cindy's red-faced response was, "You've been talking to Dot Solano, haven't you?"

Most chaplains, regardless of religious and denominational persuasion, had a good fraternal relationship. That being the case, I was not prepared for an event that happened with a civilian priest when my father died in 1978 at the age of 78. My sister Anita went to their priest and told him that since her brother was a minister, they would like for him to have a part in the service. The priest, being old school, rudely told her, "I will do the mass, and then leave. What you do after that is your business." With him out of the way, I was able to provide a service for my dad that my family felt was more Christian than the priest would have provided. There's no substitute for walking the talk! Before the service I took Mark in my arms down to view my father's body in the casket. Mark, seeing the sadness on my face, said to me, "Daddy, that's not Grandpa in there. Grandpa went up to heaven. He just left his skin down here." Rather insightful for a 4-year-old.

Later in 1995, my older sister, Ramona, died after 17 horrible years of being plagued with the dreaded disease of Alzheimer's. At this time, my sister Anita again told their current priest that she wanted me to have a part in the service. At the beginning of the service, remembering the parochial response at my dad's funeral by the old priest, I sat in a chair out of the way while the young priest prepared to perform mass. When it came time for him to do the Eucharist (Holy Communion), the young priest, apparently more broadminded than the one before, came over to me and said, "John, would you like to concelebrate the Eucharist with me?"

I did gladly, and I remember that simple gesture as one of my favorite ecumenical experiences serving with clergy of other religious expressions. This is uncommon between Catholic and Protestant clergy. Holy Communion for the Catholics is different in many ways from that for the Protestants, and that's why they allow only Catholics in good standing to partake. Among other issues, Protestants believe that the wafer and wine (or grape juice) are symbolic of the broken body and shed blood of Christ. Catholics believe that when the priest blesses the elements that they literally turn into the actual body and blood of Christ.

Too many of us don't realize that how we live our lives can influence others for good or bad—especially clergy. An example is a family that moved in next to us at Vance. As good neighbors, we befriended them and became good friends. In fact, the wife and I would arm wrestle after a few daiquiris. She took me down every time, believing to this day that I was being nice and purposely letting her do it. The truth is that she came from a farm background, was stronger than I, and did it on her own power. In time this family started attending our worship services. They ran into us some 33 years later when they too moved to Colorado Springs, and joined the church where I was serving as minister of pastoral care. They told us that we had been responsible for saving their marriage by our wonderful example of what Christians and marriage should be. One never knows what influence we might have on others without knowing.

The commander of the dental clinic, Dennis, was a good friend of mine, and one day had to do a root canal on one of my molars. Dennis told me he was going to replace that molar with a gold crown. When he went to install it, Dennis asked, "How do you like it?" I replied that it was very nice. Dennis said, "Take a good look at it. You're missing something!" Dennis had had a cross etched on the outside of the gold crown. He said, "You are going to be one minister who has his cross and his crown while still on this earth." That crown turned out to be a conversation piece, and when Dot would tell people about it at social gatherings, I had to pull my lip down and show it.

I regularly used examples from a book, *The Gospel according to Peanuts*, as sermon illustrations of Christianity, and my congregations loved them because they were so simple to understand. I was a meat-and-potatoes guy, and didn't prepare messages with deep theological issues that were above people's heads. I had been taught in my speech classes to gear my presentations to those at an eighth-grade level and to use the "KISS" method: keep it simple, Stupid!

I also used all kinds of visual aids to make a point. For instance, plugging and unplugging a lamp in their view to show that we are like that lamp, energized when we are plugged into God and in total darkness when we are not. I once borrowed a pair of crutches from the dispensary and hobbled into the chapel after everyone was seated with one of my legs all bandaged up. Everyone felt sorry for me because they thought I had broken my leg. I did that to point out how we rely on so many worldly things as crutches to bring us meaning and fulfillment instead of relying on God. As we all find out sooner or later, those crutches simply don't cut the mustard!

Another time I got a huge cardboard box from the PX (military store) that a freezer had come in. I painted it to make it look like a jail with steel bars and a cell door to point out that too many of us keep God jailed up during the week and let him out only on Sunday mornings for one hour. At the beginning of my message, I went over to the box, opened the steel barred door, and said, "Okay, God, you can come out now!" At the end of the sermon, I went over to the box again prepared to say, "Okay, God, you can go back in for another week!"

I hesitated for a little while in silence because that didn't seem right. I got so wrapped up in what I was doing that I turned to the congregation and said, "He refuses to go back in!," and with that I gave the box a swift kick and made it topple over backward, saying, "I guess we won't need that again!" Afterward one of the choir members told me, "If you hadn't kicked it over, I would have come over there and done it myself!"

I was selected for promotion to lieutenant colonel and notified that I would be going to a base on the Greek island of Crete as the head chaplain. Of course, I was elated that I would be the senior chaplain again. I was beginning to enjoy giving orders. I had learned that it was better to be number one at a small base than number two or three at a large base. Within a couple of weeks, I was notified that those orders had been cancelled, and I would be going to Torrejon AB in Madrid, Spain, to work under Chaplain, Colonel, William F. (Bill) Mattimore as the number two and as the senior Protestant chaplain.

Father Mattimore had a reputation for being tough and demanding, which I found to be true. The disappointment we felt when I was initially informed I was going to Vance repeated itself. But, again, God knew what He was doing. Although Torrejon could have been my last assignment, it, too, turned out to be a blessing in disguise. Off to Torrejon we went.

12

God's Mentor in Disguise

Torrejon Air Base, Madrid, Spain, 1979–1981

Father Bill Mattimore turned out to be everything his reputation said he would be. He was tough and demanding, but fair. He believed chaplains were about God's business and therefore should give their very best in His service. He demanded 100 percent, but he gave 110 percent. He taught me more about commitment, professionalism, and leadership than any other chaplain I worked for—and I have the scars to prove it. Under that tough exterior, Bill was very compassionate, caring, and humble. With my command of Spanish I would often go with him into Madrid and serve as his interpreter. He liked us, and we became the best of friends. We would socialize with some frequency.

Bill also had a reputation for being very generous. He proved that on numerous occasions. Once, when the assessment team from the Chief of Chaplains Office in Washington came to Torrejon, the team and all of Father's staff and their wives went to Botins in downtown Madrid, a restaurant that Hemingway mentions in his books and that he frequented when in that city. Father picked up the tab for the whole event—which had to be huge for that large a group.

As he took care of the bill, we chaplains on his staff asked him, "Bill, what's our share so we can split the cost?" He replied, "Later!" There never was a later, insisting that he had taken care of it and that was settled. Like the rest of Europe, dinner in Spain doesn't start until eight in the evening and lasts through several courses into the night.

While at Botins, Dot had a couple of glasses of wine, which normally would not have affected her. But it being that late and being on the second floor of the restaurant where the air was thin, it really hit her. She became tipsy, got sick, and had to be taken to the restroom. I couldn't believe that my beloved sweetheart was disintegrating before my very eyes. On the Torrejon chapel staff were a deeply conservative chaplain and his wife who were very judgmental. Dot was concerned about what they would think. Bill replied with clenched fist, "Just let them say something. I'll take care of them!"

Part of the chaplain's duties at Torrejon was to visit military units at the islands of Majorca, Menorca, and Seville. Personnel looked forward to our visits, and we enjoyed seeing the countryside, much of which was covered with large fields of huge sunflowers for the marketing of sunflower seeds and large herds of sheep. It was interesting to see heads of pigs and other meats displayed in the windows of restaurants for customers to see as they entered.

The negative side of being assigned to Torrejon was the bad morale. The story that expressed that sad state of affairs went like this: "Two airmen were walking along on the base dejected. One says to the other, 'You know what's wrong with this base?' The other one replies, 'No. And I don't care!'" There were two major reasons for the bad morale.

The first was the anti-American sentiment that was pretty evident in some cases. It was not uncommon for one to come out one morning and find one's black American car painted in white letters, "Go home, Yankee!" Or one's white American car with the letters in black, "Go home, Carter!" I had bought a small Spanish Siat automobile and came out one morning and discovered it missing. The police found it several weeks later about two miles away where it had been abandoned. I was lucky because in many cases those small cars were stolen, taken out of the area, dismantled, and sold for parts.

The main reason for bad morale, however, was the government housing situation. Many military personnel chose to live on the Spanish economy so they were not affected by this problem. The main part of Torrejon AB had limited base housing for what is known as "key personnel"—persons in essential positions of leadership, like Chaplain Mattimore as the head chaplain. The rest were housed 22 miles away on the other side of Madrid in the Royal Oaks Housing Area, so that made going and coming to work at Torrejon rather time consuming through heavy traffic.

Even worse, they had no chapel, Post Exchange (convenience store), commissary, or other creature comfort facilities. That made them feel like stepchildren. But not to worry! Chaplain John Solano—the hero—has arrived and he is going to solve the problem. Unfortunately, the problem was unsolvable unless all those mentioned as lacking creature comforts were provided them. So I was floundering all over the place, unable to get a handle on the morale problem.

Bill knew this and was riding me pretty hard. He was a tough Irishman from Worcester, Massachusetts, whose father had been a cop, and he had a tendency to be a bully sometimes. The courtyard between the U-shaped chapel buildings was immaculately kept by the gardener, and a restful place to relax and converse.

One day Bill confronted me when I was talking to other lower-ranking personnel and asked me about a matter that had not been addressed. When I tried to explain, he didn't give me a chance and proceeded to dress me down rather severely in front of the others. I tried to explain again, and he cut me off abruptly with the statement, "John, I am not going to stand here and get into a pissing contest with you," and walked off. (I recalled how I had done the same thing at Aviano with Jim Anderson in

1969 and how he felt about that.) I went to my office like a dog with his
tail between his legs. I sat there for about 10 minutes feeling so inadequate
and useless. In spite of working through much of my trashy upbringing
as a "no-good, dirty little Mexican" in my CPE counseling, deep down I
guess Bill made me feel that way again.

When my temper hit the ceiling, I stormed out of my office and down
the hall to his office. I barged in without knocking, walked over to his
desk, and leaned over in his face. He was shocked and surprised to see this
"raging bull" coming at him full force. I said, "Bill Mattimore, you SOB.
I have never been so demeaned in all my life. If you ever talk that way to
me again in front of anyone, I am going to beat the stuffings out of you,
and when I get through with you there is not going to be enough left of
you to bury. Do you understand me?" And with that, I stormed back to
my office leaving him in shock that anyone would talk to him that way,
especially one of lower rank.

I'm a little slow on the uptake and should have learned my lesson
when I threatened Goofus Rufous in Aviano back in 1970. That kind of
insubordination to a superior officer is a court martial–level offense, and
could have been the end of my career. But that, too, turned out to be
a blessing in disguise. Even though a preacher with 17 years of preaching about "forgiveness and brotherly love," I still had a lot to learn about
those two subjects as it applied to me personally. Like the Apostle Paul
in Romans 7:15, "That which I want to do, I do not do! And that which
I don't want to do, I find myself doing!" Apparently I had earned Bill's
respect for what was right. Bill never mentioned the incident, and our
relationship continued like brothers until his death as if nothing had ever
happened. The completion of that story comes later.

At one of the social gatherings at Torrejon, I was dancing with a young
captain's wife. At one point she said, "You really dance good for a chaplain!" I was very eager to impress her with my credentials as a former dance
instructor and said, "I should be. I used to be an Arthur Murray dance

instructor." She took the wind out of my sails when she responded, "Who is Arthur Murray?" When I told Dot what she had said, she got the biggest kick out it and told that story many times after that to her delight.

Another officer's wife asked me to dance when they were doing the limbo. That's the dance where you lean back as far as you can and dance in that leaned-back position under a stick being held by two persons, and each time they keep lowering it until everyone but the last couple is eliminated, and that couple wins. I didn't want to do it, but she kept insisting. She was not a chapel attender so finally to put her off I said, "I'll do the limbo if you promise to come to church tomorrow morning." She said she would, and we did the limbo. We didn't win, but that started her attending my service.

While at Torrejon, Dot continued her work with the OWC and the PWOC. In July 1980 Dot took a group of ladies to the PWOC conference at Berchtesgaden, Germany. They traveled by a military transport airplane known as *The Courier* because it made a circle of stops at different bases in Europe picking up and dropping off cargo. If there was room available they would also take passengers. The ladies took the plane to Aviano, Italy, and from there went by train to Berchtesgaden, Germany.

When the conference was over, they took the train back to Aviano, only to discover that the schedule for *The Courier* had been changed and was not stopping at Aviano. They were stuck. It was imperative for Dot to get back to Torrejon because we were scheduled to leave for the States to attend Keith's graduation from medical school in Milwaukee, Wisconsin, and then go to Montgomery, Alabama, where I was scheduled to perform Mike's wedding to Leigh Brawner.

Knowing she could get to Venice, Dot checked to see if there might be a commercial flight from Venice to Madrid, and there was none. The commander at Torrejon told me that if the ladies could get back to Germany, they could catch *The Courier* back to Torrejon from there. They checked with the flight scheduler at Aviano, but there was nothing scheduled back to Germany so the ladies prepared to hunker down for the duration. Dot was anxious about getting back to Torrejon, but the other ladies were glad to be stuck because they would have time to do some shopping in Aviano for some Italian souvenirs as well as get some good Italian food.

About the time they were to leave the flight line to find quarters, they heard the thumping sound of airplane wheels landing on the runway. When they asked the scheduler where that plane was going, he said he didn't know, that it was not on his schedule. It turned out to be a C-130 cargo plane from the Mississippi Air National Guard stopping for refueling and to pick up a piece of heavy equipment.

When the crew walked in, Dot recognized the southern accent and charmingly asked the pilot, "Where y'all from?" When he said Mississippi, she mentioned that two of her sons had graduated from Mississippi College in Clinton. So had the pilot, so they established an immediate bonding. When she asked where they were going, he said Ramstein AB Germany to drop off some cargo. She asked if they had room for 16 PWOC ladies to go with them. He said they did if they could be ready in ten minutes. The ladies were ready, and hopped aboard. They made all the crew members "honorary PWOC members" and pinned PWOC pins on their uniforms to prove it.

That night the ladies went to the Ramstein Officers Club for dinner. As luck would have it, the crew was in the buffet line in front of them. She heard the pilot tell another officer, "The damndest thing happened to us today. We stopped in Aviano to refuel and pick up some cargo, and 16 PWOC ladies hitched a ride with us. They even made us honorary members, they were so grateful." Dot tapped him on the shoulder and in her best southern drawl said, "And here we are again!"

The pilot asked Dot if they were sure they were going to be able to get back to Torrejon, and she assured him that they were manifested on *The Courier.* He said to let him know if they couldn't, that they would be glad to divert their aircraft and take them there. Camaraderie is found in all manner of military associated personnel, be it active duty, reserves, and even the Mississippi Air National Guard. Everything turned out fine, and we were able to keep our commitments in the States. This was one of Dot's favorite stories that she liked to tell over and over again to whomever would listen.

We are products of our upbringing, and sometimes the customs and traditions between one generation and another can cause misunderstandings and even problems. This happened with me and Mike and his new bride when they first married. Mike and Leigh started calling me by my first name and that didn't set well with me. In the Hispanic culture of my childhood, you never, ever called a grownup by their first names, much less your parents.

For example, the word for "you" in the familiar form in Spanish that is used among equals is "tu." The formal that is used as a sign of respect for elders is "usted." If you said to another of equal status, "How are you?" you would say, "Como estas tu?" Addressing one with respect you would say, "Como esta usted?" When I couldn't stand it anymore, I told Mike and Leigh, "Please don't call me John." They asked, "Why? Calling you by your first name makes us feel closer to you!" I told them about my background and said to them, "Anybody can call me John. But only my children can call me Dad. And when you do, it just makes me feel so special." Once they understood how important it was to me to be called Dad, the problem was resolved, and it was Dad from then on.

Father Mattimore was selected to be the command chaplain for Strategic Air Command (SAC), a very prestigious position, located at Offutt Air Force Base in Omaha, Nebraska. In that capacity, he would be responsible for overseeing the chapel programs throughout the 29 bases scattered throughout the United States.

Bill was so loved and appreciated that the Catholic congregation gave him a huge Lladro of David with a lamb on his shoulder for his going-away present. Lladro is a very expensive type of ceramic figurine made only in Spain. It must have cost a fortune, and he was overwhelmed. A few days later when I went to pick up him up at his temporary quarters to take him to the airport, I found him in the dark sitting in a chair in the corner, and I felt an aura of holiness when I went into the room.

I discovered that Bill was struggling with his feelings of being the recipient of such an expensive gift as the Lladro they had given him. I know from personal experience that Bill was used to giving, not receiving. Bill shared his inner struggle with me: "John, we have to be very careful that we don't get too attached to all these worldly things and make them our gods."

In Matthew 6:19–21 we find these words of Jesus: "Do not store up for yourselves treasures on earth, where moth and rust destroy, and where thieves break in and steal. But store up for yourselves treasures in heaven, where moth and rust do not destroy, and where thieves do not break in and steal. For where your treasure is, there will your heart be also." Bill not only believed this, he lived it. He gave me a very good example to try to emulate.

Why did I see this priest as a role model? Because God was using him to show me Christ-like virtues in him that I still needed to improve in myself. God has a way of using other people to do that with all of us. God has a way of doing this if we will but stay attuned to His ever loving presence.

Another person who was a giver like Bill was Dot. She would give you the blouse off her back. She also was a person to admire and a good role model for me in many ways. I remember that for years she would write birthday and anniversary cards to so many people who never responded or even acknowledged that they had received them.

You would have thought that, having grown up in such a poor environment, I would have been materialistic, but I wasn't. I fully believed what Jesus had said about earthly riches, but I also had my father as a good example for me in being content with what you have. As I mentioned previously, he was "happy as a lark" if he had a good family, a roof over his head, three meals a day, and was able to pay his bills. I admired that simplicity. I was never enamored with things or positions. My philosophy was, "If you can't eat it and you don't need it, you don't buy it!" I always thought I was frugal, but Dot often accused me of just being cheap. I stand by what Jesus said because things and fame don't last.

I once read a book by the noted Christian author John Ortberg that puts all of this into proper perspective. The title of the book is *At the End of the Game, It All Goes Back in the Box*. The book is about lessons he learned playing Monopoly with his grandmother as a young boy. He says, "When you're master of the board, you can buy this house, this car, this position, and anything your little heart desires. But at the end of the game, it all goes back in the box. You just think you owned it." Ortberg sees that as analogous to life and that is what the book is all about.

My favorite story in the book is where he says, "The executive who works from 7 a.m. until 7 p.m. daily will be greatly admired, appreciated, and fondly remembered—by his wife's next husband!" In all of my 57 years of conducting hundreds of funerals, I never saw a U-Haul trailer following a hearse.

In the latter part of my assignment in Spain, a Lutheran chaplain by the name of Jon Wuerffel was assigned to work under me. Jon was even more of a hotshot racquetball player than I, and I never did beat him. Jon had a son whose name was Danny and was Mark's best friend. They were both five years old. On occasion, Danny would sing this song in the chapel service: "I am a promise. I am a possibility. I am a promise with a capital P. I am a great bundle of Po-tenti-ality!" And "po-tenti-ality!" he was! Danny went on to play football for Florida State and become the 1996 Heisman Trophy winner. He later played for the New Orleans Saints. Danny had a higher calling than football and eventually started a Christian ministry in New Orleans, and never pursued professional football as a serious career.

While at Torrejon, Dot and I were privileged to take a pilgrimage to the Holy Land. When we visited Cana in Galilee, I remembered that this was where Jesus changed water into wine, so surely I thought they must make good wine here. Boy, was I mistaken! I bought a bottle of white wine and a bottle of red wine to take back to Spain. That night the moon was full and made for amorous feelings. Romance was in the air! I thought a little wine would make the experience even more romantic. So I opened the bottle of white wine, which was bitter and tasted horrible. I dumped it down the drain and opened the bottle of red wine, which turned out to be the same way. Wine or no wine, the moment of passion was not wasted nor denied.

I had not had a drink of alcohol since my call to the ministry in 1959, nor during my entire time as a civilian pastor, for two reasons: my tendency to drink too much, and because it was strictly forbidden by Baptists—at least in public. What went on behind closed doors might have been another matter. I was criticized by very strict Baptists who saw me drinking wine when I was a chaplain. They would ask, "How can you as a Baptist drink wine. It's sinful!" I would reply, "You will recall that Jesus turned water into wine at Cana. I put the wine to my lips and then I turn it into water!" Of course, they were not amused, but I didn't lose any sleep over it.

A joke I liked to tell about this silliness goes as follows: "Two clergy were seated side by side on a flight to a ministerial convention. One was an Episcopalian and the other a Baptist. When the stewardess came and asked them if they would like a cocktail, the Episcopalian said, 'I'll take a gin and tonic.' He turned to his Baptist friend and asked him what he would have. The Baptist self-righteously responded, 'Nothing. I'd just as soon commit adultery than take a drink.' The Episcopalian raised an eyebrow and amusingly said, 'Oh. I didn't know we had a choice!'"

In 1979 while I was at Torrejon we chaplains were a little concerned about our future in the military. A couple of liberal Harvard law students filed a lawsuit challenging the constitutionality of the military chaplaincy, arguing that having chaplains on active duty was a violation of Article III of the Bill of Rights in the Constitution, and that they should be replaced with noncombatant volunteers or contractors. For a period of time there, chaplains were on pins and needles, wondering how the ruling would come out.

When it did, the chaplains breathed a sigh of relief. The U.S. Court of Appeals determined that the plaintiffs lacked standing to bring the suit and upheld the right of the military to employ chaplains. Article 3 reads, "Congress shall make no law establishing religion or prohibiting the free exercise thereof, nor shall the right of Conscience be infringed." The court analysis described the First Amendment's Free Exercise Clause and Establishment Clause as separate clauses, and dismissed the case.

If this was a Paul Harvey broadcast, we'd say the following: "This is the rest of the story": I received orders that I was being reassigned to the Office of the Command Chaplain at SAC Headquarters, Offutt Air Force Base Omaha, Nebraska, with Father Mattimore again being my boss. As we were preparing for our return to the United States, God blessed us with a wonderful surprise. John Kilbride had been an airman who ran the junior high youth program for me as a volunteer when we were stationed at Richards Gebaur. Kilbride had left the Air Force and had gone back to New York to work for Amtrak. We had kept track (no pun intended) of each other throughout the years.

When he heard that we were coming back to the States from Spain, he wrote me asking me to send him power of attorney to pick up our car that we were shipping back from Spain to Bayonne, New Jersey, and that he would then pick us up at the airport when we arrived. Additionally, he said, "Plan to spend the Fourth of July weekend here with me at my folks' place, and I will be your tour guide while you're here." I did that, with Kilbride living up to his claim that he was one of the best tour guides in New York City. He took us to all sorts of delightful sights, including historic places like the Empire State Building and the Twin Towers by means of bus, subway, and whatever other means he could come up with to make this visit to New York City one of the best times of our lives. What a wonderful memory!

13

Building Leadership Muscles

Strategic Air Command Headquarters, Omaha, Nebraska, 1981–1984

After the incident where I threatened to whip Father Mattimore, my being assigned to the Office of the Command Chaplain at Strategic Air Command (SAC) Headquarters came as a surprise and could only have been a miracle in God's plan for me. I never apologized to him for my unruly behavior, which I should have—I still had some growing up to do. But that didn't seem to thwart the plan that God had for my life. I learned that prior to my selection, two positions had come open on Father Mattimore's staff, and the Personnel Office in the Chief of Chaplain's Office in Washington asked him who he would like to fill them. He replied, "Give me Gene Kircus and John Solano."

They said, "We can give you Kircus, but we can't give you Solano. He hasn't been overseas three years yet. You know how the system works!" The three-year overseas tours could only be curtailed for hardship reasons, that is, a need to be near family due to illness or some other critical situation. Not to be outdone, he replied, "I know how the system works. But

I also know how we can go under the table if we really want to get things done. Either give me Solano, or leave the position vacant." He got Solano, who filled the position of chief of the Budget and Logistics Division.

In that position I was responsible for overseeing construction of new religious facilities, as well as the proper maintenance of existing religious facilities throughout SAC's 29 bases. Those three years in what is called Staff Work provided me with leadership training and knowledge that could not have been secured otherwise, and which prepared me for a future assignment as a command chaplain myself. Chaplain Mattimore got me three-star-general endorsements for my performance from the SAC deputy commander the first year, and four-star-general endorsements from the SAC commander the following years and got me promoted to the rank of full colonel. Only 86 of the entire 869 chaplains on active duty at that time wore that prestigious rank. This promotion also almost earned me a black eye. This is the way Dot used to tell the story of my promotion: "This new full colonel came home feeling pompous, cocksure, and wanting to throw his weight around. He said to me, 'Woman, these are eagles on these shoulders and they demand a little more respect around here!' I squared my shoulders, and when I gave this new full colonel my steely eyed look, he knew he was in trouble. I continued, 'Boy, don't you ever forget who put you there. These are stars on my shoulders, and if you don't change your attitude, that's exactly what you're gonna be seeing!'"

This command chaplain experience expanded my leadership perspective and skills in a way that no other method could have. I was part of a team that periodically would visit the 29 SAC bases to evaluate their religious programs. We Protestant chaplains would evaluate the Protestant programs, and the priest the Catholic operation. The evaluation was a top-to-bottom assessment of the entire chapel program at each base, starting with the leadership style of the chaplain in charge to include the smallest function, all of which were essential to a healthy religious program.

Leadership style was extremely important. Where the leader was too task-oriented, we found a morale problem. The Indians felt unappreci-ated by the chief, whom they thought was heavy-handed and cared more about the work than the people who performed it. On the other hand, where the boss was too people-oriented and not mission-minded, there was chaos. There was no direction, no team spirit, and everybody was doing his own thing. The best leadership style was where everyone knew what was required of them, and the boss took care of his people and fre-quently expressed his appreciation for their good work.

Needless to say, there were good programs as well as some that needed a lot of attention to become more effective. The team would write up a report for the base commander, citing whatever deficiencies we found, with recommendations for corrections, and a window of a few months' compliance to correct the problems.

I remember one trip where the team chief, a priest, was stressing to the enlisted chapel managers the importance of their job in the overall chapel program, and the need to do it right that was so basic and insight-ful about how the piece affects the entire puzzle. To make his point, he said, "I remember once going out to say mass, only to find that the wafer and wine were not there. So there I was, ready to preach about the love of God with an urge to kill!" In this case, the Don't-sweat-the-small-stuff philosophy didn't apply. One small thing can have disastrous negative results in the big picture. It's teamwork! Even a team of horses that are not pulling together will not get to where they are supposed to go.

Some trips provided humorous events not easily forgotten. One espe-cially comes to mind. At this one base, the team members and I were having dinner at the Officers' Club with the head base chaplain and his staff. There was a three-piece combo there providing music for those who simply wanted to enjoy it or even dance. I danced a jitterbug number with one of the young ladies in the group. I was seated with the team at a table with the head chap-lain and his wife. At a nearby table sat a Lutheran chaplain from that base whose wife was from Germany and was drinking a little bit too much.

When I sat down after dancing, she hollered over at me, "Chaplain Solano." I was talking to the head chaplain and said to her, "Just a minute, please!" She rudely said, "Just a minute, hell! I'm talking to you! I want to dance with you!" I took her out on the dance floor, and because she was so tipsy she missed my extended hand during one of our jitterbug movements and fell back on the combo. When we got back to our guest quarters, one of the sergeants said to me, "Chaplain, I know that lady made you mad, but did you have to dump her on her butt?"

My experience at SAC showed me what to do and what not to do in future assignments. My leadership approach in future assignments was reliance on my staff. Shortly after arriving at a new assignment, I would say to my staff, "We have a mission to accomplish for this installation for the good of the Air Force and for the glory of God. We can do it well, or we can do it with mediocrity. How you perform will be rewarded accordingly on your performance reports. You are my staff, and I have to depend on you greatly. I can't be everywhere and see everything. I need you to be my eyes and ears. I need your inputs to make good decisions. My policy is, 'The boss should never be embarrassed or blindsided.' I will be the one to make the final decisions, but I can make them more wisely if I rely on you to help me." It worked every time.

While at SAC, one of the bases in Texas where a chapel was being built decided to eliminate the pews from money available because of some overspending that depleted their budget. It came time to dedicate the new chapel with the four-star general SAC commander in attendance as the main speaker. But with no pews to be had and no money to buy them, they were in a quandary. So they contacted me as to what to do. In my usual way, I responded, "Hang a sign in front of the building that says, 'Standing room only!'" That went over big.

When I contacted the Chief of Chaplains Office for advice, they told me they would provide half the cost of the pews if the base could come up with the rest. The Corps of Engineers told the base that was like mixing apples and oranges because pews were installed property and could not be funded from the source of that money. If the money was spent that way, they'd go to jail. The general was informed, and he said, "Baloney, fund it anyway. If they knew some of the things we've done elsewhere, we'd all go to jail." Finally, they were able to secure heavy chairs that locked into each other that functioned perfectly as pews, but were not anchored to the floor, and the problem was solved.

One never knows where God is going to place opportunities for us to learn valuable lessons. Such an opportunity presented itself in a simple racquetball court once when I was playing Gene Kircus, who was no match for me. I was riding Gene unmercifully in jest. At one point, I said to him, "Gene, since you're back there doing nothing, why don't you keep score?" He was unflappable in spite of my bombardment of insults. After the game, I said to him, "Gene, how come you don't get mad when I taunt you like I do?" He calmly replied, "John, I'm not going to let you determine how I should react." The truth of the matter is that too many of us do let others determine how we react. I had been guilty of that myself.

This assignment also gave Dot the opportunity to use her outstanding leadership skills. She served as president of the Offutt Air Force Base Officers' Wives' Club (OOWC), the biggest of the entire Air Force at the time with a membership of 1,800 members. The wife of the four-star SAC commander was the honorary chair. Because Dot had so much business to conduct in that position, they installed an extra telephone in our home for that sole purpose. Often, when Dot would call the general's wife, he would answer. Dot would tell him, "General, I wish you wouldn't answer the telephone!" "Why not?" he would reply. "I live here." She would say, "Yes, but you intimidate me!" To which he would understandably and graciously answer, "Well, I don't mean to!"

Dot's impressive resume when she took the presidency of the Offutt OWC was printed in their monthly magazine and read as follows:

OWC Experience: President, Vance; Treasurer, Keesler; Nominating Committee Chairman, Aviano; Luncheon and Programs Chairman, Richards-Gebaur; Member at Large, Torrejon; Hospital Services Chairman, Keesler; Welfare Chairman, Aviano and Vance; Scholarship Chairman, Aviano and Vance, Air Force Village Chairman, Offutt and Vance.

Other Experience: Executive assistant to U.S. Attorney in North Carolina; President, PWOC in Italy, Spain, and the European Council; Secretary and Parliamentarian, Church Women United in Enid, OK; Planned and conduced workshops, seminars, and conferences for military chapels in Europe and U.S., including Marriage and Family workshops; Representative to Omaha Church Women United.

Dot was a kind, loving, caring, and gentle person until it came to running an organization. Then she was a no-nonsense, fully in command person. She had leadership muscles and was willing to use them to solve a problem, as the following article published in the OOWC monthly magazine indicates:

Due to two complaints verbalized (one legitimate through the Member at large, one anonymous by phone to me)—and maybe others who kept quiet (no pun intended), I feel compelled to discuss a problem that has increased during our general meetings. At both the September luncheon and the September coffee, I called the meeting back to order as is one of the President's duties. If some ladies were embarrassed or offended, I'm sorry for your uneasiness,

Dot as President of Officers' Wives Club. Offutt Air Force Base, Omaha, Nebraska, 1983

Offutt Officers' Wives Club officers, June, 1963. (Dot on back row, 2nd from left)

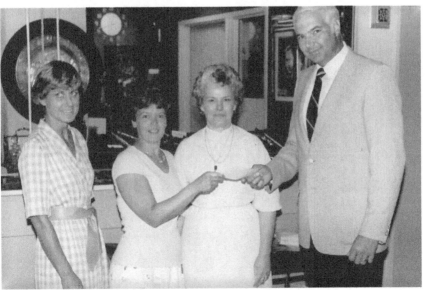

*Dot receiving a check for a charity from local civic and base
dignitaries, Offutt Air Force Base, Omaha, Nebraska*

but sorrier for the fact it became necessary in the first place. I certainly felt uneasy doing it as this is not my normal nature. It had been brought to my attention that the noise level during meetings was becoming increasingly worse, and I had been asked to try to keep better order when people were speaking from the podium so that it would not be necessary for one of our senior advisors to do so again—especially if we had guest speakers or other "outside" guests. Perhaps in order to "nip the problem in the bud" at the beginning of our fall programming, I came on a bit too strong to some of you who were not aware there had been a problem. To you

John and Dot (in front) with (l. to r.) Connie Solano, Don Solano, Mark Solano, Mike Solano, Leigh Solano. Omaha, Nebraska, 1982

I apologize. To those of you who were offenders, I ask you to please remember we do have a large club, and whereas several remarks in your own group may not sound like much, multiply that by 10–15 groups scattered around, and the "bees begin to buzz." The majority of our officers and chairman and some of our program participants are not public speakers, and when one is a bit nervous to stand before a large group anyway, it becomes even more nerve-wracking when it appears a goodly number of your audience is busy talking among themselves. One begins to wonder if what she stood to say is really worth the saying!

After three years at SAC, I received orders to serve as the senior chaplain at Travis Air Force Base in northern California. Having endured three harsh, cold winters in Omaha, we were only too glad to go to California.

14

Tempered by Fire

Travis Air Force Base, Fairfield, California, 1984–1986

Of special note in this assignment is the fact that Travis Air Force Base is situated in Solano County. The county was named after an Indian chief who was led to Christ by a Spanish missionary. The chief's original name was Sem Yeto. In 1823 the Mission San Francisco de Solano was founded by a young padre named Father Altimira. It was here in 1824 that Sem Yeto learned Spanish, reading and writing, farming, and Christianity. In baptism, Altimira renamed Sem Yeto as Francisco Solano. General Mariano Guadalupe Vallejo of the Mexican Army called him his most trusted right-hand man.

As an ally, Chief Francisco Solano of the Suisun Indian Tribe chose to protect his people by bringing Mexican influence to Central California instead of revolt and thus keep his people from being wiped out by the Mexican Army. In 1934, a 12-foot bronze statue of Solano County's namesake was erected in his memory. The statue shows the chief with an open, uplifted hand signifying peace, as apparently Indians were known to do. All he has on for dress is a loincloth. The statue stands outside the site of the old county library.

Ever the jokester, on occasion for fun, I would present myself with uplifted hand in front of Dot with only my jockey shorts pulled tight to look like a loin cloth pretending to be Chief Solano. I never did learn that she was a perfect match for me in being witty. Dot would simply reply, "Never in your wildest dreams!" Of course, everything in Solano County bore that name, but I was the only human being in the county with that name. I liked to boast that the county was named after me.

Not long after our arrival, Dot and I were at a social function where the editor of the local paper was in attendance. He met and talked with us briefly, and that week there was a short article announcing the arrival of the new senior chaplain at Travis with the headline reading, "Solano Comes to Solano." When I left two years later I had become well known (a lot due to the bad racial publicity mentioned later), and the local paper printed a two-page spread showing pictures of me in various situations of ministry with the huge headline, "Solano Leaves Solano."

Because of my hazel eyes and light complexion, people would mistake me for being of Italian descent. When I would correct them, they would ask what the name Solano meant. I looked it up in the large Merriam-Webster Dictionary and found the following: "A hot, oppressive wind off the Mediterranean coast, especially off the coast of Spain." When I would tell them that with Dot within earshot, she would wryly say, "Yeah, windy. Most appropriate for describing John!" When asked about my ancestry, I would tell them that my family was so poor that our main concern was with survival, not lineage. While stationed in Italy, I discovered that there were some Solanos in the southern part who had probably come from Spain.

"Besides," I would add humorously, "you have to be careful about how far back you trace your ancestry. Two fellows did that and one said to the other, 'We traced our family tree and found some of our ancestors hanging by their necks!' The other replied, 'We did that too and ours was worse. We found some of our ancestors hanging by their tails!'"

I didn't know of any of my kin who might have been hanging from their necks or their tails, but I did know about a couple of my relatives who had had a run-in with the law. My mother's sister-in-law had a daughter and son whom she had taught to steal from department stores. The boy was especially mean. Once when those two children and my sister Anita and I were picking mulberries from a tree, the boy purposely urinated on us from above. He was later involved in criminal activity and was killed in a shootout with the police in front of the Denver courthouse.

My mother also had a brother, Paul, who was sentenced to life in prison for getting in a fight with two brothers in Springer, New Mexico, and one of the brothers that he hit real hard bounced against the wall of a building and died from a brain hemorrhage. Paul was charged with involuntary manslaughter and imprisoned at the penitentiary in Canyon City, Colorado. His incarceration was at the time of World War II, and being a model prisoner and having served five years of his sentence, was offered a pardon if he would consent to serve in the Army. He did, and upon discharge lived an exemplary life until his death.

I was told that many years before I was born, there had been bad blood between the Italians and the Mexicans in the Pueblo, Colorado, area, where one of my uncles on my father's side lived. My uncle fell in love with an Italian, and they married in spite of her brothers' warning not to do so. Later on, the brothers put out a contract on them both, and they were shot and left to die on the side of the road.

At Travis I had a very effective staff that provided an outstanding chapel program—except for one of the priests. The priest's normal routine on the job was wandering around and doing very little else. It was joked that he must have had a degree in MBWA, which stands for just that: "Management by Wandering Around."

Serving under me was my right-hand man, a chief master sergeant by the name of Henry (Hank) Kras. Hank was the cream of the crop. He was well educated, smart, and had a whole lot of common sense. He ran a tight ship, but he did it with kindness, gentleness, and all the many Christian virtues with which he was gifted. He had degrees in higher learning and could have been a commissioned officer but chose to remain in the enlisted ranks because that's where he felt he could do the most good, and really because he felt that's where God wanted him to be. I learned a lot from him.

One of the main things I learned from him was how to remain calm under pressure. He was well matched by a wonderful wife who was a schoolteacher. He and I became the best of friends, playing racquetball and socializing frequently. Hank was later assigned to the Chief of Chaplains Office in Washington to serve as the senior enlisted advisor for all of the chapel managers in the entire Air Force worldwide. I like to think that my recommendation might have had something to do with his selection.

Our secretary was a woman named Irene. She had a fairly good figure for a person in her 60s. But she had the oddest blond-looking wig that looked like a haystack. Among her other duties, it was her job to take notes at our staff meetings. One day she didn't show up, so I went to look for her. I found that she had slipped off her chair and was sprawled on the floor with her legs spread apart. Her wig had slipped off her head and was half resting on her face over her nose. Every time she breathed in and out, the part of the wig over her mouth would move in and out. She was pitiful and funny looking at the same time in that position. It turned out that she was on a special medicine that had to be adjusted, and once that was done she was okay.

Because I had been selected to the rank of full colonel, the month after we arrived at Travis I received a VIP cardboard plaque to place on the windshield of my car so we could drive all the way down to the flight line for the Fourth of July fireworks celebration, while the "peons" had to park a long distance away and walk. We felt so important. but *we* turned out to be the peons! At the end of the fireworks display, because of the huge walking crowd, our vehicle was routed through a gate in another part of the base and around the city of Fairfield, and it took a whole hour for us to get back home. The next year when I received my VIP plaque, I threw it away, and we chose to watch the fireworks from a hill where the hospital was located that overlooked the flight line.

While at Travis, an incident that I didn't see coming blew up in my face. Shortly before reporting to Travis while on one of the evaluation visits to SAC bases in California, I left the team and visited Travis to apply for housing and to get a briefing from the chapel staff. While there, I discovered that a new chapel costing $1.8 million was being built. Nearby was an old wooden World War II–era chapel where the black congregation held services—cold in the winter and unbearably hot in the summer. I also discovered that the black congregation said they had been told that the new chapel was being built strictly for them. Upon my return to Offutt, I informed the command chaplain as well as the Chief of Chaplain's Office. Both informed me that chapels were not built for special groups alone, and for me to correct the problem as soon as I could.

I reported to Travis in June and started working the problem with my black chaplain. Knowing that the style of black worship didn't lend itself to simply 45 minutes, which was a worldwide standard time limitation for Catholic and Protestant services using the one facility during prime time, I was willing to offer them all Sunday afternoon if needed. I saw it as a scheduling problem, while I would find out, much to my regret, the black congregation saw it as a racial problem. I would also discover that the power bloc of this congregation was the choir, which was made up of many liberal-thinking students from nearby Berkeley who had no connection with the base with the exception of fellowship and membership in the choir.

On September 8 I had my staff assembled at a Catholic retreat center in another location off base where we had gone to plan the next year's chapel program away from the need to answer telephones. Two days after, I received a phone call from a chapel manager who had remained at the chapel to answer telephones, who told me, "Chaplain Solano, the local paper called and would like a statement from you. There is a group of blacks from the base at the local newspaper office accusing you of being a racist." It was ludicrous that I, who had been subjected to discrimination in my youth, would be a racist.

From that moment throughout the next three days, it was bedlam. The wing commander, a full colonel in line for a possible selection to brigadier general, was running scared. So he called the base commander and me and told us that the blacks had called a meeting with the press that night to air their grievances, and that the base commander and I were to attend to help answer questions. When we walked into that small chapel that night, 300 angry blacks were singing, "We shall overcome," and wore signs on their lapels saying, "Same old shit again!" The meeting became somewhat of a shouting match.

The Associated Press picked up the controversy going on that night, and the next day it was all over the press with the headline, "Chapel Racist Problem at Travis AFB, California." For three days it was chaos with unpredictable results, but with the support from my higher-ups as well as my wonderful staff, I managed to keep my cool and stuck it out. I was the one in the hot seat!

Sometimes it gets lonely up at the top. As much as I liked it, this was one time when I was wishing I wasn't the center of attention. Reporters would call for a statement from me just to say they had contacted me and cover their butt, and then they would misrepresent the problem and print whatever they wanted in order to sell copy. The *Washington Post* called for a statement, and the problem even made the overseas military newspaper, the *Stars and Stripes*.

But I had learned well at SAC headquarters and worked the problem wisely with the help and cooperation of my staff. I got all of my staff together to discuss every possible solution, and by the process of elimination decided on the best possible outcome. Travis had some good, committed black Christian volunteers operating the chapel programs, so I got all of the leaders together to discuss the problem for resolution. I took them through the same scenario I had taken with my staff, already knowing what the outcome would be.

But they didn't know that, so they came to the same conclusion believing it was their judgment of the problem that had brought them to that decision. They sensibly saw that it was a scheduling problem and not a racial problem. The problem resolved itself in three days. The papers quit hounding me because there was nothing of an inflammatory or sensational nature to print and sell copy.

The other thing that compounded the problem was that the black chaplain was an alcoholic and I didn't know it. The wing commander saw that he was having blackouts at a wedding he performed and told me to watch him more closely and get him to the alcohol rehab unit at the hospital. To make a long story short, I finally had to call him in, confront him about his drinking, and ordered him to go to the rehab unit where I would meet him. When he was released from rehab, I said to him, "I never saw you drunk." He replied, "Boss, you never saw me sober!" That addiction has destroyed so many good lives.

Another problem I encountered was when the Chief of Chaplains Office called me and asked, "What's this about you and Jack [my senior Protestant chaplain] not being able to get along?" Jack and I had not had any problem getting along that I knew about, so I told them I didn't know what they were talking about. They said Jack had called complaining that we couldn't get along and wanted to be reassigned. I said I would talk to Jack and get back to them. When I confronted Jack about the matter, Jack replied, "I'm unhappy here and would just like to be reassigned. I know we don't have a problem. But I thought it wouldn't hurt you and it would probably help me if I told them that."

I called the chief's office and informed them what Jack had said. I went on to say, "With that kind of attitude and conniving, underhanded behavior, he's going to be ineffective to me. So grant him his wish and get him out of here!" And they did. It turned out that because I was junior to Jack in time in the service but superior to Jack in rank, Jack resented that.

The 22nd Air Force Commander, Major General Don Brown, a devout Catholic who was a good friend of Father Mattimore, and I became good friends. He also became my racquetball partner. Dot continued with her work in OWC, PWOC, and even as a Red Cross volunteer and became good friends with the general's wife as well. Travis was part of the Military Airlift Command (MAC), located in Illinois, which was responsible for all carrier transport airplanes worldwide.

One day the MAC command chaplain came for a visit, and General Brown arranged with the command chaplain for him and us to come to his house for cocktails and then dinner at the Officers' Club. The plan was for General Brown to pick up the command chaplain at the Distinguished Visitors' Quarters and then us at our home in his staff car. With the command chaplain in the front seat, we got in the backseat. I asked the general, "General Brown, do you mind driving around the housing area for a little while before we go to your house?" "Not at all John, why?" the general replied. I answered, "So that I can wave at my friends. It isn't often that I get chauffeured around by a two-star general." Dot simply shook her head.

After two years at Travis, I received orders to be the senior chaplain at Kadena Air Base, Okinawa, Japan. I was third pick. Some chaplains, after being selected for full colonel, develop an "I'm-special" attitude, and feel that they are entitled to prestigious assignments of their own choosing, which Kadena was not. Two of these chaplains turned down the assignment and chose to retire instead. When I was called to take the assignment, I saluted smartly as I had always done, and took the assignment without question. It turned out to be our second-best assignment in my career, Aviano having been the best.

Our transfer to Okinawa was the easiest we ever had. Chaplains at Travis were allowed to put on the flight suit and travel anywhere the plane was scheduled to go with the crew in what was known as "MAC Mission observer flights." Knowing I was going to be assigned to Kadena, I arranged to go on a flight that was traveling there.

Instead of staying with the first crew for the required crew rest in Hawaii, I stayed with the plane and the relieving crew and went straight to Okinawa. I arrived there when they were having the celebration of the Annual National Prayer Breakfast, which I attended. Thus I was able to meet all of the squadron commanders. I received a briefing from my staff, took the house and furniture that the senior chaplain was vacating, and bought two cars from two chaplains who were rotating back to the States prior to my arrival.

In the interim, General Brown one day told me he was going to Okinawa, and was there anything I might want to send on his plane. We sent pots and pans, sheets, and other items we would need to set up housekeeping for the three years we would be there. Most of the other household goods would be stored in the California area until our return back to the States.

15

Teamwork Is the Answer

Kadena Air Base, Okinawa, Japan, 1986–1989

We arrived at Kadena on a Thursday. I got my driver's license on a Friday, and we moved into our house on a Monday. Easiest move we ever had. Kadena had a large chapel program with thirteen chaplains, all go-getters with the exception of two. There were at least that many enlisted airmen and numerous hired musical directors to perform the large program. I found out that the program was being superbly operated and had enough sense to stay out of the way of my staff and let them do their job. They made me look good, and we received all manner of commendation for the operation when assessment teams from headquarters in Hawaii made their visits. Three of those chaplains working under me went on to achieve the rank of full colonel and serve in important positions as well in later years.

The black congregation had heard about me being accused of being a racist at Travis, so they were a little apprehensive about me coming. Once they got to know me, they realized I was not a racist and everything went well. Chaplains throughout the Air Force were assigned to specific units so that personnel in those units could use his or her services if need be.

One of my less effective chaplains (we'll call him Joe) was assigned to the Air Rescue Squadron. One night, a crew was practicing low-level exercises in a helicopter, and due to human error the helicopter crashed with all the crew perishing. Joe did the memorial service with the base commander, a devout Catholic, and I seated in the front pew.

At one point, Joe said, "Don't think of them as being gone, they've just gone TDY." The base commander was shocked, turned to me, and asked, "What in the hell is he trying to say?" I replied, "I don't know, sir. I'll ask him after the service." TDY means "temporary duty" where one goes to another base for a short period of time and then comes back to his permanent duty station to resume normal duties. PCS means "permanent change of station," where you leave one base for your new assignment and sever all ties with the base where you have been. When I asked Joe what he was trying to say when he said, "They have gone TDY," he answered, "That we believe in the afterlife and would see them again." I said, "Joe, you picked the wrong analogy. They didn't go TDY, they went PCS. They aren't coming back!"

My senior Catholic chaplain was somewhat of a jokester like me. His name was Bill. One day a Japanese wife who was a member of his congregation asked him if he would do the funeral for her husband, a retired sergeant who professed to be Baptist. Chaplains worldwide were frequently called upon to do funerals for retired personnel whether they were church affiliated or not because it was considered an entitlement along with other veterans' benefits. When Bill got back, I asked him, "Bill, what does a Catholic priest say for a Baptist at a Catholic funeral?" Bill lowered his head to look downward, cupped his hands over his mouth, and hollered out as if he were hollering into the abyss, "Good luck!"

Our secretary was a Japanese national whose name was Kimiea and who was of inestimable value to us (like Rita Urbani in Aviano), not only because she was capable and efficient but also as an interpreter. Dot and I were often invited to her house for Japanese meals. When I left Kadena, she fondly told me, "Chaplain Solano, you were not only my boss. You were my friend!"

Playing racquetball for 17½ years almost daily, my body began to show signs of wear and tear, so I took up the game of golf instead. After playing a round of golf, I would call Dot and tell her to bring the jug, and she and I would sit on a bench facing the China Sea, sip wine, hold hands, and watch the sun disappear below the horizon in majestic splendor. As a song in our times used to say, "Memories are made of this!"

One of the most interesting things about Okinawa are the "love motels" that sit atop a hill overlooking the city. Lit up at night they look like Las Vegas. When you first hear that they are "love motels," you assume that they are brothels, but they are not. They are legitimate. Since homes in Okinawa are so small, there is little privacy for lovemaking, so couples rent these motels for overnight purposes. The wife of one of my chaplains surprised her husband by renting one for the celebration of one of their anniversaries, and she said they were decorated very ornately to make the event suggestive and memorable.

Okinawa depends highly on rain so they welcome typhoons. We experienced a water shortage one year when we were there, and the guiding instructions for flushing toilets was, "If it's yellow, let it mellow. If it's brown, flush it down." When I take off my hearing aids at night, I am as deaf as a fence post, and one time I slept through the entire night as a typhoon threatened to blow the house away. In the morning Dot asked me, "How could you sleep through all that blowing?" I replied, "What blowing?"

Our fourth son, Mark, was 12, and he began to show a little rebellion. He kept getting bad-behavior slips from one of his teachers. While on vacation in Hawaii visiting our Army physician son, Keith, who was stationed there for his first residency, I read a book by James Dobson where he said his mother had straightened him out by threatening to follow him to every one of his classes if he didn't get his act together. So I decided to try that tactic on Mark. I donned my fatigue uniform and did just that. The next day, someone asked Mark if that was his dad following him around to all the classes the day before. When Mark said, "Yes," they asked him what I did on the base. Mark answered, "He's the exterminator!"

Midway through our tour, the three of us caught a military plane to Clark Air Base in the Philippines that regularly carried supplies from base to base throughout the Far East. From there we caught another plane that went from Clark to Singapore for food supplies they took to troops stationed at Diego Garcia, and we were able to spend 10 wonderful days in Singapore before taking the same route back to Kadena. Mark later became an accomplished guitarist, and it was in Singapore that he bought his first guitar.

In my role of senior chaplain we were privileged to attend many functions at the base and wing squadron level. While at Kadena, I was also privileged to go to bases in Oson, Korea, and Guam to be the speaker for several functions. When I was in Guam, one of the Guamanian generals in attendance at the head table asked me, "Chaplain, do you know what the letters G-U-A-M stand for?" I said, "Tell me!" The general said, "*Give Us American Money,*" and burst out laughing. Electricity is known to suddenly go out in spurts in Guam. Just before I got up to speak, the lights went out. There was still a shred of daylight remaining, so I proceeded to the podium. About the time I began to speak, the lights came back on. The title of my message was, "You Are the Light of the World!" Only God could have provided that kind of visual aid for the topic.

I had a Southern Baptist chaplain by the name of Jimmy who had been reassigned to a base in California. In mid-1987, we came to the States to visit friends and relatives. When we boarded the plane in Raleigh to head back to Okinawa, Dot complained about feeling sick. We had a nine-hour layover in Los Angeles and were to meet Jimmy and his wife at the airport so we could spend some time together. By the time we arrived in Los Angeles, Dot was very sick and running a fever. I briefed Jimmy and said, "There's no way she can make it across the Pacific in this condition. I'm going to have to leave her with you and let you ship her to me later." Mark and I continued on to Okinawa as scheduled.

Fortunately we were able to locate her luggage without any problem. Leave it up to God to take care of everything when you're in a pinch. This couple was still in temporary quarters, but they kept her, got her well, and sent her on to Okinawa when her health improved. It turned out that Dot had a urinary tract infection. Only in the military do you find that kind of camaraderie. Knowing this kind of bonding existed, Dot's father used to say, "You're the only people I know who can go from one end of the United States to the other without paying a motel bill."

Kadena had a communication site on the northern end of the island of Okinawa, known as Okuma, which was adjacent to a resort area on the beach. I had to supply a chaplain to go there every Sunday to conduct worship services for the personnel on site. One Sunday, I decided that Dot, Mark, and I would go there, preach, and enjoy the beach for the weekend. Unfortunately, it rained the entire weekend so there was not much opportunity for beach time. The Kadena Post Exchange (PX) was having a contest for the best essay on the topic, "Why I Am Proud of My Military Family." Besides myself, Keith and Don were also on active duty. Since we were stuck inside and Dot had nothing to do, she decided to enter and write.

The prize was $100 and she won. She asked me if she could apply that $100 on anything in the PX, and I said, "Of course." Well, she did—as a down payment on a diamond ring. In later years, she jokingly would show off her $100 diamond ring, which obviously cost much more, and in which she delighted in having gotten one over on me.

Kadena turned out to be one of the most joyful experiences we had in our entire Air Force career. Those two chaplains who had turned the assignment down just don't know what a blessing they missed. Maybe I just didn't have sense enough to know the difference.

Toward the end of our 38-month tour, I received notice that I was being reassigned to serve as the command chaplain for the Air Force Communications Command at Scott Air Force Base in Belton, Missouri, not too far from St. Louis. Dot and I had heard about the military resort area in the Philippines called Baguio, so we decided to catch *The Courier* military plane that normally went to Clark as we had before and spend a week in Baguio before our rotation to the States.

On our return to Clark, much to our regret, we discovered that the route had been changed and there would be no plane going back to Kadena, as had happened when we were in Spain and Dot and the other ladies got stuck in Aviano. We checked to see if there was anything going to Okinawa from Manila commercially, and no luck there. So we were stuck, and our going-away party was to be held in a few days. I called and told my assistant chaplain at Kadena to go ahead with the party since it was already planned and video it so we could view it later. Fortunately, the Clark base commander had been the base commander at Kadena previously and, after making a few calls, discovered that there was a small plane going to Kadena that would be able to take us back.

The night before we were to leave, we had dinner with the commander and his wife at their quarters. He said he would pick us up at our visiting quarters and take us directly to the flight line to catch the plane early in the morning. Just about the time we were about to board, Dot asked the commander, "Don't I have to have my passport stamped before I leave?" He replied, "Don't worry about it. You'll be back in the States in a week or so, and nobody will know the difference." As far as Dot's passport was concerned, she entered the Philippines, but she never left it. As I said before, leave it up to God to work things out when you're in a pinch.

The going-away party for us was a blast. Typical of my roasting was a letter from the former base commander's wife that she asked to be read. It went like this:

As we all know, Chaplain Solano is truly a people person. When he comes to a new base, he quickly wants to get acquainted with the community. He's also been told that he resembles the Mexican American actor and star of the TV program, *Fantasy Island*, Ricardo Montalban.

Soon after John arrived at Kadena he went visiting all over the housing area to make himself known. He came to this house where a most attractive brunette came to the door. She said, "Oh, Ricardo Montalban, how good to see you." "No, no," John said, "I'm John Solano, the new base chaplain going around to introduce myself."

He went to another house where a beautiful redhead came to the door, and the same scenario repeated itself. He went to a third house where a gorgeous, voluptuous blond in a transparent negligee came to the door as did the other two. When she said, "Oh, Ricardo Montalban," Chaplain Solano answered, 'Welcome to Fantasy Island.'"

And with that, we packed up and headed for Scott Air Force Base in Missouri.

16

At the Mountaintop

Air Force Communications Command,
Scott AFB, Belton, Missouri, 1989–1991

The assignment as the Air Force Communications Command (AFCC) chaplain was a joyous experience for me, but one of hardship for Dot and Mark because I traveled a lot throughout the United States, Europe, and the Far East as the representative of the AFCC commander, a two-star general, visiting communication squadrons to ascertain the morale and welfare of the troops. The headquarters for Communications Command had always been considered what they call a "tenant organization," meaning that they shared space on a base that was actually the headquarters for another command.

At Scott, the AFCC was the main command and had had their own building built strictly for them. When they had the dedication ceremony for the building, a former commanding general was invited to attend. After the ceremony, I went up to him and introduced myself. I said, "General, I'm Chaplain Solano, the command chaplain. I was one of your chaplains at Richards Gebaur when you were in your prime." The general

AFCC Command Chaplain, 1989-90, Scott
Air Force Base, St. Clair County, Illinois

replied, "Huh. I thought I was still in my prime!" (My memories of Scott at this time would turn out to be a whole lot different and better than I had experienced here when I was a private 40 years earlier in 1950 and flunked out of Air Traffic Control Tower Operator School.)

In my travels, I was accorded VIP treatment everywhere I visited, including having my visit posted on the marquee at the gate of the bases visited with the notice, "WELCOME, CHAPLAIN, COLONEL, JOHN O. SOLANO, AFCC COMMAND CHAPLAIN." But I never let it go to my head or define who I was because I knew that once you retired you went to the end of the line just like everybody else, regardless of rank.

Following is a story that I used to tell that illustrates how silly those who try to impress others with status really come across. The story is about a lieutenant colonel newly promoted to the rank of full colonel. (Believe me, there is quite a difference in the protocol and treatment accorded a full colonel as opposed to a lieutenant colonel.) An office was assigned for the new colonel appropriate with his new rank. Having just settled into his new office, he heard a knock at the door. He picked up the telephone and said to the person at the door with authority, "Come in!" There stood an airman with a canvas bag in his hand.

So full of himself and itching to impress someone with his new status, he pointed to the phone indicating that he was talking to someone of importance and said to the airman, "I'll be right with you. I'm talking to the general!" The phone conversation went like this, "Yes, general. You can depend on me, general. Be assured that I will take care of the matter right away, general." Finishing the conversation, he put the telephone on its cradle and said to the airman, "Now what can I do for you, son?" The airman said, "Sir, I'm from telephone maintenance. I'm here to connect your telephone." What fools we mortals be.

At this time, Keith was stationed in Belgium as an Army doctor. During one of my visits to Europe, Keith picked me up in Germany and we were able to spend some quality time together in Belgium before I had to return to the States. My rheumatoid arthritis was giving me a fit. At one of the squadrons I visited in Germany, one of the sergeants said to me, "My grandmother used to take a jigger of vinegar every day and it really helped her with her arthritis. You ought to try it, Chaplain!" I told Keith that story and asked him, "What do you as a doctor have to say about that?" Keith replied wisely, "If it works, I'm not going to knock it!"

On another visit to England, I started showing signs of sickness while having lunch with Chaplain and Mrs. Gene Kircus in England, and was taken to the emergency room. Gene was the senior chaplain at Lakenheath AFB. I was evaluated and it looked like I would have to be admitted to the hospital there for treatment. They took me off the manifest of the military aircraft that was scheduled to return me to the States. I got to feeling better as the day went by, was placed back on the manifest, and was able to catch my flight back to the States. However, once back at

Scott, the symptoms I was experiencing returned and I was hospitalized for one week.

On one of my visits to a base in Colorado Springs, I was given a tour of Space Command in what was then called Cheyenne Mountain, a huge underground-looking cave inside the mountain that was built on massive coils to sustain the shock of the blast of any force available by the enemy

Belton, Missouri, the year before my retirement from the Air Force as chaplain, with more than 32 years of active duty, in the rank of full colonel

at that time. That was a sight to behold, and you couldn't help but wonder what a horrendous task that must have been to drill into all that massive rock, and then have to cart it away. It was mind-boggling, to say the least.

Scott proved to be a trying time for Dot and me because Dot was diagnosed with having breast cancer in one breast. Dot's first response was not, "Why me?" Her deep faith is seen in this statement to me: "Honey, it seems selfish for me to ask God to perform a miracle and make this cancer go away. What I can do is ask God to give me the power of His presence and the courage to face whatever all of this brings."

The country was in the midst of a breast enhancement craze. The bigger the "watermelons," the better the lustful attraction. Admittedly, God provided women with breasts for the primary purpose of feeding the child. Without a doubt breasts play a very important part in the sexual relationship as well. All in all, a woman's breasts have a very crucial role in defining femininity.

But the craze that swept the nation became ridiculous to the point that breast size became the main characteristic of femininity. So many women were having their breasts enlarged to become sexier—and often just to be sexier than their friends and neighbors. Plastic surgeons made tons of money, hand over fist. The sizes of enhancement ranged from "Pikes Peak" to "Mount Fuji" to "Mount Everest"—the more cleavage the better.

Bosoms were in your face everywhere on television. They sold every manner of merchandise besides bras: automobiles, vacations, furniture, you name it—the "boobs" had milked the market dry. (Pun intended.)

Mastectomies can bring about very serious adjustments for the husbands as well as the wives, and some husbands who saw breasts as the sum total of their wives were not able to deal with it. We had known of numerous cases where husbands who apparently considered wives without breasts to be less of a suitable sexual mate jumped out of the marriage, leaving the wives to deal with the matter by themselves. Apparently the vows, "for better or for worse, in sickness and in health," didn't include the loss of a breast.

We had also recently had a friend who was going to have a mastectomy to save her life as well. Her remark to me before the operation was, "They may be attached to me, but I am not attached to them." That statement turned out to be false because she later realized that her breasts had defined her femininity more than she had thought. It took many months for her to work through the depression she experienced because of that loss and learn to live without them.

I share all of that because the scenes I just mentioned couldn't help but be on Dot's mind and make her wonder how different she would be in how she saw herself, and even more importantly in how differently she thought I might see her as my sex partner. I sensed this, because in discussing the matter she said, "You've always been such a boob man."

Dot was more to me than a couple of "fleshly boobs," and the thought never, ever entered my mind that I would ever see her any differently. And I never did. If anything, I loved her even more because I realized I could have lost her. Saving her life was far, far more important than saving her breasts. *Big deal!* You don't throw the baby out with the bathwater.

I assured her as emphatically as I could that it didn't matter, and never having lied to her (except when we were courting and I told her I was 22 instead of 18, but that was before I became a Christian), she was convinced. I stand before God and tell you that our sex life never suffered one bit.

Since the chances were high that cancer could also appear in the other breast, we decided to not take chances and to have a mastectomy done on that one as well. That was a smart move because she became a cancer survivor and lived for 27 more years. The method by which they did postop chemotherapy and radiation kept her from losing her hair or from sickness that often comes from that type of treatment. Dot became very instrumental in starting breast cancer support groups for other breast cancer survivors at every place we relocated after that. In spite of her bout with cancer and caring for Mark on her own while I was gone so much, Dot did a superb job keeping the home front on an even keel without me, as always. "John who?"

In 1991 Communications Command was told that due to budget constraints it had to downsize by eliminating some nonessential positions. One of the first slots to go was the command chaplain's position, so I had to be reassigned somewhere else. The senior chaplain at Kirtland Air Force Base in Albuquerque, New Mexico, was retiring, so they assigned me there to replace him.

17

Time to Hang It Up

As with all the other assignments, Kirtland turned out to be an enjoyable assignment for us. This was probably due to the ever-positive attitude that God had blessed me with and a helpmate who adjusted fabulously to whatever life brought our way without complaint. At each base, when I was notified of a new assignment, I was asked, "Is that a good assignment?" I would reply, "If it's not, I'll make it a good one when I get there," and I meant it. The difference between how you see things and circumstances as "good" or "bad" is attitude. If you don't like the channel, change it!

When we were stationed in Aviano 24 years earlier, one of the ladies in the PWOC said to Dot, "I hate your husband!" When Dot asked why, she responded, "Because nobody can be that happy all the time!" Dot told her, "Well, I can tell you that he is that happy all the time." Dot was famous for telling me two things that described me to a *t*. She would say, "If God had ever put a serious thought in your mind, you might have amounted to something." The second thing was, "You don't have sense enough to be unhappy." I thought they were compliments, but sometimes I wondered.

Ever looking for a story to make people laugh, I had a story that addressed the subject of optimism that I liked to tell. It was about a man who had two sons who were completely different. One was a total optimist and the other a total pessimist. Their father wondered how they could be so extremely unlike. *Surely*, he thought, *there must be a smidgen of similarity in dispositions in each of them.*

So he decided to find out by putting them to a test. To the pessimist he gave a brand-new Rolex watch, and to the optimist he gave a bag of horse manure. Then he stepped back to see what their reaction would be. The pessimist looked at his watch, and walked away mumbling, "Huh, he gives me this expensive watch that will probably break and I'll have to spend a lot of money to fix it." Then he looked over at his optimist son on his knees digging into the bag of manure for all he was worth, saying, "Come out of there, pony! I know you're in there somewhere."

Actually, by being happy I was simply trying to live the lifestyle we are asked to live in I Thessalonians 5:16–18: "Be joyful always; pray continually; give thanks in all circumstance, for this is God's will for you in Christ Jesus." After such an underprivileged beginning, what did I have not to be happy about? I had a perfect mate, a good family doing well, and more importantly I had a working relationship with the Lord that He had so graciously given me, known as a "new birth." I had seen many sour-looking people who claimed to be Christians but who looked like they had been baptized in vinegar juice. I was not about to be like them.

I had met Father Boyle, the senior Catholic chaplain in the rank of lieutenant colonel at Kirtland, previously at a chaplains' conference in Menlo Park, California. When he knew I was coming to be his boss, he asked me if I would deliver the homily (sermon) at the Catholic mass on Saturday evening and Sunday morning the week after my arrival. I did, and that little gesture established me as the senior spiritual leader of that community. It was another wonderful ecumenical experience like the one I had with the young priest previously at my sister Ramona's funeral. If we humans could only see our similarities instead of our differences and capitalize on that with love, understanding, and compassion as the basis of our relationships, we would be so much better.

I had a good staff, and the chapel program ran smoothly. In fact, the senior sergeant, Bob, went on to become the chief Air Force enlisted advisor to all chapel managers worldwide in the same manner that Hank Kras had done when he worked for me at Travis. Bob also credited me for recommending him to that position.

Base housing turned out to be a bummer. Quarters were adequate, but small. Not what you would expect for those in the rank of full colonel. The house we had at Dickey Goober when I was a major was much larger by comparison. This was in the area called "Colonels' Row," where all of those houses were of the same size and built by the Army during World War II. The movers delivering our furniture had to pop out the entire window in the master bedroom to get the triple dresser in because the hallways were too small to allow them to do that. Our house was cooled with a "water cooler" that blew air through wet filters that were pretty typical in the West during this time.

Next to us lived a wonderful couple. She was Catholic and he was Protestant and very much involved in the Protestant program. One night at a party in the Officers' Club they were singing "How Much Is That Doggie in the Window?" I chimed in, and she jokingly said, "John, you ought to sing that in church from the pulpit sometime!" I took the dare and said, "I'll sing it if you'll come to hear me do it!" She did come, and I explained to the Protestant congregation the arrangement and sang, "How Much Is That Doggie in the Window?" to loud applause.

While at Kirtland, my oldest sister died in La Junta, Colorado. On the way there for the funeral we were to pass through Springer, New Mexico. The map indicated that my place of birth was 22 miles east of Springer, just across the Canadian River. Since I had no recollection of Taylor Springs whatsoever, I decided to go there, and I told Dot and Mark,

"Let's go to Taylor Springs and see where 'this famous man' was born."
Mark was driving. We passed the Canadian River and then some, but no
sign of Taylor Springs. Mark said, "Dad, you were never born. There is no
Taylor Springs!"

So we turned around and went back. A few miles up the road we saw
a small sign about two feet by two feet with the words "Taylor Springs,"
indicating that the few adobe ruins that surrounded the area was all that
was left of my birthplace. We stopped so that we could take a picture of
me pointing to the small sign. Dot pointed out one particular mound
of adobe ruin and said, "That looks like where a chicken coop might
have been. That's probably where you were hatched!" It reminded me of
the story Vance Havner, an evangelist from North Carolina, used to tell
about where he was born. He said, "The place where I was born was so
small that I was born between 'litter barrel' and 'resume speed.'"

I was born on March 31, 1932. Dot used to tell me that we must have
lived so far out in the boonies that by the time my father got to Springer
to register my birth he was so confused that he told them I was born on
March 31 instead of April 1 when it actually took place. Seeing what was
left of Taylor Springs only confirmed what she had said. The truth may
be that it was never recorded, because when I went on the mission trip to
Brazil in 1965, the only proof of my birth that I could offer for a passport
was my baptismal certificate from the Catholic church in Springer. And
that was not too uncommon in those days. In many cases, the only proof
some people had of their birth was what was recorded in the family Bible.

One big concern at Kirtland was the fact that many of the chapel orga-
nizations were run by retirees, which was not common on most bases,
because sometimes their views were not in sync with the times. In time, I
slowly took action to correct this by getting more active duty personnel
involved. When I was about to retire, the senior Protestant chaplain, Ken,
informed the chaplain coming to replace me so that he would be aware of
that problem and what was being done to correct it. That chaplain, Bill,

apparently not agreeing with my decision, told Ken to keep that from happening until he came and took charge. I told Ken to tell Bill, "I'm still in charge. And we'll continue by my decision until I'm gone."

This was a bad move on my part because I later found out that Bill was vindictive and kept Ken from being promoted to the next rank because of that incident. When Ken saw me at a later time, he said, "I found out what you meant when you left and told me to 'watch your number six.'" It was a warning to "be careful!"

Kirtland was a time when Mark, who was 18, again gave us some heartaches. He would do his school assignments, but then hide them under his mattress and not turn them in. His grades in school were atrocious. He was running around with the wrong crowd. (Sometimes the acorn doesn't fall too far from the tree.) In his senior year, the principal called us in for a conference one day and told us it didn't look like Mark was going to graduate, so they assigned him to a special ed school. Mark was smart, buckled down, and completed the necessary unaccomplished work in a few weeks and graduated.

That graduation ceremony was something to behold. They had a mariachi band, and some of his fellow graduates looked like they had come from the lower district of the city. Some were pregnant, tattooed, chains hanging from the waists of baggy pants, and so on. I had bought Mark several late-model cars while at Kirtland and he wrecked every one of them.

On one occasion while Dot and I were visiting our former daughter-in-law in Hawaii, Mark called me from Kirtland asking if there was gas in the propane grill because he was preparing to grill for some friends. I, somewhat irritated, asked Mark if he had checked the gas container, to which Mark responded in the negative. Shortly thereafter Mark called again and talked to Dot, asking her how long to cook the potatoes in the microwave—that some of his guests would soon be there. I told him to take some responsibility and not call back. Later on, the base commander, a good friend of mine, called and told me that the security police were called to my house because Mark and his friends were partying too loudly. Since they were underage and drinking, they were taken to the guardhouse and locked up. While there, one of Mark's friends set off the fire alarm by taking a cigarette and letting the smoke filter up into the alarm box. After Mark graduated, he decided to attend a culinary school in Atlanta, Georgia, so I took him there, left him with another car I had bought for him, and flew back to Albuquerque—anything to get Mark away from the crowd he was running around with. As stated earlier, Mark finally got his act together, earned a bachelor's degree from the University of North Carolina in Wilmington, and became successful as a consultant, earning a six-figure salary.

I retired with 32 years, five months, and two days of active duty. Dot had always told me that she wanted me to put her back in a Cadillac before she died. I bought her a beautiful, white 1992 Cadillac Sedan Deville as her well-deserved retirement present. (Unlike what I thought back in 1950 when she strutted around town in her father's Cadillac, she really did look like "Miss-It-on-the-Stick" in this one.)

By the time of my retirement, our third son, Mike, was a captain in the chaplaincy stationed at Grand Forks Air Force Base in North Dakota. He and his family came for the retirement ceremony that was held in the chapel and presented the prayer. Mike and I were the only father-and-son chaplains who were on active duty at this time.

Mike told a favorite story of his that took place when we were stationed at Vance 16 years before:

One night I came home with my face all bloodied. There was this guy up the street kissing his girlfriend out in the carport. My buddy and I decided to throw pine cones at them from the bushes where we were hiding. He came over and took issue with us and we got into an argument, so he punched me in the face. He was older and bigger than I was. When I got home, Dad was getting ready to go to bed. When he saw my face all bruised and bloodied, he wanted to know who hit me. When I told him, he was furious and stormed out the door with me in tow. I stopped him and told him, "Dad, at least put your pants on. You're in your shorts." Dad was so mad he was ready to hang the guy that hit me, but the fellow and I talked Dad into not pressing assault charges.

At my retirement ceremony, Mark blew the general's mind with his rendition of "The Star-Spangled Banner" on his guitar, Jimi Hendrix style. After the ceremony, the general, who was never a chapel attender, said to me, "John, I'm sorry I never attended chapel. But I was always much too busy." I was retiring and had nothing to lose, so I answered, "Jim, any excuse is as good as another. When you're too busy for God, you're too busy!" and with that I walked away, leaving the general stunned that this colonel had talked to him so disrespectfully.

As had been done at our other going-away parties, a large number of people expressed their appreciation for our ministry by saying many nice things about us, especially about me since I was the one being retired. When it came time for me to make my remarks, one of our sons turned to Dot and said, "I hope he doesn't tell that Hershey's Chocolate story." But because it typified so much of my life, I did tell it.

I said,

I grew up in the poorest of conditions in La Junta, Colorado. We had no indoor plumbing. Our water supply came from water delivered to a cistern dug in our yard, and our toilet was a "two-holer" in our backyard. I didn't realize it then, but we were better off than I thought. Some people only had a "one-holer"! Montgomery Ward and Sears catalogs were the equivalent of today's toilet tissue.

Our playground was the city dump, where a poor, sheltered

6-year-old discovered all kinds of fascinating things he had never seen before. It was an "Alice in Wonderland" paradise. One day I saw a gallon can covered with brown paper. I picked it up and saw some brown gooey stuff oozing out of a hole at the top. I smelled it, and it smelled sweet. I tasted it, and it tasted good. That was my first introduction to Hershey's Chocolate Syrup. In later years when Dot and I attended social functions dressed up in our fancy duds and were served ice cream with chocolate syrup on top, I would turn to her and say, "Honey, I've come a long way!"

As stated earlier, I only completed the ninth grade in high school, dropped out of school, lied about my age at age 16, and joined the Air Force under fraudulent enlistment. I later earned an undergraduate college degree in psychology and a master of divinity degree. The rest is history. Many people reviewing the story of my success would probably say, "John's a self-made man!" But there is no such thing as a self-made man. I am who I am because of the values instilled in me by my parents; and the influence of teachers, fellow chaplains and chapel managers, and other coworkers.

My special thanks to Father Bill Mattimore, who is here tonight, who taught me more about being a good chaplain than anybody else. And most of all, I am who I am because of my children, my beloved wife, and especially my Lord and Savior, Jesus Christ. I thank you all for coming, and I bid you well.

My story may seem extraordinary to the person who has failed to see the tremendous possibilities that reside and remain untapped within each one of us. I have read that studies show that most human beings only use 10 percent of their potential in a lifetime. Like Louie Zamperini, thousands more have succeeded against more insurmountable odds than the ones I had to push up against. Take the life of Mary Kathlyn Wagner, for example—a girl born into a rugged set of problems.

Her childhood unfolded during the Great Depression, and her father was bedridden with tuberculosis. Mary took care of him, kept the house, did the chores, and cooked the meals without skipping school. Her mother worked 14 hours a day, seven days a week managing a restaurant and receiving a paycheck far below what a man would earn in a similar position.

Mary longed to become a doctor, but funds weren't available for college. She married a man with whom she had three children, but he cheated on her and abandoned them. She married another man, who died of a heart attack a month after the wedding. Her third husband died of cancer. Mary herself was struck by a strange paralysis that affected one side of her face.

But Mary never let her problems define her. Her mother had told her over and over, "You can do it, Mary, you can do it!" Taking those words to heart, Mary carved out a sales career and eventually founded a little cosmetics company you might know—Mary Kay, which is now one of the world's largest direct-selling companies. "For every failure," Mary once said, "there's an alternative course of action. You just have to find it. When you come to a roadblock, take a detour."

(Fast-forward to September 2016: I have just finished two books that address the issue of self-improvement at any age. The first is by Derek Doeprek, *Break through Your BS*. "BS" standing for "belief systems, "blind spots," or just plain "bull——" excuses. He says that any of these can keep us from self-improvement and self-actualization and limit our dormant potential. The other book is by Tony Robbins, *Awaken the Giant Within*, which deals and expands on the same line of thinking. The content of these two books has revolutionized my thinking and future immensely. I give this example: I'm six months short of 85 years old. I am a successful person in character in every regard, obviously from my retired Air Force rank and civilian ministerial history career-wise, and well off financially. That explains where I am today. But is that the end of the line for me? Absolutely not. I have been motivated to move beyond that reality for personal gifts, possibilities, and opportunities to become better. I want to make as much of this philosophy to grow and to motivate others to empower themselves to tap those inner resources for themselves, either on a one-on-one basis or in a group setting.

I did this by compiling a booklet on motivational thinking that I supplied to the elderly residents at the independent living facility where I live. I add the text from this booklet here, thinking that it might motivate the reader as well, because motivation is something we all need at whatever age or stage in life.

The LAST of Life, the BEST of Life

By John O. Solano, Chaplain, Colonel, USAF, Retired

Reading a number of books by motivational speakers in recent months has me convinced that we, at whatever age in life, especially those in the sunset of life, have the God-given power within us to choose to be more of who we believe ourselves to be. One of the definitions of "retire" is "to take that which has *outlived its usefulness* and put it on a shelf." I refuse to see myself in that fashion, and I pray that you who read this will too.

RECOMMENDED BOOKS

Work through Your BS, by Derek Doperk
Awaken the Giant Within, by Tony Robbins
The Grace and Truth Paradox, by Randy Alcorn
Keys to Success: The 17 Principles of Personal Achievement, by Napoleon
Hill
Little Book of Big Quotes, by Zig Ziegler

Grow old along with me!
The best is yet to be,
The last of life, for which the first was made:
Our times are in His hand
Who saith, "A whole I planned,
Youth shows but half; trust God, see all, nor be afraid!"

Robert Browning, the great poet, wrote these famous words to his beloved Elizabeth at the age of 52, three years after her death. Perhaps he was dreaming—wishful thinking, because he was so deeply in love with his wife. Literary experts believe the meaning of this poem was that a person is not measured by his or her work capabilities, but by the character molded by time and life.

There is tremendous evidence that productivity and achievements continues into old age. Here are a few examples:

GOLDEN ACHIEVEMENTS

Pierre-Simon Laplace, 18th-century astronomer known for his investigations of the solar system, worked on his astronomy until he was past 70, saying, "What we *know* is nothing, what we *do not know* is immense."

John Milton wrote the 10-volume *Paradise Lost* at age 57, 13 years after becoming totally blind.

Ludwig van Beethoven composed his *Ninth Symphony* after he became deaf in the fifth decade of his life.

Grandma Moses began painting when most people retire.

LETTING THE INSIDE MATCH THE OUTSIDE

(A commentary from *The Student Bible,* New International Version)

Is everyone a hypocrite? "Almost *all of us live two lives*: what people see *outside* and what is really going on *inside*. In school we learn what outward signs of attention will please the teacher. At a job we learn to "put up a good front" whenever the boss happens to stroll by. As if putting on masks, we style our hair, choose our clothes, and use body language to impress those around us. Over time, we learn to excel at *hiding* truly serious problems.

People tend to *judge* by *outward appearances*, and so can easily be fooled. Acquaintances are often shocked when a mass murderer is arrested. "He seemed like such a nice man!" they insist. The *outside appearance* did not match the inside reality. *Chapters 5–7* in the *Gospel of Matthew* announce that the time has come for us to change not just the outside, but also the inside. In Jesus' day, religious people tried to *impress* each other with *showy* outward behavior. They wore gaunt and hungry looks during a brief fast, prayed grandiosely if people were watching, and went so far as to wear Bible verses strapped to their foreheads and left arms.

In his famous *Sermon on the Mount*, Jesus blasts the *hypocrisy* behind such seemingly harmless practices. God is not fooled by appearances. We cannot fake behavior to impress him. He knows that *inside the best of us* lurk dark thoughts of hatred, pride, and lust—internal problems only he can deal with. Jesus goes on to present a truly radical way of life, *free of pretense.*

FOOD FOR THOUGHT

The pleasure principle: Our behavior is motivated by what brings us pleasure and reward, and avoidance of what brings us pain and punishment.

WE HAVE SIX BASIC NEEDS

1. *Certainty.* We need to know we are safe and secure.
2. *Variety.* We like to be safe and secure, but we need some challenge, a little bit of a risk. Otherwise, if things were peachy all the time, we would get bored and stale.
3. *Connection.* We were not meant for isolation. We need to be connected to others, to nature, and to our Creator.

4. *Purpose.* There needs to be meaning for who we are and what we do.
5. *Growth.* Everything in life is moving and growing. If it doesn't, it wilts and dies.
6. *Contribution.* We need to leave a legacy that who we were and what we accomplished made a difference.

GROWING GRAY GRACEFULLY

Growing old gracefully occurs when one has made peace with his past and present life and has hope for the future. Successful aging is based on the capacity to master life's changes and stresses. Learn to live in the moment, it's all we have. The past is gone, let it go. You have no control over what the future will bring, so get off that rocking chair!

LOSSES IN AGING CAN SUCK THE LIFE
OUT OF YOU IF YOU DWELL ON THEM

A major cause of stress at any age is loss—and losses multiply as people grow older. One great loss the elderly have to grapple with is loss of self. Realizing that the capabilities we spend a lifetime honing are no longer sharp is quite a blow.

Loss of control over oneself and one's life is hard to take. Seeing friends and family members of the same generation begin to die is a significant loss. Questions like "Who was I?" "Who am I?" and "Who am I becoming?" are not uncommon.

OTHER LOSSES THAT AFFECT OUR LIVES

Loss of intimacy. Both physical and emotional intimacy, found in sex, touch, and physical closeness, are diminished.

Loss of respect. Moral standards and traditional virtues are being de-emphasized. With all these changes, the elderly may be made to feel invisible, outdated, and marginalized in a world they don't fit in anymore.

Unfortunately we define ourselves by what we *have* and what we *do*.

With age, we may lose our standard of living and meaning found in one's life work. Elderly people may feel disposable and disregarded when they are no longer economically productive.

Loss of health and well-being. With increasing age, the likelihood of health problems increases. Health problems can reduce our ability to do things we used to enjoy doing. Feelings of anger and resentment are not uncommon.

Loss of future. There is an old saying that goes, "Everyone wants to go to heaven, but just not today!" What one thinks about life after death plays a significant part in how one deals with loss of life.

Aging people must eventually come to terms with loss, even the loss of the person they used to be, and find consolation in the new person they are becoming. If we look back we will see that our lives have gone through certain stages of life—schooling, work, family, empty nest, and so on. Hopefully they have all been meaningful, and we shouldn't rob them of their richness by regretting that they are gone.

Eventually retirement and old age roll our way. Each of these stages is, in its own way, another new beginning. Entering old age is a transition of major proportions, and with it comes a tangle of ailments and emotions that need to be dealt with. The secret of doing that well is left up to each of us to discover.

WHEN DOES END OF LIFE BEGIN?

When the *physician* says, "I'm sorry but there's nothing more that we can do for you."

When the *patient with chronic* illness says, "I don't want to do this anymore."

Christina Puchalski, MD: "All too often people die in hospitals or nursing homes, alone and burdened with unnecessary treatment—treatment they would have refused if they had the chance to talk about their choices with their physicians long before the deathbed scene.

"Physicians are often trained with the mindset that death is an illness that demands curing. So when the patient reaches the terminal condition, physicians are often ill equipped to contend with this different dynamic."

Also, faced with possible lawsuits, doctors protect themselves by prolonging life as long as possible. An article in *Readers Digest* titled "How Doctors Die" pointed out that when doctors discover that they are terminally ill, they do not subject themselves to means of prolonging life in the same manner that they prescribe for their patients.

RELIGIOUS FAITH CAN BE GOOD MEDICINE

As an older person grapples with the reality of death and dying, spiritual growth may or may not occur. A strong spiritual framework can make a difference in how we cope with death.

Faith can play an important role in how we deal with this transition if we apply it. Those who believe the Bible's message of redemption and resurrection through Jesus Christ have faith in life beyond the grave. They have a purpose for living that transcends their own problems and circumstances.

State of mind—attitude—is crucial to how we handle old age. Those who are content with what they have (living in the moment) and are optimistic about the future feel more in control of their own lives. With faith, a person expects that good will ultimately come out of bad situations.

Romans 8:28: "All things work for good for those who love God and are called according to His purpose." Ecclesiastes 7:1: "The day we die is better than the day we were born."

Faith puts one in touch with the love of God—even in the face of great loss. There is a close connection between spiritual well-being and physical and emotional well-being—seeing ourselves as a whole (the medical field calls this "holistic treatment").

The problems and ailments of old age can test our spiritual foundation, yet times of suffering and pain can result in spiritual growth. (James

1:2 4: "My brothers and sisters, whenever you face trials of any kind, consider it nothing but joy, because you know that the testing of your faith produces endurance, and let endurance have its full effect, so that you may be mature and complete, lacking in nothing.")

No matter what our age, having the proper perspective on ourselves—that Christ died for our sins once and for all, the just for the unjust, to bring us to God—can help us give up the baggage that keeps us bound to the past.

The secret of *growing gray gracefully* is the same as growing gracefully at any age—it can only happen if God is in the picture. Every phase of life—youth, adulthood, old age—all have trials and tribulations peculiar unto themselves, and God can help us maneuver through them gracefully if we allow Him. That secret has three requirements: (1) We must experience God's *presence,* (2) We must obey God's *principles,* and (3) We must fulfill God's *purpose.*

Studies have shown that people who have placed their faith in Jesus Christ for salvation face the end of life differently than those who have no assurance about where they will spend eternity. Believers view death as a great new beginning—exchanging a life of pain or sorrow for eternal life in the wondrous presence of God.

But that does not mean dying is easy. Many of us do not fear death itself but rather the dying process. We worry about the possibility of a long illness—of being hooked up to tubes—having uncontrolled pain—being kept alive by artificial means—being a burden to the family—and dying alone. For most people, these fears are never realized, so it is needless worry.

MAKING ETHICAL TREATMENT DECISIONS

Medical technology has extended people's lives, but that also means that elderly people and their families face end-of-life decisions their grandparents didn't have to make.

Ecclesiastes 3:12: "There is a time for every event under heaven—a time to give birth, and a time to die." While Christians need not fear death, today's medical advances can place believers in a moral dilemma as we ask this question: "When is it time to allow nature to take its course and let loved ones go home to be with the Lord?"

PRACTICAL END-OF-LIFE MATTERS

We live in a world of personal denial when it comes to death. Everybody else is going to die, except us. We just don't want to think about it, and because we don't, our affairs are too often left undone and cause a lot of uncertainty and confusion for our loved ones left behind. Get your affairs in order so that your loved ones won't have to guess about what to do.

As a minister of 57 years, I have seen the confusion and heartache that matters left undone can cause. As a result, I have completed all of my estate planning with a DNR, Will, Power of Attorney, Trustee, when and where to have a memorial service, where my ashes are to be inurned, and I have outlined a list of 18 items that my executor only has to follow closely by going down the list to get my earthly life business finalized.) Make it easy for them by reducing the guesswork!

LIFE AFTER DEATH

Is there life after death? Some people believe there is, while others believe that this life is all there is. The book titled *Heaven* by Randy Alcorn and the movie *Heaven Is for Real* and some out-of-body experiences in recent years have sparked a renewed interest in heaven.

Major faith groups differ in what they teach about heaven, or the lack thereof:

1. *Islam* believes that there are heavens and hells, and we go to the one designed for how good or how bad we are.

2. *Judaism* has no absolute belief about the afterlife or heaven, but there is a hope in Sheol, a place of purification where the spirit goes for one year, and then awaits the final resurrection.

3. *North American liberal Jews* tend not to believe in an afterlife at all. However, the *Orthodox Hasidic Jews* wholeheartedly believe in reincarnation for those who could not complete their life purpose in one lifetime.

4. *Hindus and Buddhists* believe that the soul perfects itself by reincarnation (over multiple lifetimes) until we get it right, and then the soul, the Atman, merges with Brahman (or Nirvana—which is enlightenment for Buddhists).

5. *Confucianism* believes in no god per se. (Not really a religion.) It is a *sociophilosophical movement* aimed at bettering society. The ethical teachings of Confucius, Chinese philosopher and teacher, emphasize devotion to parents, ancestor worship, and the maintenance of justice and peace. God is not a core concern of Confucianism.

Confucianists have found no problem delving into Taoism or Buddhism or even Christianity or Islam. They can convert and embrace the others and still remain a Confucianist.

Confucianism uses the Chinese lettering for heaven, but that can mean sky or nature. It does not take a firm line on religion. One does not have to believe in God to be a Confucianist. Nor does faith in God prevent you from being a Confucianist.

6. *Christianity* believes in an afterlife, with heaven or hell as our final resting place. Plus, Catholics also being Christian, believe in purgatory, a place of purification.

However, it needs to be said that many liberal Protestants believe metaphorically in heaven and hell as a state of mind, as do many Unitarian Universalists.

CLOSING THOUGHTS

There are support groups for alcoholics, (AA, Al-Anon), drug addicts, eating disorders, gamblers, breast cancer survivors, and many others, where the need for sharing common problems can be dealt with in a confidential, therapeutic setting.

Why not a support group for the elderly? Do the elderly not have problems and issues that could and should benefit from discussing them in a confidential and trustful setting with other persons facing the same things? As a pastoral counselor for over 57 years, I know this venue to be extremely therapeutic for my counselees.

I now take the reader back to the time of my retirement in 1992. A few months before I retired, a lady from Florida called me and asked me if I would visit her father, a retired Navy chief petty officer who was terminal in a local nursing home. Because of many other administrative duties, the senior chaplain normally assigned visitation duties to lower-ranking chaplains, but because she had asked me personally I decided I would go visit the chief. What a blessing that turned out to be.

His name was Charles. When I visited enough times to believe that we had established a solid relationship and knowing he was dying, I asked him, "Charles, how is it between you and the Lord?" He answered, "It's okay!" I said to him, "I want it to be better than that—I want it to be A-Okay." The routine of our visits went something like this: We would visit, then I would read Scripture and pray. When I would get to the door about to leave, I would turn around and ask, "Charles, how is it between you and the Lord?" It never failed—he would answer, "A-Okay."

I went to visit him one last time before I left to go to Phoenix to talk with a church that wanted to consider me to be their pastor. When I got to Charles's room, I found him in a semicoma. I didn't know whether he knew that I was even there, but I went through the same routine, visited for a while, read Scripture, and prayed. Just about the time I got to the door and was ready to leave the room, I heard this deep, labored guttural sound, "Aaaaaaaaaaaaaaaaaaaa———Oooooooooooo———kkkkkkkkk kkkkkkkkkaaaaaaaaaayyyyyyyyyyyyyyyyyy!"

That made chills run up and down my spine! As the Apostle Paul rightly says in Romans 8, "There is nothing in this world or in the world to come that can keep us from the love of God which is in Christ Jesus." That being true, a little ol' coma doesn't stand a chance!

I have no doubt in my mind that my being an Air Force chaplain was always in God's plan for my life. My early days of living in a low-income environment and under discrimination was fairly typical of so many servicemen and servicewoman who entered the military for reasons similar to mine who came from comparable situations. We could commiserate!

With my wayward life as a young airman, I could identify and counsel with troubled airmen who were going through the same thing I had been through. "Been there, done that!" Additionally, if a commander had had it with an undisciplined, troublemaking airman like I used to be whom I was counseling and was ready to throw the book at him, I could intervene, tell the commander about my background, and say, "Where would I be today if someone had not given me a second chance?"

On the other hand, if I was counseling a young airman with a lot of potential and big dreams, but no self-esteem, I could ask, "Do you think I'm a success?" When the airman responded to the obvious with, "Of course!" I could say, "Well, let me tell you about where I came from. You have more going for you than I did. And if I can do it, you can too!"

Even more, the opportunities that my long chaplaincy career gave Dot as my coworker, and who ministered as much as I did in so many areas and in so many ways throughout the United States and many foreign countries, could never have been possible for her in civilian life. And that can also be said of our four sons, who went on to become well-educated, productive, patriotic citizens of this great United States that God has blessed so much. As I alluded to in the beginning, this story is truly more about God and Dot than it is about me. I am simply the recipient of their wonderful, enduring, freely given unconditional love and influence.

PART V

What Next?

18

A Short-Term Sabbatical

Warner Robins, Georgia, 1992–1996

Dot and I had jointly bought a house in Warner Robins, Georgia, with Dot's parents. Her father put down the large down payment, and we made the monthly house payments and paid for occasionally needed maintenance with her parents living there rent free, and with the understanding that we would acquire possession of the home when I retired. By the time of my retirement, Dot's mother was deceased, her father was in a nursing home, and the house was being rented.

We decided to put our household goods in storage and spend four months with Keith, who was then stationed at an Army post in Vicenza, Italy. Keith had graduated from the high school at the Army post there and had previously been assigned there as the physician for the 509th Airborne Battalion. Earning an MD degree is no small achievement, but it never went to Keith's head. However, being with the 509th did. In those days, wearing the maroon Berea was pretty special, and when he did he strutted like John Wayne.

Those four months in Vicenza with Keith were a vacationer's dream.

He could not do enough to wine and dine us. It was payback time! He would take us to the best local restaurants to eat, and even arranged for us to have a romantic ride in a gondola in Venice while he watched lovingly and admiringly from the bridge above.

Keith also arranged for us to join him in attending a performance of *The Nutcracker* at the famed La Scala Opera House in Milan. We looked forward to this privilege with great anticipation. That proved to be a bummer because La Scala is formed in the shape of a horseshoe. Those seated at the curvature of the horseshoe opposite the stage had perfect view. But those seated in the boxes on the side where we were sitting had to keep leaning out and peering toward the stage to see, and more times than not, the persons in the box seats next to ours were doing the same thing and blocking our view.

Keith had two cars, so we borrowed one of them to go to Aviano to visit old friends there and then hop on military aircrafts going to Wiesbaden, Germany, and Incirlik, Turkey, where we visited chaplains who formerly had worked for me. While in Turkey with our priest friend who had worked for me at Kirtland, we visited Antioch, where followers of Christ were first called Christians. During this time, Dot's brother, a retired dentist, and his wife visited us in Vicenza as well. We took them to Florence and other touristic sites.

When I was stationed in Okinawa in 1987, my base commander (the one mentioned earlier being a devout Catholic) heard me speak at one of our patriotic functions. He turned to Dot and said, "He's a hell of a speaker!" While we were visiting with Keith five years later, that commander was now a two-star general and commander of the Flying Wing at Luke AFB in Arizona. He had his aide track me down all over Italy until he found me, because he wanted me to come to his base and be that year's national prayer breakfast speaker, which I did.

I used the book of Esther as the basis for my message. In that story there is a lot of deception, where Mordecai and his young cousin whom he has raised as his daughter from childhood are among the Jewish captives who have been brought to Babylon from their homeland as captives. To make a long story short, the present queen displeases the king during a drunken orgy, so he gets rid of her and takes Esther to be his new queen, with Esther keeping secret under Mordecai's command that she is a Jew.

One of the king's henchmen plots the elimination of all the Jewish captives and gets the king to consent to their demise. Mordecai finds out about the plot and tries to convince Esther to get the king to rescind that order. She flatly turns him down because she knows she'd be risking her own life. Mordecai reminds Esther that she also is a Jew and could be done away with as well.

Being a person of strong Jewish faith, Mordecai finally convinces Esther with this plea found in the book of Esther 4:12–14: "Do not think that because you are in the king's house you alone of all the Jews will escape. For if you remain silent at this time, relief and deliverance for the Jews will arise from another place, but you and your father's family will perish. And who knows but that you have come to royal position *for such a time as this*."

I used as my text the last phrase of that passage, "For Such a Time as This," preaching to a full house (who would not have attended a gathering sponsored by the two-star general?) of Air Force personnel of all ranks, including many, many high-ranking officers. My main thesis was to try to get the thought across that God has a purpose for all of us to accomplish His will in the moment in which we live—much like He did with Esther—and that we were living in the moment "For Such a Time as This."

Who would ever have thought that a little ol' Latino nobody from the dumps of La Junta, who was once one step ahead of the law, would be given such an important platform to proclaim the good news to the glory of a loving, caring, merciful God? Dot was right when she often said, "People wonder about God's miracles. I'm married to one!"

When we finally settled in Warner Robins, I stayed busy playing golf and making improvements on the house while Dot settled back to being a devoted housewife, preparing gourmet meals for the family, entertaining, and doing her best to keep me on the straight and narrow. We were able to spend a lot of quality time with Dot's brother and his wife. Another big plus was the fact our second son, Don, was the commander of the communications squadron at nearby Robins Air Force Base and we were able to visit with them often. (Whether that was the same squadron that I had gotten in so much trouble some 40 years before I didn't bother to investigate. Some things are better left alone.)

During our time in Warner Robins, I served as interim pastor for the Mount Calvary Baptist Church in Cary, Georgia, and the Limestone Baptist Church in Cochran, Georgia. I was never good at remembering names, so I took the Mount Calvary church directory, and while watching TV, would place the face with the name. I would greet them by their given name, and they thought I'd hung the moon. However, one Sunday morning a lady shook hands with me as she was leaving after the service, and I couldn't for the life of me place her name. She sensed it and said, "You don't know my name, do you? You'd better. I'm the one who signs the checks!" Needless to say, I didn't forget her name again.

While at Mount Calvary I took a month of leave, and we had the privilege of visiting Mike and his family, who were then stationed at Aviano as a chaplain as well. The deacon at Mount Calvary gave me a large stuffed envelope as a gift and told me we were not to open it until we were on the airplane. When we opened it, we found it full of love letters from all the church members telling us how much we had meant to them and how much they loved us. Nothing could have been more treasured than that. Four times in Italy, what a rare treat!

Both churches were pretty conservative in their beliefs. At Mount Calvary, they had ordained a seminary-educated female into the ministry, but only so that she could serve as a hospital chaplain in Macon. They would not allow her to preach because they thought that was biblically unacceptable. They also had a very devout male Christian who sang in the choir and served in other programs in the church as a volunteer, but they would not ordain him as a deacon because he had been divorced.

Because the head deacon knew that I had won the admiration and confidence of the congregation, he asked me to address these two issues during my last few weeks there. I did this, pointing out that the only "unpardonable sin" that I knew that was biblical was refusing the gift of salvation that God offered in Christ, and that when Paul wrote to Timothy about "a deacon being the husband of one wife" that he was talking about bigamy, not divorce. I told them that it seemed to me that Southern Baptists thought the "unpardonable sin" was divorce and keeping women from speaking in the church.

Fortunately, this kind of prejudiced mentality didn't exist in the military at this time. In the military they were more concerned about merit than gender. In 1994 Lorraine Potter, an American Baptist chaplain who had risen up the ranks to full colonel, was elevated to the rank of brigadier general (one star) as deputy chief of Air Force chaplains, and the next year was promoted to major general (two stars), where she served until her retirement a few years later. In the year 2015 there was a female serving as chief of the Navy chaplains with a two-star rank as well. We visited Mount Calvary several years later and discovered that the fellow previously mentioned had been ordained as a deacon. The woman had left the church, so that was no longer an issue.

The previous minister at the other church, Limestone Baptist, was absolutely against dancing, and he preached against it. His favorite expression was, "A bended knee and a dancing foot just don't go together." I came along and blew their minds by telling them that I was a former Arthur Murray dance instructor.

Dot was not altogether happy in Warner Robins because it was no longer the town of her childhood—it had grown by leaps and bounds.

1993

So on a visit to Keith in Aurora, Colorado, I asked Dot if she thought she would be happy in Colorado Springs, and she said she certainly would be happier than she was in Warner Robins.

Keith was about to complete his second residency in nuclear medicine at Fitzsimons Army General Hospital in Aurora near Denver and be reassigned to the hospital at Fort Carson in Colorado Springs to set up a nuclear medicine clinic there. Another factor that influenced our move to Colorado was the fact that Don and his family had been transferred to Guam from Warner Robins.

So we looked for a place in Colorado Springs, bought a house, and moved there in 1996 to be close to Keith. I felt this was God's will and told the real estate agent to get the house on the market, and that it would sell in two weeks—and that's exactly what happened.

PART VI

Your Ways Are Not My Ways

19

Who Authorized Retirement?

Colorado Springs, Colorado, 1996–2013

The years in Colorado Springs turned out to be among the best in retirement for us, except toward the last when Dot's health became an issue. I also had some health issues. My days of racquetball had taken their toll. I had to have my second knee replacement, and when I was in the recovery room the nurse detected an irregular heartbeat. I had never had any heart, cholesterol, or weight problems so I was unconcerned. However it turned out to be very serious. It was determined that the main artery, what they call "the widow-maker," was 98 percent clogged and three days later I had triple bypass surgery. Undetected, it could have been fatal, but the good Lord just wasn't through with me here on earth just yet.

Another incident that year could have been my demise. Dot and I had been to San Antonio to visit Mike and his family. On our return trip to Colorado Springs, we decided to go by and visit one of my former chaplains and his wife who lived in the Austin area. On the way for about 50 miles there was a girl in her 20s, who we surmised was a college student, with whom we would take turns passing back and forth.

As we approached the bottom of an incline I saw an 18-wheeler with the cab staying in its lane, but with the tractor trailer angled across our lane that was unmistakably going to hit us head-on. I said to Dot, "Honey, say your prayers. I don't think we're going to make it!" At the last minute, and in the nick of time, the truck driver straightened out the trailer that had blown two tires on the left side. When we reached the top of the hill we discovered what had saved us was her death. The car of the girl who had been passing us was sheared in half as well as her face. It was a horrible sight to see—brain matter everywhere. I couldn't get that image out of my mind for several weeks.

Because of my commissioned military service, I had entitlement to the GI Bill that I could use for educational purposes if I so chose. Dot told me that I should work on my doctorate. I replied, "What do I need a doctorate for at this stage in my career?" Instead, I elected to enter the University of Colorado at Colorado Springs and study fine arts—fun stuff like painting, drawing, sculpting, and photography. I was in my mid-sixties and in time everyone knew I was a minister as well. But as far as the rest of the students in their 20s were concerned, I was just one of them.

With my arthritic fingers, I must have destroyed more film than anyone else trying to thread the film in the small sprockets in the darkroom for developing. When it came to doing print sheets after the film was developed, I didn't do much better. After a few failed attempts, I finally came up with what I thought was a pretty good product. I asked my lab partner, who was a female around 20 and who knew I was a minister, "What do you think of my print sheet?" Her answer was not what I was expecting. Just as natural as someone else would say, "I think it's great!" she said, "I think it's a kick-ass print sheet!"

For one of my class assignments, I had to go to the library to do research for a paper. When I asked the student librarian where the card catalog was, the student looked at me as if I had come from another planet. He told me, "We do things by computer now!" I took two semesters in computer education, but that turned out to be a waste of time—the reason being that the computers in the classroom were current ones, and the one I had at home was quite dated and I was too cheap to buy a newer one. It was like trying to apply the lessons learned driving a Cadillac in the classroom to driving a Model T Ford in real life.

Since we had traveled so much in our lifetime, the desire to travel some more got to us, so we decided to visit Father Mattimore in Hawaii. The bishop had assigned him to the St. Georges Parish in Walmanella at the end of the island of Oahu. Father was now a monsignor. My former commander at Kadena had been promoted to the rank of four-star general by this time and was commander of all Air Forces in the Pacific. He arranged for us to stay in the general's quarters right on the beach.

They were magnificently furnished with the best of the best and a hot tub outside. The view of the beach, the blue water, and the surrounding area through the huge picture window in the living room was spectacular and breathtaking. We were living like we were somebody. But we were only allowed to stay there for five days, and then we would have to move to Hickam's Air Base Distinguished Visitors Quarters. Our son Don was a squadron commander in Guam who was coming to Hickam on TDY. I told Don to bring his golf clubs and to take a day of leave in conjunction with his TDY so that we could play golf, and Don did. However, I found out that I had blown it.

When we moved over to Hickam there were no tee times left. What to do? Ever the smart one, Dot said, "Why don't you call the Protocol Office and tell them you're the general's guest and I'll bet they'll come up with one." I did, and sure enough, one just happened to be available. On the day of play, they matched us up with a Mormon couple from Hill AFB in Utah. At one point, the woman asked Don, "Is your father a general?" He replied, "Naw. He's just a colonel. He just thinks he's a general!"

Later in time we had a chance to visit Don and his family in Guam. We were to arrive at the time that their church was having their annual

Sweetheart Banquet in one of the fancy hotels down on the beach, so Don got tickets for us to attend. The traffic in Guam is atrocious, bumper to bumper at all times. The night of the banquet was made even worse due to construction on the last leg of the road leading down to the beach area.

Traffic congestion was so bad that we didn't make the banquet on time and finally had to turn back, and ended up celebrating our Sweetheart Banquet at McDonald's. But we were all together and that's all that mattered. We had to cut our visit with Don short because one of my knees was hurting me so badly I could hardly stand it. On the trip back, we had a long layover in Los Angeles, and I spent ten agonizing hours on a lounge chair in the USO in the airport. A few weeks later, I had a total knee replacement.

Although I had served as a Southern Baptist in the Air Force Chaplaincy, we decided to join the 1,800-member Sunrise United Methodist Church in Colorado Springs because we liked the pastor, Jim Calhoun, who was a fellow Georgian, and also because the church was close to where we lived. When Calhoun left a year later, he was replaced by Marv Vose, who became a good friend of mine.

When the minister of pastoral care resigned, Marv asked me if I would take the position. I said I wasn't interested—that I was retired, was enjoying golf, and didn't want to be tied down. Marv then asked me to take it for two weeks on a part-time basis until they could find someone permanently and I consented.

I guess I had been listening to what I wanted to do, but not what God wanted. I knew this was where I was supposed to be because when Marv had announced the other person's resignation, the Holy Spirit clearly told me, "He's going to ask you to replace her!" I ignored it because I wanted to be free to do my own thing now that I was retired. I felt I had paid my dues.

Now, why would I have heard that voice were it not for the fact that it was meant to be? That position was perfectly suited for me due to my previous CPE training and hospital experience. I loved it, saw the valuable contribution I could still make in the Lord's work, and that two weeks turned into 15 years when I finally retired in 2012.

If a congregant was scheduled for surgery at 7 a.m., I was there at 5 a.m. to read Scripture and offer prayer. I would visit the sick in the homes or hospitals, and do follow-up at home either by phone or email. That half-time position actually turned out to be full-time. Only the pay remained at half-time, but that was okay because my military retirement pay was more than sufficient for our needs.

In addition, Marv asked me if I would start a more traditional service in the theater chapel for those who were more inclined to that style of worship. I did so and kept that service operative until my retirement. At my going-away party, person upon person stood up and lovingly stated, "He was there for us when we needed him!" That seminary professor was right: "Eloquent preachers will soon be forgotten, but loving, caring pastors will long be remembered!"

Marv and I had a wonderful working relationship, and he pretty much let me run things as I wanted. We would go out to lunch every week—mostly to a local Mexican place. We later found out that the place had been raided for selling illegal drugs. The news of the raid was in the local papers, and one of the other staff members asked me, "John, did you know about the raid and them selling drugs?" I answered, "Knew about it! Where do you think Marv and I went to get our high?"

The immigration problem was getting a lot of attention at this time. One day at lunch Marv asked me, "John, what do you think about this immigration problem?" I said to him, "Wat do I tink about theeese imogration problem? Wat ees eet about theeese imogration problem dat yu doon't oonderstand, gringo? Wee gonna tak over!" I didn't know how prophetic I was being.

As is true in large churches, the church staff doesn't always know everybody, but because of the staff's visibility everybody knows the church staff. One day shortly after I became part of the Sunrise Staff I found a note in my inbox. It said, "There is a church member by the name of Salvatore who thinks that you and he might have crossed paths in the past somewhere in the Air Force. He wants you to call him."

I called him, and this is what he told me: "You probably don't remember me, but I remember you. Thirty years ago when you were the hospital chaplain at Keesler Air Force Base in Mississippi, you came to visit me often. I was just eighteen, sick as a dog with the flu and had just received a 'Dear John' letter from my girlfriend. I was so depressed I didn't know what to do. Your visits, reading of Scripture, your prayers, and your words of encouragement pieced me back together and put me on the right road to a personal relationship with Christ. We need to get together to renew our acquaintance."

We got together alright. But not in the way that he had wanted. Salvatore was in the basement of his home working on his computer and watching television when he, like millions all over the world in shock, saw the unbelievable, infamous events of September 11, 2001, unfolding before our very eyes—four commercial planes manned by terrorists toppling the Twin Towers in New York City, attacking the Pentagon, and bringing down a plane in Pennsylvania, killing over 3,000 innocent people. Salvatore ran upstairs shouting to his wife, "Sheryl, Sheryl, turn on the television. You won't believe what's happening in New York City." On the way down, Salvatore had a massive heart attack, and I did his funeral service. That's how Salvatore and I came to meet for the first and last times after not seeing each other for 30 years.

Some of my most interesting memories were weddings and funerals, of which I conducted hundreds over a 54-year period. No matter how well you planned them, they didn't always turn out that way. Of course, the most special ones were the weddings I did of my sons and grandchildren.

On one of my visits to my cardiologist, Dr. Paul Sherry, he asked me if I still did funerals in retirement, to which I said I did. He asked me if I would do his mother's who was not expected to live long. She had

Alzheimer's and was living in a skilled living facility. I said I would, and could I visit her? When I went there for the first time, she stared into space and would not even acknowledge my presence or anything I said.

Remembering that Paul said she spoke Italian before she spoke English, I said to her, "Senora Anna, yo sono Cappellano Solano, y amico da suo filio, Paolo, capice?" which means, "Ms. Anna, I am Chaplain Solano, and a friend of your son, Paul, do you understand?" I never cease to be amazed at how wonderfully God works! The Apostle Paul says in Romans 8:38–39, "For I am convinced that neither death nor life, neither angels nor demons, neither the present nor the future, nor any powers, neither height nor depth, nor anything else in all creation, will be able to separate us from the love of God that is in Christ Jesus our Lord."

I had used that Scripture when I did my sister Ramona's funeral. She had also had Alzheimer's—for seventeen years. God used what little Italian I knew for Paul's mother and I to connect from my world into hers— both of us in His world. When she heard me speaking in Italian, Mrs. Sherry got a twinkle in her eyes and smiled from ear to ear. The response was the same every time I visited Mrs. Sherry after that when I spoke to her in Italian. I did her memorial service when she died, as well as the wedding for Paul's daughter.

No matter how well these services were planned, it appeared that there was always something wrong that would happen that at the time might seem upsetting, but which made each one more unique and memorable. At the rehearsal of my first wedding, when I went to ask the father of the bride, "Who gives Jane to be married to Bob," I was nervous and said, "Who gives Jane to be buried to Bob?" Knowing I was a jokester, they thought I had done it on purpose to relieve the tension.

Forty years later at another wedding, I found out that mistakes could still be made, no matter how much experience you've had. The daughter of one of our parishioners had gone to Ecuador to do mission work. While there she met and fell in love with a young man. She taught him workable English, and they decided to marry, the wedding to take place in Colorado Springs. They thought it would be nice to have a bilingual ceremony because the parents of the groom knew no English. So they asked me to do the wedding. Since I hadn't spoken Spanish on a regular basis since my days in college, I was a little rusty.

I translated the ceremony as best I could, and then took it to the Spanish professor at the local university to polish it up. I decided to go through the entire ceremony in English and Spanish so that the parents of the groom, who knew no English, would be familiar with the actual wedding. On the night of the rehearsal when it came time for the vows to be exchanged in Spanish, I meant to ask the bride, "Andrea, repite despues de mi!" which means, "Andrea, repeat after me!" Then I meant to ask Andrea to say to her groom, "Carlos, prometo amarte," which means, "Carlos, I promise to love you." Instead I got confused and told her to repeat, "Carlos, prometo amatarte," which means, "Carlos, I promise to kill you." Those knowing Spanish were initially aghast, and then broke out in laughter. I was glad that it happened at the rehearsal and not at the wedding ceremony.

After so many years of counseling people, there comes a time when a minister thinks he's heard it all. Not true! This happened to me when I was providing premarital counseling for a couple whom I did not know personally, but was doing the wedding as a favor for a good friend of mine. The last question I always asked at the conclusion of every last counseling session was, "Where are you spiritually?" It was an open-ended question intended to provide a testimony of whatever relationship they personally had with God, if any. Throughout the years I had heard so many different answers that I thought I had heard them all.

The groom-to-be replied, "I am studying all religions, to see which one I like best." I'd heard that one before so I was not surprised. But her answer blew me away. She said without hesitation, "I believe in the separation of church and state!" I must have come across as too religious because they got another person to perform the ceremony and dismissed me. My friend later told me that no mention of God whatsoever was made at the ceremony. One of the interesting things about liberal Colorado at this time was that anyone could perform a wedding ceremony. You didn't have to be a Justice of the Peace or a clergyperson.

From the current divorce statistics at this writing, that union in all probability didn't last. One sermon that I heard from another minister hit the nail on the head. He said, "Marriages last because (1) they believe that God *brings* them together, (2) so they allow God to *build* them together, (3) so the result is that God *binds* them together. Those that don't last are influenced by the Hollywood model of (1) 'Hook up,' (2) 'Shack up,' and (3) 'Break up.'"

There was another wedding that I conducted as a favor for my real estate agent friend for a couple I didn't know. It was held out in the country at a popular tourist attraction that was built in a western-style motif, corral, barn, animals, and all the rest. They had an open bar for those in attendance before we got there, and by the time my agent friend and I got there, it was obvious that the booze had been flowing. Needless to say, that turned out to be a disaster. But, the good book says, "Judge not, that you be not judged!"

Another interesting wedding was the one that I did for the son of a family that had been members of the church for a long time, the mother in the choir and the father serving as an usher. It was a cold day when the couple came to my office. The bride-to-be was wearing a topcoat that concealed what was a surprise at the end of the session. She said, "Oh, we forget to tell you I'm expecting next month." I was tempted to say, "Good. We can have a wedding and a baptism at the same time!" But I didn't. A judgmental minister would have stopped everything right there and told them that he would not be able to perform the ceremony because the child had been conceived in sin out of wedlock.

But I remembered the story of Jesus who dealt with the judgmental, self-righteous, noncaring legalists who brought the woman caught in the act of adultery who wanted her stoned. Jesus didn't accept her adulterous behavior, but loved her with compassion and forgave her. I had been guilty of similar sinful behavior myself in my days before becoming a Christian, but the Lord took pity on me and now I was a "sinner saved by grace." Jesus said to her accusers, "He that is without sin, let him cast the first stone" (John 8:7). I didn't have any stones of self-righteousness to throw!

Situations like these were pretty common in 2019. So many were already living together without the benefit of marriage, and many others already expecting by the time they decided to wed. Even same-sex marriage was legal and accepted by a sizable segment of the world.

One of my most interesting weddings was the one I did for the son of one of my Jewish golfing buddies in Denver. The son was Jewish, and the bride was Southern Baptist. Talk about opposites! When I was asked to do the wedding, I wondered how that would go with these two faiths having such a great difference in how they view Christ. I thought I would be doing the wedding jointly with a rabbi, but found out I had the whole enchilada. Actually, they combined parts of both religious traditions, and it turned out to be a very nice wedding after all.

Funerals are a time of loss, sorrow, and heartache. But I found them to be one of my most enjoyable and blessed of ministries. It is a time when people feel hopeless and helpless—a time when a minister should be at his best in offering faith in God and hope for life after death. It's a time, of all times, when God's representative should be what I was fond of calling "the presence of God with skin on it." I found that these times were my forte—I was at my best. My CPE training in 1963 and my personal relationship with the living Christ and love for His people had prepared me for this awesome ministry.

I once conducted a funeral for the two-year-old child of a military family. The child had gotten sick so the mother took him to the local

Army hospital emergency room, where they treated him and sent him home stating that he would be alright. Two days later the child died at home. Her only consolation was that the father, who was stationed in Afghanistan, had been home on leave a few months earlier to celebrate the child's second birthday.

While preparing for the memorial service, I comfortingly said to her, "I wish I could tell you why these unfortunate things happen. But I can't. You'll have to wait until you get to heaven and ask God." She said emphatically, "You can bet your life I will!" (Two things we were taught in my CPE training that you never say in such circumstances: (1) "I know exactly how you feel" (you really don't), and (2) "The Lord giveth and the Lord taketh away" (that does nothing for God's image as a loving and caring Heavenly Father).

Two services that I conducted deserve special mention. Oftentimes I was asked to do services for relatives of members who were not affiliated with our church, or any church for that matter. This is a time when people need the church, so there's no way or reason to refuse. I, ever the humorist, used to tell the story about this rich lady whose dog died, so she consulted several ministers to do the service. But all refused, saying that they did not conduct funerals for animals. The last person was a Baptist minister who said the same thing. The lady said to the minister, "You were my last hope. I guess I'll just have to do it myself. I was even willing to pay $1,000." "Oh," replied the minister, "you didn't tell me your dog was a Baptist. Of course, I'll do the service!"

While planning the order of service for a funeral/memorial service (funeral being where the body is present, memorial where it is not—interment meaning burial of the body, inurnment meaning disposal of the ashes after cremation), I always included a spot where loved ones could eulogize the deceased. It was at the part where the bulletin showed, "Remembering So and So." While preparing for the service of a member whom I had never met because she never came to church, I said to the daughter, "You and a few other family members can say things about your mother at this point."

I noticed that she displayed a little bit of discomfort. This had happened many times because many people are nervous about speaking in public. In those cases, I would tell them to write something out and I would read their sentiments for them. Her husband was out in the hall on his cell phone answering an official call. When he came in, I told him what I had told her. He said, "Well John, Ms. 'So and So' was a very difficult woman. I don't know what we would say." Needless to say, that part of the service was scrubbed.

What terrible memories some of us leave with our children. Without a doubt, we are a fractured humanity in need of God's redemption. The following story shows the opposite, where the child leaves terrible memories for his parents.

I conducted a memorial service for a retired army sergeant whose son was in prison at the state penitentiary in Canon City, Colorado. He obviously was not a model inmate because he was brought to the church in Colorado Springs for the service in an orange prison uniform, hands and feet shackled with two prison guards with weapons holstered side by side. Later on he was released from prison and in time got in trouble again. One day he was being chased by two patrol cars in Missouri when he rammed his car under an 18-wheeler and was killed. His mother told me that she believed he had done it purposely because he vowed he would never go back to prison again.

Another memorial service that I conducted had to be one of kind. It was for the son of a member whom I didn't know. He was 52 years old, alcoholic, and had lived a pretty shady life. The mother told me the minister who had married them wanted to say a few words at the beginning. It was a last-minute request, so I didn't even have a chance to talk with this minister about what he would be doing. I couldn't believe what I heard this minister say about the deceased.

He went on and on about how bad this dude was as if his behavior was a virtue. Typical of his remarks was the story about the time when the deceased was being chased by several police cars, and the only way they were able to catch him was to hem him in. I was always taught that if you can't say something good about somebody, don't say anything.

I discovered early on that you had to be careful about letting people randomly speak at these services who were not part of the program. They could eat up your sermon time by not knowing when to quit, and an overly lengthy service took away from the good feeling that you wanted to leave with those attending. One service that I conducted shows how a well-meaning gesture by the uninformed can turn out to be a disaster.

At this particular memorial service, a female friend of the family who had a part in the service at one point asked anyone in the congregation who wanted to say something about the deceased to come up to the podium and do so. They came out of the woodwork! Each one kept saying the same thing. The service went on and on for one hour and forty-five minutes. People became jaded and bored. It went on so long, I saw many people frequently looking at their watches.

A wonderful reception had been planned in the church annex with large amounts of food. When the service ended, most people went home. They had had enough. From then on, I limited the number to eulogize to three or four with me calling the shots.

One of the good things that came from this incident was the fact that the widower was very generous in the amount of money he gave to the church for his wife's service. This enabled my wife, who was in charge of all receptions, to buy some nice, much needed silver items for future receptions. The husband later became one of my congregants, and we also became the best of friends, playing golf together regularly. He also turned out to be a person who ministered to me with his Christ-like traits of kindness, generosity, patience, gentleness, and caring. And most of all, he laughed heartily at my corny jokes.

I always took pride in being quick-witted and being able to concoct a quick comeback in a moment's notice. But one day when he and I were going to play golf at the Peterson Air Force Base Golf Course I met my match. When we showed our identification to the female guard at the gate, I jokingly said, "It's too nice a day to be working. Come on and join us in a game of golf." She immediately responded, "Didn't anybody call you? They were supposed to call everybody who had a tee time. There was a shooting at the golf course and the golf course is closed." She came across as being dead serious and we were convinced. Then she smiled, knowing she had hooked me, and I realized I had been had. Bob got the biggest kick out of that incident and never let me live it down.

The reason for my retirement from the church was due to Dot's declining health that had been caused by the fusion of the five lower vertebrae in her back that caused her to worsen in later years. A fine Christian neurosurgeon, who later did cervical spinal stenosis surgery on Dot's neck, told us that the fusion of five vertebrae should never be done because it's too invasive—that he disagreed with the surgeon who did surgeries of that nature. He said the fusion of three was fine. He added that the fusion of five vertebrae was more lucrative, and that's the reason it was popular with this particular surgeon.

But we have been so conditioned to believe that doctors are all-knowing gods that we trust them completely and swallow what they tell us hook, line, and sinker. We were victims of that trust and paid dearly. A few years later that surgeon was killed in a skiing accident in Canada at the age of 52.

When the wrongful back surgery was performed, I was given permission to stay with Dot in the Intensive Care Unit overnight and sleep in a reclining chair. Because Dot was so restless and creating a lot of noise, I was unable to sleep. I moved the chair close to her bed and took her hand. Apparently knowing the feel and security of my touch, she calmly settled down and we both got a good night's sleep. Unfortunately, too many of us have yet to discover the importance and power of touch.

Many people think that, when a person comes to know Christ, an instantaneous transformation of perfection takes place then, as well as immunity from the world's trials and tribulations. This belief was being widely spread by "health and wealth" evangelist preachers on television who claimed that coming to Christ would provide precisely that. Some even falsely promised that abundance of material things would also come from a surrendered life to Christ. It appealed to the greedy appetite for possession of things in all of us.

We need only look at the Bible to see that this is not so. Jesus said, "If anyone would come after me, he must deny himself and take us his cross and follow me. What good is it for a man to gain the whole world, and yet lose or forfeit his own soul?" (Luke 9:23, 25).

A look at the Bible tells us that those who followed Him in person, and in later times, experienced times of worldly difficulties, not a life of peaches and cream as many financially well-heeled preachers would have us believe. Judas betrayed him, Peter denied him, and the rest of His followers either scattered to the winds or remained hidden in the shadows when He was arrested and later crucified. Some were imprisoned, stoned to death, burned at the stake, and even crucified upside down.

Life's problems and suffering, like death, come to every human being in one form or another, but they do come. Even the Apostle Paul, who is considered the greatest Christian who ever lived, had his struggle staying on the straight and narrow. Listen to his confession in Romans 8:15–17 and 24: "I do not understand what I do. For what I want to do I do not do, but what I hate I do. And if I do what I do not want to do, I agree that the law is good. As it is, it is no longer I myself who do it, but it is sin living in me. What a wretched man I am! Who will deliver me from this body of death? Thanks be to God—through Jesus Christ our Lord." That initial relationship with Jesus is simply a "new birth," as Jesus said. From then on, our task is to grow into His likeness by faithful, daily discipline to develop and maintain an intimate relationship. I say that to point out that struggling to be Christ-like is not easy and not without its frequent stumbling and failings. It's the natural fabric of humanity!

There is documented statistical evidence that shows that all families are dysfunctional to one degree or another. It's not a matter of kind, but of degree. It's also a matter of much pain to the entire family, not only the main actor. In fact, a well-known Christian author by the name of John Ortberg deals with this dysfunctional problem in a book titled *Everybody's Normal Till You Get to Know Them*. This problem was evident in our family as well. And I ministered to so many with this problem.

In 2007, the alcoholic son of the financial director at our church took a shotgun and blew his head off. At their home when I was counseling with the family, the mother said, "I know this may sound awful, but I'm at peace with knowing where he's at. We never knew when the phone rang whether he'd be in jail or the police calling to tell us to come and get him. It was very disruptive and painful to the family." I worked with this family to try to make sense out of this suicide, and in time God used our counseling sessions to draw them closer to Himself.

Soon thereafter, the wife of a retired alcoholic Army major whom I was counseling called me to inform me that her husband had just died and would I come to the house. A month before, they had called me late at night when they were having a domestic dispute. I left them and went home in the wee hours of the morning. I must have been so tired that I forgot to turn the car off and about an hour after I went to bed Dot woke me up asking if I had left the car running. I went to the garage adjacent to the house, which by then was filled with exhaust fumes, and quickly opened the garage doors and windows throughout the house until I felt it was safe to close them. It's a wonder we didn't all die from carbon monoxide poisoning.

As soon as the man's wife called about his death, I went to the house as fast as I could. I saw blood everywhere. His body had swollen so much from cirrhosis of the liver caused by his drinking that his stomach had exploded. His memorial service turned out to be a wake-up call for those in attendance who might have had a drinking problem knowing that it could also happen to them. Alcoholism had become a huge problem by the year 2019, especially among our youth, and the astronomical cost in revenue and human suffering and misery is mind-boggling. Even worse, this addiction has been compounded by the drug epidemic.

At the time of this writing, Colorado and Oregon had legalized the use of marijuana for medicinal purposes so we have yet to see what kinds of problems this will present to society. Other states, hungry for added revenue, were seriously considering doing the same. In less than a year in Colorado we began to see evidence of how "uncontrollable" this had become, and the destructive direction that this mistaken decision would probably take us.

I know from personal experience because of my propensity for drinking in the early years of my life that alcohol can be so destructive. Some argue that it's a genetic thing while others blame it on the culture, while still others judge it as being a sin, and not a disease as many claim. What I do know is that on Dot's side of the family, they can take a cocktail or two and leave it at that. On my side of the family we drink it until it's all gone.

We have all heard the saying "God works in mysterious ways, His glories to behold!" Our fourth son is proof of that. He had always been a church attender, even having served as an acolyte. But, like many who grow up in churchgoing families, once he left home to be on his own he discontinued that practice. His friend was a drug user and went into a Christian rehab for treatment. When he was released he went into great detail explaining to my son all the religious things that took place at that rehab facility.

As a result of that conversation, something of a miraculous spiritual awakening took place with my son. He called me full of excitement and said, "Guess what, Dad? I discovered that Jesus is real," and he went on to tell me how it had happened. He said, "Isn't it amazing that God would use a druggie for me to have this wonderful experience when you couldn't do it from the pulpit?" Yes, sir. "God works in mysterious ways, his glories to behold!"

The rest of this personal story includes life in independent living facilities. One day in June 2010 Dot and I were visiting a friend in an Air Force retirement facility in San Antonio, Texas. I saw what a place like that offered for us in our present circumstances, with Dot's declining health becoming an issue. That visit turned out to be another God thing. I clearly heard God's voice say to me, "Sell your home and find a place like this where Dot needs to be." I had the same feeling when we sold our home in Warner Robins in 1996 and moved to Colorado Springs. So when we got back to Colorado Springs, I called our real estate agent friend and told him, "Put the house on the market. It will sell in two weeks."

That next Thursday I had a meeting with the senior pastor at the church and shared that information with him. At the conclusion of the meeting we ended with prayer. He led in prayer, "Lord, it is John's feeling that this is your will and that their house will sell in two weeks. If this is so, so may it be. Amen." It came time for me to pray, and never shy, I said to the Lord in prayer, "Lord, I believe our house will sell in two weeks. But if you want to get it sold in one week, it won't hurt my feelings." It sold in one week.

The agent and I were playing golf on Saturday when he got a call from his secretary. He said to me, "I think we have a bid. Be prepared for a lower bid, and maybe them asking you to pay the closing costs, as well as asking you to remove the wallpaper in the TV room, the master bedroom, and the guest bedroom." None of that was asked, and the buyers paid cash.

Dot and I moved into Liberty Heights Independent Living in Colorado Springs, a beautiful, modern, up-to-date facility with five levels, but none on top of each other. The apartments were all on tiered ground so that everyone could see the gorgeous Pikes Peak, the rest of the picturesque mountainous landscape, and the unique Garden of the Gods directly across. We had wonderful gourmet meals, frequent entertainment, an exercise room with all manner of exercise equipment, an Olympic-size swimming pool and Jacuzzi, and even a certified lady who did massages. We were living the big time—a far cry from the city dump of La Junta, Colorado, for this dirty little Mexican!

Our apartment was located directly across from the Air Force Academy football stadium on the first level. Seeing that majestic view every morning was heavenly. Even getting that apartment, a plum, was evidence of God's handiwork on our behalf. So convinced was I that the house would sell in one week that I went to the marketing person and selected the apartment I just mentioned before the house even sold. The following week, she called and said another person wanted that apartment, and that if I wanted to keep it, I would have to pay a month's rent in advance. "Fifty-six hundred dollars for an empty apartment? No way, Jose!" I told her to let it go. She showed us another apartment on the same first floor level on the extreme side of the first floor, but the view was obstructed by the parking lot in front, trees and a flagpole. But I had no choice but to take that one.

I called the following week and asked if those people had taken the apartment we initially wanted. She said no, but that there was another lady from Florida who was interested. I resigned myself to living in the second apartment because living is living. A few days later, I received another call: "You must be living right. The lady decided to take another apartment, so if you still want that first one you can still have it!" I think this was the one the Lord wanted for us from the beginning, but was putting me to the test to see how I would handle the apparent disappointment. There were two other retired Navy chaplains and their wives living at Liberty Heights, but I conducted most of the memorial services for the residents who died and delivered the prayers at special functions in my uniform. The Navy chaplains had retired and they wanted to leave it that way.

God's gift of never meeting a stranger made me a winner with these residents as I endeavored to minister on a one-to-one basis each day by being humorous, encouraging, supplying a kind word, a smile, a touch and a hug, and all manner of friendliness. The opportunity for this kind of personal ministry is so needed among these persons in the sunset of life who have suffered so much in their lifetime, been widowed, are lonely, and can no longer define themselves by what they have had or what they did.

They are all old and they all know they are going to die soon—and frailty is an everyday reminder of that. I would try to make it a point to know each person by name and to sit at different tables for meals to try to know the residents on a more personal basis. Even my silly jokes were well received and therapeutic. By this time Dot's health kept her from much social involvement, which was heartbreaking because she had always been my faithful companion and so actively involved.

One day I sat with a certain couple, and while engaged in conversation the issue of health came up, as it did often. The husband, Bob, told me that he had incurable cancer, but that so far it was under control. I asked who their doctor was. The wife said, "It's a funny name like Salamo or something like that." I asked, "Is it Solano?" She must not have known my last name because she answered, "Yes, is he your doctor also?" I told her, "He's my son!" She replied, "Bob likes your son, but I don't." When I asked her why, she said that she didn't like Keith because he had told her husband that he was going to die. Keith didn't tell her that, but like so many of us we expect doctors to be miracle workers. Bob had incurable cancer, and Keith was just being honest when he told him that there wasn't much else that could be done for him medically. Bob did die about six months later, and I did his memorial service.

By this time Dot had limited mobility, walked with a walker in our apartment, but went to the dining room and attended a few social functions in a motorized wheelchair. When medical personnel discovered she was Dr. Solano's mother, she received special treatment. Once when she was taken to the emergency room, the doctor was rather aloof in her treatment at first. He didn't have much bedside manner. Later when I told him my son was a doctor, and would it be okay if Keith called him so he could tell Keith what her problem was and what treatment would be prescribed, Dot suddenly became a person instead of a case. This was absurd—everyone should be treated with that same care and courtesy no matter who they are.

Dot had several hospitalizations and stays in rehab facilities and almost died in July 2012. She said she was very tired so I asked some friends who were visiting to help me get her in bed. When we placed her in bed she complained about not being able to breathe, her lips were turning blue, her skin felt flabby, and she gave every indication that she would die at any minute. She was able to hold on long enough for the paramedics to get her to the emergency room.

Here I have to give great credit and express my deepest admiration to the doctor described two paragraphs above. He was a true caring professional, fully taking charge and calling and directing every appropriate procedure needed to save her life. He moved here and there like a gyro in motion monitoring every phase of the

Liberty Heights Independent Living.
Colorado Springs, Colorado, 2011

long, laborious procedure to the point of sweat visible on his brow. God used this Jewish servant in His ministry of healing to save his Christian sister. It's quite possible that he had just had a bad day or was preoccupied when I first thought him to be "aloof," and I just misread him.

Keith was a well-liked and respected physician. When nurses realized he was our son, they would speak highly of him, saying that he was not like other doctors who made them feel like they were above them. When I mentioned that to Keith, he replied wisely, "Dad, my nurses are my first line of defense. The nurses who have hands-on care with the patients all the time can give me a lot of personal information about the patient that is not in the patient's chart." The military had taught him well.

We had moved to Colorado Springs to be close to Keith, but now after 17 years the Lord felt it was time for us to move to another location. In July 2013, I again heard the Lord clearly say, "I want you to move to Wilmington, North Carolina, where you can enjoy the company of Mark and his family, and where you're to spend the rest of your days on this earth." I visited Wilmington to locate an independent living facility similar to Liberty Heights in Colorado Springs, and to write the final chapter of our lives on earth. We found a place comparable and made our final move.

When Dot and I left for Wilmington, we were given a going-away party at Liberty Heights, which was not customary and which was held for us in the large activities hall with a packed house in attendance. We were lavished with all manner of kudos and fun roasting, not only for my official ministries, but for the love, care, and compassion we gave to each other on a one-on-one personal basis. The following poem, which was written and read by the president of the Resident Council, captured their sentiments:

OUR IRREVERENT REVEREND

At Liberty Heights we have a prize
He's somewhat short of a major size
But he makes it up in a mighty tide
For his humor is known both far and wide.

Now John Solano is his name
And saving souls is his game
But prior to that there was some doubt
As to what would happen, opined a scout.

From all reports he was a rounder
By some definitions he was even a bounder
But fate intervened and it would reach
By meeting Dot, a Georgia peach.

So life was changed, and John recanted
His old habits were quickly slanted
Away from sin to the straight and narrow
And he's been there since, straight as an arrow.

Now John is a Chaplain, Air Force type
Who toiled around the world, with all manner of hype
But he counseled wisely and left a fine mark
To those he met, for he said, "hark."

"I have found the Way, and it's exciting
I used to have a spirit, that was somewhat biting,
But now I am changed, and gentle and meek
And if you don't believe me I'll whop you on your cheek."

So that's the story of our friend John
Who faced the world and found it fond.
He's added much to Liberty Heights
By his wisdom, humor, and doing what's right.

—Jack Houser, February 2013

PART VII

Til Death Do Us Part

20

What Will Be, Will Be

Wilmington, North Carolina, 2013–2015

Having clearly received a message from the Lord to move to Wilmington to be close to Mark and his family, we moved on September 8, 2013. The apartment in Wilmington did not have a garage where we had a lot of things stored, nor a storage room like the one in Colorado Springs. I rented space with a trucking company and sent a lot of stuff to Mark, who could gladly use it. The rest we gave away to the church and those persons who helped us pack and move, and come to find out we really could do without a lot of that stuff.

Two months later, the senior independent living facility where we lived in Wilmington had their second annual "Academy Award" presentations. The residents were asked to nominate fellow residents for awards in different categories. God continued to use the gift that He gave me "to easily relate to people" and make them feel special, and that earned me one of the awards. I was awarded a small plastic "Oscar" with the inscription "2014 Brightmore Oscar, Best Animated Personality." The award of my presentation, as well as the others, was broadcast on two of the local television evening news.

The move turned out to be a true blessing for me, but not so for my beloved Dot. I enjoyed playing golf, and being close to Mark and his family. Since Dot was sick a good deal of the time, she could not see and spoil the grandchildren as much as I did, and that broke my heart. She was entitled to that grandparent blessing as much as I! But when her health allowed it, she was included in all the family gatherings. Unfortunately, declining health meant this didn't happen often.

The move turned out to be a bummer for my beloved sweetheart. Dot only got to spend a week or so occasionally with me in our senior independent apartment. The remainder of her life was in the hospital or rehab facilities. Six days after we moved into our apartment, she became sick with a urinary tract infection (UTI) that turned into other complications that landed her in the hospital for a few days, followed by a 16- to 20-day period in a rehab facility, and then she came home to be with me for a week or two. Then the same thing would occur again. This happened over and over again four times during the next seven months until other, more extreme measures had to be taken.

Caregiving can be a grueling, demanding, and very exhaustive task. A UTI can cause a person to lose all strength, have delusions, and experience other side effects. That happened with her. When the delusions would come on, she would repeat, "Help me, help me, help me," as well as "I hurt, I hurt, I hurt," and "I'm afraid, I'm afraid, I'm afraid!" When I would ask her what I could do to help, where she hurt, and what was she afraid of, she could not answer clearly because of her confusion. This drove me bananas. As we all know, it takes time for one to get an appointment with the doctor, and I encountered this many times before I could get her on antibiotics.

In the meantime, hearing that constant refrain over and over night and day and feeling helpless wore me out. I wanted her to quit that never-ending refrain and get well. I was scared of losing her and wanted so badly for her to be normal again. In my helplessness, I often would even scold her telling her that she wasn't trying hard enough to get better. That would only compound the problem because she would tell me I didn't understand and didn't care. Then I would feel guilty and have to apologize for being so stupid.

Sometimes her strength was completely depleted and I had to manhandle her to get her from her lounge chair to the wheelchair or to the bathroom. I had to take care of her every personal need—and that means "every personal need." I remember reading the book *Tuesdays with Morrie*, where Morrie, who had Lou Gehrig's disease, believes that the most degrading thing that could happen to him would be for somebody else to have to "wipe him." Dot and I loved each other so much that wiping her was never humiliating to either one of us. Her recurring illnesses would become so bad that I had no choice but to call 911 and have the ambulance take her to the emergency room where she was hospitalized time and time again. I was her primary caregiver for over five years.

Caregiving brings with it ambivalent feelings of all descriptions that wreak havoc on a person. By this time Dot was pretty much wheelchair-bound. There were many times when I wasn't up to the task and didn't feel like doing it and then I'd feel guilty. But instead of giving up, I forced myself, remembering the vows so many of us had said, but never kept, "in sickness and in health—'til death do us part!" I also knew that Dot would do the same for me were the shoe on the other foot, and I leaned on the Lord for His strength. In my more clear moments I would realize that taking care of her was not a burden at all, but a real blessing—a gift from God! How could it not be so for this woman whom I loved for 64 years with all my heart, and had been so instrumental in helping me to get on the straight and narrow?

When I prayed for God to perform a miracle and heal her, and He didn't, I found comfort in the words of the Apostle Paul in II Corinthians

12:8–9, where he refers to a physical problem that he suffered with all of his life and pled with the Lord to cure him. He said in that Scripture: "Three times I pleaded with the Lord to take it away from me. But he said to me, 'My grace is sufficient for you, for my power is made perfect in weakness.'" Paul found that last verse to be true as seen in verse 10 where he says, "For when I am weak, then I am strong!" Not only was that promise made to Paul, but also to us who also found it to be true as well. "When things look down, look up!"

Dot's roller-coaster health changes just described went on from September 14, 2013, until April 7, 2014, when it became necessary for us to admit her to Liberty Commons Skilled Living on a permanent basis so that they could keep her healthy with 24/7 care. We had tried home care where a nurse and physical therapists would come in and try to restore her back to health, but that was simply putting a Band-Aid on the problem.

After 64 years of being together, having to place her in another facility permanently was heartbreaking to both of us, and drove us to tears time and time again until we came to accept the fact that what has to be has to be. The facility being only twelve minutes away made it convenient, and I would visit her daily and take her to eat at the Brightmore dining room where I lived or a restaurant of her choice three days out of the week. At the Mexican restaurant she would enjoy a plate of enchiladas topped off by a Corona beer. Then we would spend time together in my apartment. Those few hours together may not seem like much, but they were precious quality time that we cherished.

She did well until October 2014 when a series of events caused her to be hospitalized for a 16-day period. After that, she didn't seem to have the energy nor the will to bounce back. Finally on December 8, 2014, she was placed under hospice care. In the ensuing weeks she began to eat or drink very little, and slowly began the process of leaving her earthly body in exchange for one eternally in heaven. When Dot's health became so badly deteriorated, I informed Mike and Marcia Conway, dear friends in

Colorado Springs, by email of our situation. Marcia, knowing that I was also a dear friend of their son, David, a Colorado State patrolman, felt led to send the email to Dave expressing her heartfelt sorrow for us.

Dave's response captures in a nutshell the basis of our long marital bliss and the influence that God and Dot had on my successful life—words that seemed so appropriate to our then current circumstance. David wrote,

Oh Mom, don't look at the pain. John doesn't see the pain, he sees his education. God drew something on the blackboard for John. John is reading it for the first time with understanding. Yes, it is a tough lesson, but John understands the answer. John grew up as a very rough piece of coal. Dot found that piece of coal, and with the guidance of God, [Dot] brought [John] to an unparalleled craftsman, "God." God put the piece of coal, "John," through heat and pressure and made him into a diamond. But God isn't finished, diamonds must be cut and polished. So while this part of John's life is being held to the buffing wheel, and that will get hot and sting, the end result is so much worth the trouble. When God is finished, John will be a spectacular diamond worthy of the crown God has already set aside for him. I only hope that I could hold up to the Master's hand the way John has, for his suffering has in itself an inherent nobility. God's angels are preparing for Dot's arrival. When God's work has been accomplished through Dot, Dot will receive her crown and it too will be glorious, for she brought John to God. Sadly her body will fail, but that has always been God's plan. Who are we to question how or why a body must fail, it's the way it does. Every tear will be wiped away and in that I stand on solid Ground.

The following story is told in jest, but clearly shows how most of us feel in times of intense suffering: Once when Mother Teresa was making rounds visiting the sick, one of the patients asked her, "Mother Teresa. Why am I suffering so much?" In her sweet, tender way she answered, "Well, you remember that Jesus suffered and he said that we would suffer as well." Not finding that answer satisfying, he asked again, "But why am *I* suffering like this?" She again answered in this manner, "My son, because the Lord loves you!" He told her, "Mother Teresa, tell the Lord not to love me so much!"

The question many people ask is, "Why does God allow suffering if He's as loving, caring, and merciful and forgiving as the God we see in Jesus?" Books by the hundreds have been written trying to give an answer that satisfies the question, but to no avail. Rabbi Harold Kushner even wrote a book titled *Why Do Bad Things Happen to Good People?* that speaks to the question that baffles so many of us. Suffering is suffering and too often confuses even more those who believe themselves to be good people. For example, there are good Christians who believe that when they become Christians they will be immune to all the trials and tribulations of this world, only to shockingly find out that it is not so. Randy Alcorn in one of his books calls the gospel many preachers preach—that when you become a Christian you will be successful and immune to trials and hardships—"health and wealth Christianity."

Then there are those Christians who believe that their suffering is punishment from God for their bad behavior, which of course contradicts the gospel. If Jesus suffered by His death on the cross for our sins, why would He turn around and punish us for sins that He has already paid for? Double jeopardy!

The struggle for answers as to why we suffer is best seen in the book of Job in the Old Testament. The devil convinces God that the only reason that Job, the most righteous and wealthy of men of his time, loves God is because God has given him everything to make his life a paradise. "But take it all away from him," says the devil (paraphrased), "and see how he turns on you." Job is the only one who can prove the devil wrong, so

God allows Job to be tested and the devil takes everything away from Job, including his health, and Job suffers horrendously. But Job rises to the task and remains true in his love for God, and that is the lesson the book attempts to teach those who wonder about the whys of trials and tribulations, including suffering.

But no matter how many answers we get, we find them only partially satisfying intellectually until it happens to us personally. We all claim to have a strong faith when everything is going in our favor like Job's life was. But will our faith hold up to the test when the storms of life kick us in the teeth? In Job, we see ourselves in his agonizing ordeal—and hopefully will see ourselves in the end the way he did as well. As the *Student Bible* (NIV) puts it,

How could it happen? All at once the world came crashing down on a single innocent man, a man named Job. It was the ultimate in unfairness. *First,* raiders stole his belongings and slaughtered his servants. *Then* fire from the sky burned up his sheep, and a mighty wind destroyed his house and killed his sons and daughters. *Finally,* Job came down with a horrible, painful disease. "What did I do to deserve such suffering?" he wailed. Sooner or later we all find ourselves in a position somewhat like Job's. Our world seems to crumble. Nothing makes sense anymore. God seems distant and silent. At such moments of great crisis, each one of us is put on trial. In a sense we become our own actors in a contest like the one Job went through. This book records every step in that process with unflinching honesty. Job's life stands as an example to every person who must go through great suffering.

I was no stranger to pain, suffering, and death—I had been immersed in it in my work as a hospital chaplain, and in my many years as a pastor in churches. But seeing my beloved Dot suffer so much for so long was heartbreaking, and I have to honestly admit that there were moments (fleeting as they might have been) when I felt like Job. As the old saying goes, "Surgery is minor surgery when it's being done to you, but its major surgery when it's being done to me."

This suffering was personal for us. It was like my remembrance of the memorial service I had done for Al Gurganus, a dear friend who was more like a brother. Seeing the urn with the ashes of dead persons on the altar hadn't bothered me in memorial services that I had previously done. But with Al it was personal. Seeing my good friend reduced to ashes in a small container affected me in a way that it never had.

In Dot's situation, even with my strong faith in God, I was only human and couldn't help but wonder on occasion, *Why is this happening to my wonderful Dot? Why is she suffering so much? Why couldn't it have happened to me instead? Isn't God listening?* The questions kept coming like tumbleweeds in the western prairie. God must have thought I could handle it or He would not have allowed it. Randy Alcorn, in his book *If God Is Good, Why Is There Suffering and Evil?*, says God placed us on this earth to become like Him, and that everything that happens to us He either allows or causes so that we can grow into His likeness.

Dot's end-of-life journey hit me pretty hard, but having dealt with death in my 54 years of ministry and Dot having been in such poor health for over a period of so many years, it came as no surprise to me. I had seen time and time again that death many times can be a blessing. If there's no quality of life, why do we want to remain in such a state?

I remembered the words of my mentor of long ago, the Reverend Broadus Jones, "John, I am not afraid of dying, but I am afraid of suffering." Immersed in this long-term suffering period we came to personally believe that, indeed, death can be a blessing. And yet hope for recovery was never far away. I had seen two different persons in the hospital on different occasions in the past where I would have said they weren't going to live another day—yet they lived for several more years. And that gave me hope that Dot might miraculously be healed. But we tempered this on-again, off-again thinking with the fact that it's all in God's control.

In time we resigned ourselves to the inevitable, and Dot and I openly talked about her death. We decided to turn this sorrowful event into a blessing, and that it turned out to be! We fully trusted in the promise of Jesus, "I am the resurrection and the life. He who believes in me will live, even though he dies; and whoever lives and believes in me will never die" (John 11:25–26). We Christians believe that "This is our Father's world," but in reality it is only temporary—we're just passing through. (Wouldn't it be something if we found ourselves in eternity and came to the realization that this earthly life was just something that we dreamed? Haven't you ever entertained crazy thoughts like that? Don't lie now!) We have the promise of a better life being in store for us in eternity.

That promise reminds me of a story about President Teddy Roosevelt. A missionary and his wife came home from India on the same boat with President Roosevelt, who had been hunting in India. The missionary was depressed because here was a tremendous gathering to welcome the president back home from a hunting trip while the return of the missionaries, who had done such great work for the Lord, went unnoticed. He mentioned this to his wife, who suggested that he take the matter to the Lord in private prayer in the confines of his cabin. When he came back, she asked, "What did the Lord say?" He replied, "The Lord said, 'You're *not home yet!*'"

There is no scientific way to prove that this promise of Jesus is true or not true, just like there is no scientific way to prove that love exists. You can only believe it on faith, experience it, and examine the results of such wonderful truth.

For me, the following story that I often used at the conclusion of my many funeral and memorial services captures what we Christians believe about what's beyond the grave. I have preached it passionately for 54 years because I personally believe it to the point that I trust it completely. The story goes like this:

A sick man turned to his doctor as he was preparing to leave the examination room and said, "Doc, I'm afraid to die. Tell me, what is on the other side?" Very quietly, the doctor said, "I don't know!" "You, a Christian believer, do not know what is on the other side?" The doctor was holding the handle of the door. From the other side came a sound of scratching and whimpering. As the doctor opened the door, a dog ran into the room and leaped on the doctor with an eager show of recognition, love, and joy.

Turning to the patient, the doctor said, "Did you notice what my dog did? He's never been inside this room before. He didn't know what he would find inside when he entered that door. He knew nothing except that his master was here, and when the door opened, he came in here without fear of what he would find. I know little of what is on the other side of death. But I do know one thing. I know my master is there, and that's good enough for me!"

Early in my ministry I read something that I believed to be true and embraced it as a foundational truth. It read, "You're not really prepared to live until you are prepared to die!"

A poem by Helen Lowrie Marshall that has meant so much to me expresses that trust in this fashion:

THE SONG AND THE ECHO

A song we sing. We cannot know
How far the sound of it will go,
How long its echo will be heard,
We can but pray that every word,
Each note in this, the song we sing,
Will find its resting place and bring
Some little measure of repose,
Some strength, some happiness to those

Who hear our song. If just one smiles
To hear its echo down the miles,
Then we should be content: and know
Our song was meant—God willed it so."

Unfortunately too many of us live as if death is for someone else, it's never going to happen to us. But I have seen, and experienced it myself, that death for those of Christian faith can turn death into a blessing for this life, and hope for the life to come. Several incidents caused our situation to move in that direction. One day shortly after Dot was placed under hospice care, Mark and I were riding together to go visit her when I suddenly broke down and cried uncontrollably. Mark asked, "What's the matter, Dad?" I replied, "Something just hit me like it never has before. I have been preaching about the love of God for over 50 years, but I just this moment understood what that means. It just came to me that if I, as a human being, can love your mother, another human being, the way I do, I can only imagine how much more God must love me that He would do for me what He did in the person of Jesus Christ."

The hospice personnel were outstanding. I had seen this kind of care before in many other death situations during my 54 years of ministry, so I was not surprised. They kept Dot as comfortable and as pain free as possible, and I spent as much quality time as possible at her bedside as I could. This was done not only because of my devotion and love for her, but also because aide assistance in assisted and skilled living facilities in all the eight different places that I had her over this time period in Colorado Springs and in Wilmington in some cases proved to be mediocre at best.

As a result, I had to monitor her care in order for Dot to get the necessary attention she needed and deserved to remain healthy. Being so groggy from her medicines, my sweetheart didn't know when she wet her diaper or soiled herself, and this kept her from pressing the call button for assistance. And of course, this produced problems with even more complications. I can only imagine how patients are treated who don't have an advocate there frequently to oversee the matter. Many of the aides did the minimum required, and some of the nurses seemed to lose the motivation that initially led them to this healing ministry and became simply pill pushers. I have to be honest and admit that most were committed and professional and took their job seriously. And it's easy to see the ones who simply see it as a job versus those who truly see it as a calling from God.

My beloved Dot got to the point where she couldn't feed herself or care for herself because she lacked the use of her arms. Often I would come and she would make an effort to blow her nose, but the boogers just wouldn't come loose. In the early days of our marriage, having to pick her nose for her would have been disgusting and unthinkable. In this situation, I gladly became her "boogie" man. I was only too glad to still have her in that moment and loved her so much that I would do for her what she couldn't do for herself and praise God for allowing me to do such a small thing for someone that helpless.

I was reminded of the Scripture in John 13 where Jesus washes the disciples' feet. Verses 13–17 read as follows: "When he had finished washing their feet, he put on his clothes and returned to his place. 'Do you understand what I have done for you?' he asked them. 'You call me Teacher and Lord, and rightly so, for that is who I am. Now that I, your Lord and Teacher, have washed your feet, you also should wash one another's feet. I have set you *an example* that you should do as I have done for you. I tell you the truth, no servant is greater than his master, nor is a messenger greater than the one who sent him. Now that you know these things, you will be blessed *if you do them*." With that kind of an example by my Master, could I do any less as His servant?

Dot and I spent a lot of time reminiscing about all the wonderful blessings we had enjoyed during our many years of marriage—two lovebirds walking down memory lane hand in hand. Periodically I would sing for her the song I used to sing to her from our early years of marriage that was so precious to both of us. "Too Young," made famous by Nat King Cole, began, "They try to tell us we're too young." I would sing the entire song and Dot would lovingly smile in agreement.

Latin genes are hard to keep under wraps, and time and time again I would repeat the romantic words in Spanish that I wooed her with when we were courting, "Ah, querida mia. Tu eres todo mi Corazon! Sin tu, la vida es nada. Con tu, la vida es todo!" In English that means, "Ah, my beloved, you are my heart. Without you, life is nothing. With you, life is everything." The hymn "Precious Memories, How They Linger" rang so true and blessed our hearts.

She slept a good deal of the time, but would stay awake long enough for me to read the day's devotional, read Scripture, sing hymns, and pray together. I had preached living in the moment for all of my 54 years of ministry, but now I listened to my own preaching and started practicing it. In time the discipline of "living in the here and now without thinking about the inevitable" became a mainstay. The reality of Dot's death made me do a lot of soul searching that forced me to see some things that I thought had been resolved within myself, but really hadn't. Some were painful memories that I didn't like! We have more trash buried in our subconscious and unconscious than we realize or care to admit. It's stinky down there!

In my clowning to amuse people, there was a question that I sometimes used in order to make a humorous point and make them laugh. I would ask, "Do you know why Cleopatra never went to see a psychiatrist?" When they would answer no, I would say, "Because she was in *de-Nile*!" I found out that I was in denial about many things. There's a saying that goes, "Though sticks and stones may break my bones, words will never hurt me!" As we all know, that's the biggest lie ever told. Wounds from sticks and stones will naturally hurt for a while, but you'll get over it. Words can cause hurt that can last for a lifetime if not resolved. They can also bring healing if forgiveness is asked from a truly contrite heart and lovingly given. I found that there were some unresolved "unforgiving issues" that needed to be put to rest.

Because we're all dysfunctional in one way or another, in 54 years of counseling I heard story after story where parents and children suffered with pain and separation for long periods of time because neither party would take the initiative to reach out to the other for the necessary forgiveness for hurts committed, and forgiveness is the only thing that can mend a relationship in the right way. Even if we ask God and receive His forgiveness, the relationship still remains unresolved until the one injured and the one doing the injury give each other that blessed gift of forgiveness.

In my lifetime I have heard people say many times, "I may forgive, but I won't forget!" The way that is said is not forgiving. You can remember the incident, but you have to let go of the anger and animosity that it has created. Holding ill will toward another is like you drinking poison and waiting for the other person to die. In Luke 23:33 we see this episode recorded: "Then they came to the place called the Skull, there they crucified him, along with the criminals—one on his right, the other on his left. Jesus said, 'Father forgive them, for they do not know what they are doing.'" *That's forgiveness!*

In Acts 7:59 we find another model of forgiveness: "While they were stoning him, Stephen prayed, 'Lord Jesus, receive my spirit.' Then he fell on his knees and cried out, '*Lord, do not hold this sin against them.*' When he had said this, he fell asleep." *That's forgiveness!*

It's a known fact that Senator John McCain from Arizona was brutally tortured by his North Vietnamese captors while he was imprisoned for five years. He still visibly showed the results of that permanent damage by the way he walked and with twisted limbs out of joint. In Matthew 5:43–45 we find these words of Jesus about how we should behave toward our enemies: "You have heard that it was said, 'Love your neighbor and hate your enemy.' But I tell you: *Love your enemies* and pray for those who persecute you, that you may be sons of your Father in heaven. He causes his sun to rise on the evil and the good, and sends rain on the righteous and the unrighteous." I have no knowledge about McCain's religious beliefs or how he felt toward those who tortured him. I do know that I would have a hard time forgiving those who tortured me as badly as they did him.

How can one forgive a person who does such monstrous, painful tor-turous things to you? Louie Zamperini did. After Louie came to know Christ under the ministry of Billy Graham, he wrote a letter to the very person who brutally beat him into submission almost daily for those hor-rible years that Louie was in captivity. To Watanabe he wrote that, as a result of being a prisoner of war and enduring unwarranted and unrea-sonable punishment at Watanabe's hand, Louie's life after the war had become a nightmare. He said the tension of stress and humiliation, more than the pain and suffering he had endured, had caused him to hate with a vengeance. He said his rights, not only as a prisoner of war, but also as a human being, had been stripped from him under Watanabe's discipline. He struggled to maintain enough dignity and hope to live until the end of the war. Although the nightmares he endured after the war had caused his life to crumble, he credited a confrontation with God through the Evangelist Billy Graham to his committing his life to Christ. Love had replaced the hate he had for Watanabe. "Christ said, 'Forgive your ene-mies and pray for them,'" he wrote.

Louie told Watanabe that he had returned to Japan in the early 1950s and was graciously allowed to address all the Japanese war criminals at Sugamo Prison. "I asked then about you, and was told that you probably had committed Hari Kari, which I was sad to hear. At that moment, like the others, I also *forgave you* and now would hope that you would also become a Christian," he wrote.

Louie carried the letter with him to Japan hoping to meet with Wata-nabe, but that was not to be. CBS contacted Watanabe and told him that Zamperini wanted to come see him. Watanabe practically spat his reply: The answer was no.

When Louie arrived in Joetsu, he still had the letter. Someone took it from him, promising to get it to Watanabe. If Watanabe received it, he never replied.

Watanabe died in April 2003.

That's forgiveness!

While in her last days under hospice care I asked my wife, "Do you love me?" She quietly responded, "Uh-huh." I asked, "How much?" With a foggy mind she said, "2.2x2." Typical me, I said, "And there were times when you wanted to love me with a two-by-four, right?" Again, she emphatically said, "Uh-huh!" One time the hospice nurse asked her how many boys she had. Dot replied, "Five!" referring to me as the fifth one, of course.

In those final days, Dot would occasionally wake up from her long naps troubled from a bad dream that she had had. I surmised that in that stage in the dying process the person probably has a hard time distinguishing what is real and what is not, at least from a worldly point of view.

(I have had two experiences like that, although not while dying. One was in 1958. I was sleeping next to Dot when I woke up and saw the full moon shining through the venetian blinds. For some reason my heart started racing out of control and that terrified me horribly. I saw myself tumbling in outer space without any control and that frightened me even worse. Then I convinced myself that it didn't matter because as a Christian I was tumbling with Jesus and that was okay. That calmed me down, and as a result of that experience have been unafraid of death ever since.

I had a similar experience in April 2018. I woke up and felt that I was alive in two dimensions, in this body and as a spirit standing side by side. I struggled to try to decide which was the real me and tried to combine the two images together. It took some time for me to do that, all the time not really caring which was which because I believed them both to be real and felt comfortable in both. Some would say I was being delusional, and that's okay for them to feel that way. "Not their circus, not their monkey." For me those two experiences were spiritual blessings that I cherish.)

I would reassure her that everything was okay, and she would calm down and go back to sleep. I had recently read a truism that I applied to our situation: "We are all addicted to trying to control life (playing God), which is uncontrollable. What we can do, and must do, in order to maintain our sanity, is to manage the way we deal with what life brings into our lives in the best way we can."

I treasure our last days together on this earth as much as any of our 64 years together. They were moments of openly talking about her death, our faith and hope in life after death, reminiscing about the special moments of our life's journey, holding hands, learning to live in the moment, praying and singing hymns, and savoring the final moment to the fullest. Those moments were held in the highest regard because the reality of their finality was weeks or days away, and they would be no more.

The death of your loved one can make you realize in a way you never did before that all of life is precious and a gift from God, whether it's 87 years in a personal life; 64 years of wonderful, loving companionship with your beloved; or even just one moment—it's all eternal life in the eyes of God, who is eternal life, "everlasting from everlasting." As the Bible says, "A thousand years to God is like the twinkling of an eye."

It would be untruthful and dishonest if I were to leave you, the reader, with the impression that dealing with Dot's death was a piece of cake for us because of our Christian faith. It was not! Faith in Christ still has its home and its workings in this fleshly body. I can assure you that it was far from a piece of cake. We questioned, we doubted, we cried, we grieved, we got angry, we ran the gamut of our emotions just like any other human beings will do in similar circumstances, faith or no faith.

The difference in us having faith in Christ is that we always came back to the promises of our Living Savior, renewed our hope, and unquestionably believed and felt that he was there "walking hand in hand with us through the valley of the shadow of death" exactly as He has promised to all who trust and believe in Him.

Being the fighter that she was, Dot lasted 80 days under hospice care. One day in February when I was reading the Scripture that the author had selected for the devotional of that day in the Methodist *Upper Room*, I noticed what Dot had written on the margin of her Bible regarding that selection. Looking through her Bible you would see similar notations that she made throughout the entire Bible, a practice I think she picked up from her mother.

The Scripture selection for that devotional was Psalm 46, which reads in the first few verses, "God is our refuge and strength, an ever present help in trouble. Therefore we will not fear, though the earth give way." Next to that last phrase she had written the word "body" referring to the sunset of life. If the word "body" were substituted for the word "earth," it would read, "God is our refuge and strength, an ever present help in trouble. Therefore we will not fear, though the *body* give way." Further down in verse 10 of that Psalm appear the words, "Be still and know that I am God."

At the bottom of the page in her Bible she had written, "European PWOC theme when I was President in 1970–1971. Hymn was 'Be Still My Soul.'" The first verse of that hymn reads,

> *Be still, my soul: the Lord is on your side:*
> *bear patiently the cross of grief and pain;*
> *leave to your God to order and provide;*
> *in ev'ry change he faithful will remain.*
> *Be still, my soul: your best, your heavenly Friend,*
> *through thorny ways leads to a joyful end.*

How appropriate for our present situation, I thought.

More than once when I left that depressing place where Dot lived with slobbering, gaunt, bed-ridden, wasted human beings, many in a grotesque fetal position who seemed to be in another foggy existence, I wondered how Dot had been able to stand being there 24/7 for those long ten months and admired her for her courage and tenacity. I thought, *If I were she, I would have asked the Lord to come get me quick*, and would have felt fully justified. She dealt with her death as a true warrior. I can honestly say, "Not only did Dot show me how to *live the right way*, she also taught me how to *die the right way*."

And that brings us to an important question that we hardly ever think about but probably should. As Max Lucado wrote,

> What kind of remembrance will we leave behind? When you are in the final days of your life, what will you want? Will you hug that college degree in the walnut frame? Will you ask to be carried to the garage so you can sit in your car? Will you find comfort in rereading your financial statement? Of course not. What will matter then will be people. If relationships will matter most then, shouldn't they matter most now?

In writing this story, I have endeavored to share what I remember about the life God gave Dot and me to share with each other for the ultimate purpose of using those lives in a joint ministry to glorify His blessed and holy name. Regardless of differences in gifts, talents, or life pursuits, I firmly believe that everyone of us has the one common purpose claimed in Ephesians 2:8–10: "For it is by grace you have been saved, through faith—and this not from yourselves—it is the gift of God—not by works, so that no one can boast. For we are God's workmanship, created in Christ Jesus to do good works, which God prepared in advance for us to do."

The following words are taken from a favorite hymn of ours titled "Trust and Obey":

When we walk with Lord
in the light of His Word,
What a glory He sheds on our way;
While we do His good will,
He abides with us still,
And with all who will trust and obey.

Trust and obey,
For there's no other way
To be happy in Jesus,
But to trust and obey.

Whatever glory our lives in joint ministry have accomplished, it is because we simply believed the truth of those words and we trusted and obeyed—something every one us can do if we will. That hymn could have been written about us, but it wasn't. It was written for us and for the thousands upon thousands who have also heeded those words since they were first written in 1887.

As I stated at the outset, I knew that writing our story in the first person was risky because of the possibility that I might come across as egotistical and self-centered. I decided to take the risk trusting that the Holy Spirit in your heart and mine would connect in brotherly love and understanding and prevent that from happening. The primary intent, which I honestly and firmly convinced He placed in me to do this, was to encourage you, the reader, to allow Him to do with your life the same thing that He has done in ours. I also have to confess that had Dot written this like she had planned long ago, this book would have been much better written.

Take a good honest look at yourself, and compared to us, you probably have more going for you than we did at the beginning. The same God who worked through us can also work through you—God has no favorites and we're all his children, whom He loves beyond our wildest imaginations! Dot and I were nothing more than human vessels used in God's service and whatever successes were accomplished, it was through His presence and power and to Him be the praise and the glory. He deserves the credit!

One day when Tim Tebow, the 2007 Heisman Trophy winner, was being interviewed he was asked how he wanted to be remembered when he's gone. He replied, "I don't want to be remembered as a well-known football player. What I want people to remember about me is, 'That he loved the Lord Jesus Christ, and did his best to make a difference.'" That's the way Dot will be remembered because she *did* make a difference. Will Rogers was fond of saying, "I never met a man I didn't like." It can be said of Dot that "she never met a person who didn't like her." Legacies don't get much better than that.

The son who really took it the hardest was Mark, the could-have-been-an-abortion case, whom she called "My Joy Boy," because they were so close. But Mark has also grown deeply in his faith through this agonizing experience, and he, too, will be a better follower of Christ because of his mother's death. Life on this earth comes and ends, for "from dust we came, and to dust we must return." But for those whose trust is in the living Son of God, the resurrected Christ, this is not the end of the story.

The end of this earthly story, and the beginning of the heavenly story, is summed up in the words of the Apostle Paul, "For me to live is Christ, to die is gain" (Philippians 1:21)—and also words from the 23rd Psalm: "The Lord is my Shepherd, I shall not want. . . . Even though I walk through the valley of the shadow of death, I will fear no evil for you are with me . . . and I will dwell in the house of the Lord forever," as well as in the words of that beloved hymn, "When we all get to heaven, what a day of rejoicing that will be. When we all see Jesus, we'll sing and shout the victory!"

Jesus was once asked which was the greatest of all the commandments. He responded, "You shall love the Lord your God with all your heart and with all your soul and with all your mind. This is the first and great commandment. And the second is like it: You shall love your neighbor as yourself" (Matthew 23:37–39). The vertical beam pointing upward to God, and the parallel beam of the cross pointing in both horizontal directions are symbolic of that command.

The wedding vows repeated by this loving couple 64 years ago, "'Til death do us part" have become "Hasta luego, mi amor, mi Corazon, mi vida" (Until then, my love, my heart, my life). Three loves made in heaven? Without a doubt!

Epilogue

When Dot and I married 64 years ago we exchanged rings and vowed, "'til death do us part." There is a plaque on our kitchen wall that reads, "I can't promise you that I will be here for the rest of your life. But I can promise you that I will love you for the rest of mine." She lived up to her part of the bargain, and I fully intend to live up to mine. I shall continue to wear my ring as well as hers until I die as a symbol that—"death will *not* part!" and as a symbol of our eternal union. I firmly believe that the love she and I had for each other was a godly love that came from God himself, and since Jesus has already conquered death, the grave is not going to be the victor. I believe with my whole heart that this separation brought by her death is simply an interlude—that when I die we will be reunited and we will continue that love relationship into all eternity in one form or another.

That belief is unsubstantiated by anything I have read or heard to make me think that—until I came across a book referred to me. That book is titled *Heaven* and is authored by a biblical scholar named Randy Alcorn.

Christians often refer to verses 1–5 in chapter 21 of the book of Revelation in support for the existence of heaven.

Then I saw a new heaven and a new earth, for the first heaven and the first earth had passed away, and there was no longer any sea. I saw the Holy City, the New Jerusalem, coming down out of heaven from God, prepared as a bride beautifully dressed for her husband.

And I heard a loud voice from the throne saying, 'Now the dwelling of God is with men, and he will live with them. They will be his people, and God himself will be with them and be their God. He will wipe every tear from their eyes. There will be no more death or mourning or crying or pain for the old order of things has passed away.

He who was seated on the throne said, "I am making everything new."

The question "Is there life after death and what is it like?" has been around since the dawn of man. An Indiana cemetery has a tombstone more than 100 years old with the following epitaph:

> *Pause, stranger, when you pass by;*
> *As you are now, so once was I.*
> *As I am now, so you shall be.*
> *So prepare for death and follow me.*

An unknown passerby scratched these additional words on the tombstone:

> *To follow you I'm not content,*
> *Until I know which way you went.*

Which *way* you went? Yes, the *way* appears to be an important consideration. Do we find out whether there is or is not an afterlife by way of Islam, Judaism, Buddhism, or Hinduism, whose tenets we mentioned earlier? We have the free will to choose whatever satisfies us personally, and no one person has the right to impose his or her way upon another.

I have chosen my way to be the way of Christianity. I base my belief on the promise of Jesus in John 14 where Jesus says, "I am the way, the truth and the life. No one comes to the Father except by me!" "I go to prepare a place for you, and if I go I will come again and receive you unto myself that where I am there you may be also." When I die I have no doubt whatsoever that I am going to heaven to be with Jesus! My choice is simply my belief based on my Bible and my own peace of mind as a Christian and as a Christian minister—nothing more. It is not my intent to convince or offend anyone—or to demean other views.

I was curious about what others might think about heaven, so I set about asking a multitude of people to get some idea. I discovered that most had the same view about heaven: a complete lack of knowledge and a whole lot of uncertainty. When I asked one lady to describe heaven for me, she said, "Heaven is whatever a person wants it to be." In my view this lady is grossly mistaken. Heaven is what God has made it to be—no matter what people want it to be.

I also discovered that a large majority feel comfortable simply answering, "I don't know what heaven is like, but I know that Jesus will be there and that's good enough for me." That was my position as well, and I still stand by it. However, the more comprehensive concept of heaven that I found in Alcorn's book *Heaven* has caused me to expand my view considerably. I feel led to share that concept of heaven in this manuscript simply as information and not to impose that belief on anybody else. I do it because to me it is so commonsensical and because I have come to believe it and embrace it as my own. I say again: this is simply *my* testimony!

This commonsense view comes from Alcorn's 25 years of biblical research, the reading of over 100 books on heaven, and as a teaching professor at a seminary. The book is in its second edition and has sold over 1 million copies. I know some will be thinking, *That's just his opinion. What makes him think his is the right answer?* Twenty-five years of research, reading hundreds of books on heaven, and teaching the course on heaven in seminary is more than "just his opinion." Without reading the book, I might have said the same thing. But unless a person reads the book he is in no position to judge it from misinformation, bias, hearsay, speculation and even worse, ignorance.

I'm a practical person. If I have a problem with my heart, I'm going to seek the advice of a cardiologist who has studied and knows about hearts—not a proctologist! I want to be well-informed before I trust something that important. I trust Alcorn because of his impeccable credentials, reputation, and 25 years of research. Even with our theological education and many years of ministry, most of us ministers are midgets in comparison to this scholarly giant who has devoted his life to this topic. The inside flap of the book calls it the most comprehensive and definitive book on Heaven today. "Randy invites you to picture Heaven the way Scripture describes it—a bright, vibrant, and physical New Earth, free from sin, suffering, and death, and brimming with Christ's presence, wondrous natural beauty—and the richness of human culture as God intended it," it reads.

Rather than a vision of Heaven as a realm of disembodied spirits, clouds, and eternal harp strumming, this book about "real people with real bodies enjoying close relationships with God and each other—eating, drinking, working, playing, traveling, worshiping, and discovering on a New Earth as God created it. It is earth as he intended it to be."

Be assured that Alcorn's beliefs are not pie-in-the-sky, nor something he simply made up. He supports every claim he makes with Scripture references from Genesis to Revelation and refutes arguments he has received by support of Scripture as well. Where he can't back up what he claims by Scripture he admits to speculation—but then relies on common sense from all of his study and research. He says clearly throughout the entire book that heaven will be like this earth but without any evil at all. It will be a holy place with holy people in it. Those holy people are us Christians! There will be animals, trees, flowers, and all the rest once it is restored to its original state as it was in the Garden of Eden. Thus he tells us to appreciate and acquaint ourselves with the best in this earthly life because it's going to be more of the same, but in a much more perfect state.

I know this is thinking out of our comfort zone, but think about our 10 fingerprints as an example. Each fingerprint is unique. Not one is like the other nine, and not one is like that of any of the billions of human beings whom God has ever made since he first created Adam and Eve. Now if that isn't mind-boggling, I don't know what is! If God can take those tiny, little bitty lines in each finger and arrange them with that kind of uniqueness and precision, restoring us and earth back to its original condition is going to be a piece of cake.

Since there is no other person on this earth like you or me, why would God not want to perfect us instead of destroying us and starting all over again? God has more sense than that. I already have an identity—a special DNA. I don't need another one. I was made in the image of God by God himself. Now all I need is restoration! That restoration process is already in the works. It started 66 years ago when I had a new birth experience with Christ and the Master Carpenter started reshaping me into His likeness. That restoration will continue in the afterlife! Thinking of my old farmer friend again: "I ain't as good as I ought to be, but thank the Lord I ain't as bad as I used to be." I'm a work in progress!

Alcorn says it's important to understand that the Greek word for "new" where it speaks about the New Heaven and the New Earth in the book of Revelation means to make what is now existent "renewed"— "restored" not "new" as in a replacement.

He uses Jeremiah 18:1–8 as an example of the new earth restoration:

This is the word that came to Jeremiah from the LORD: "Go down to the potter's house, and there I will give you my message." So I went down to the potter's house, and I saw him working at the wheel. But the pot he was shaping from the clay was marred in his hands; so the potter formed it into another pot, shaping it as seemed best to him." [Same clay, just a pot transformed into a much better product.]

"... Like clay in the hand of the potter, so are you in my hand, Israel. If at any time I announce that a nation or kingdom is to be uprooted, torn down and destroyed, and if that nation I warned repents of its evil, then I will relent and not inflict on it the disaster I had planned."

Alcorn claims that God will take the present earth and restore it to its original condition as the potter did the pot and not destroy it. If God made a mistake in creating this present earth, what's to keep him from making a mistake again? To destroy it is to admit that God failed in the original creation of this earth, and God does not fail. Alcorn also emphasizes over and over again that we will be bodies in some form or another and not disembodied and simply spirits. If God had wanted to make us simply spirits he would have at the beginning. But he points out that God made earth first and then he made man. He took of the earth and created a body and then breathed His Spirit into it and man became a living being.

Body and spirit go hand in hand here on this earth, and body and spirit will go hand in hand in the new restored earth. This may be a poor analogy for what he is saying but think of yourself as a teenager—then as an adult—and now as an old person. Your appearance has changed, but you are still the same person you've always been—and still recognizable as that person. Is it not conceivable that this is what will happens to us in the afterlife?

Another argument he makes for the importance of bodily form is that of Jesus coming in human form and not simply as a disembodied spirit. Alcorn cites Luke 24:36–45 as only one of many examples to show Jesus in his recognizable original body after his resurrection when he appears to two of the disciples on the Road to Emmaus.

While they were still talking about this, Jesus himself stood among them and said to them, "Peace be with you." They were startled and frightened, thinking they saw a ghost. He said to them, "Why are you troubled, and why do doubts arise in your minds? Look at my hands and my feet. It is I myself. Touch me and see; a ghost does not have flesh and blood, as you see I have." When he said this, he showed them his hands and feet. And while they still did not believe it because of joy and amazement, he asked them, "Do you have anything here to eat?" They gave him a piece of broiled fish, and he took it and ate it in their presence. [Spirits without bodies don't eat fish!]

In John 20:26–27 we see another example where Jesus is in bodily form—somewhat different, but recognizable as the Jesus they had known for three years.

A week later his disciples were in the house again and Thomas was with them. Though the doors were closed, Jesus came and stood among them and said, "Peace be with you." Then he said to Thomas, "Put your finger here; see my hands. Reach out your hand and put it into my side. Stop doubting and believe."

Instead of focusing on what is wrong with this world, we are told to focus on what is good, that is, the church, generosity, kindness, the advancement of technology, art, music, space exploration, and on and on, concentrating on the goodness of what is now because it is going to be a zillion times better than we can imagine.

Now I want to explain why this concept of heaven has been so meaningful to me. Many people who saw me so effervescent after my wife's death wondered, "How can he be so happy and jolly since his wife just died?" I want to answer that question by recounting her death and how I dealt with it. Just before midnight on the night of February 26, 2015, the hospice nurse called me to tell me my beloved wife of 64 years had just died. I went with my son to the facility where her death took place and saw her still-warm, lifeless body before me. She was dead. That I knew for sure.

What I didn't know for sure was where she had gone to. Like so many who have been through similar ordeals, it was obvious that she had vanished. Was she disembodied? Had her spirit gone to be with God? What did her spirit look like? Was her spirit in a sleep state until the Second Coming? Was she in a ghostlike form? Would I see her again? It was nebulous thinking! The questions were maddening and unsatisfying. Then I read Alcorn's book, and I'm no longer plagued by those questions.

This is how I now think based on his book. My thinking has changed dramatically because his view makes more sense to me and brings me more comfort than what I believed before. Here's what I think happened to my wife when she died. I share this only to answer the question of my being "jolly" and "happy." At the moment she died she went to what Alcorn calls the first heaven, the intermediate heaven, or paradise. He uses all three terms interchangeably. There she will have faced the first judgment, which is acceptance or denial of salvation offered by God in Christ Jesus. And I know the answer to that one! When it was determined that she had accepted Jesus and is one of His, she was allowed to stay there in some bodily form enjoying the company of Jesus and all other Christians, and not simply sleeping.

Those who come there who have denied Jesus will immediately be sent to hell. Whatever else hell means, it means separation from God. If they are separated from him here, they will be separated from him there. Why would they want it to be otherwise? No interest for him here, why interest for him there? Throughout my 57 years of ministry, people have asked me, "What about those who have never heard of Jesus, what will happen to them?" I am not God and I don't have the answer to that one. I can only describe what my Bible tells me and what I personally believe. Beyond that it's up to each person to believe whatever they want to believe.

Alcorn goes on to say that at the Second Coming of Christ those of us Christians who remain on earth will be brought together with those who are in the first heaven like my wife and will live forever in some bodily form in what he calls the "eternal heaven," which is also the new restored earth. There is debate as to whether this will be the thousand-year reign or not. At any rate, we will live with God forever in the way that He initially wanted to live with Adam and Eve in the original Garden of Eden. Both humanity and the earth will be restored anew in the Second Coming. At that time we will again be judged, this time on our works as Christians so that we can be rewarded accordingly. There will be work because God told man to care for that which he had created. Alcorn says we will recognize each other and enjoy each other, but in a state of perfection.

Sounds too good to be true—but no more than the forgiveness of our sins by the crucifixion of the human Jesus who died and was resurrected and who is the hope of our resurrection as well. That's why they both can be called the good news. "With God, and by God, all things are possible." To know that my wife of 64 years is at this moment in Paradise in some bodily form and enjoying those wonderful Christians we knew who preceded her in death is of more comfort to me than to think that she simply vanished—is in a mummified state somewhere sleeping—simply a spirit, or me having no idea whatsoever. And that is my reason as to why I was happy and jolly in the midst of her death.

Still another reason is that our life of 57 years of serving Christ as a team was full of meaning and purpose. We knew for what we were created—and that purpose for her was complete on this earth on February 26, 2015. Meaning and purpose are so important to a satisfied life. And since the world didn't give it to us, the world can't take it away. In *Man of La Mancha*, Don Quixote says, "The tragic thing is not that man died, but that he never really lived. We really lived, and we lived it to the fullest!" *There are no regrets* to keep me from being jolly and happy!

Of course, Alcorn's ideas can be considered a totally radical concept from what we normally believe about heaven but since he backs up everything he claims with Scripture references from Genesis to Revelation, he presents a credible argument. His view of heaven brings me more comfort—and I can only speak for myself—than I could have imagined!

The reading of Alcorn's book has given me a new appreciation of myself, others, life after death, heaven, and many other things that have been a mystery. I am aware that I will be accused of swallowing the bait, hook, line, and sinker. And that's okay! I have only myself to answer for. My accusers can live with their question marks while I naively live jolly and happy — and very much at peace with this life and the assured life to come!

This story has been about the three loves made in heaven that were meant to be —the exceptional love that Dot and I shared that could not have been possible without the divine love that came to us from God through Jesus Christ in the form of His Holy Spirit. My intent from the beginning to the end of our life story has been to honor her memory and to glorify God. I pray that I will not have failed in that intent. *To God be the glory!*

Made in the USA
Middletown, DE
13 February 2023

24560916R00159